POSTHUMANITY

POSTHUMANITY

Thinking Philosophically about the Future

Brian Cooney

ROWMAN & LITTLEFIELD PUBLISHERS, INC.
Lanham • Boulder • New York • Toronto • Oxford

ROWMAN & LITTLEFIELD PUBLISHERS, INC.

Published in the United States of America
by Rowman & Littlefield Publishers, Inc.
A wholly owned subsidiary of The Rowman & Littlefield Publishing Group, Inc.
4501 Forbes Boulevard, Suite 200, Lanham, Maryland 20706
www.rowmanlittlefield.com

PO Box 317
Oxford
OX2 9RU, UK

British Library Cataloguing in Publication Information Available

Library of Congress Cataloging-in-Publication Data

Cooney, Brian, 1943–
    Posthumanity : thinking philosophically about the future / Brian
Cooney.
      p. cm.
    Includes bibliographical references and index.
      ISBN 0-7425-3292-5 (hardcover : alk. paper)—ISBN 0-7425-3293-3
(pbk. : alk. paper)
      1. Technology—Social aspects. 2. Technological forecasting. 3.
Technological innovations. 4. Virtual reality.   I. Title.
    T14.5.C667 2004
    306.4'6—dc22

                                                                2003024479

Printed in the United States of America

∞™ The paper used in this publication meets the minimum requirements of
American National Standard for Information Sciences—Permanence of Paper
for Printed Library Materials, ANSI/NISO Z39.48-1992.

For my first grandson, Jacob Zatlukal,
b. February 3, 2003.
May he have a blessed future.

CONTENTS

ACKNOWLEDGMENTS

I want to express my thanks to Centre College for funding a sabbatical and three summers of research and writing for this book. Thanks to Jennifer McMahon for her comments on part of my manuscript, and to Kelly Becker for his patience and generosity in commenting on two earlier versions. The book is better for their suggestions, but they are not responsible for any of its weaknesses. I used an earlier version of this book as one of the texts for a philosophy senior seminar in the spring of 2002. The students in that course did much to help me get a better focus on many of the issues covered in *Posthumanity*. For their spirited discussion and valuable comments, I want to thank each of them: Katie Clyburn, Carter Conley, Leann Dikes, Erin Greenwell, Matt Haberfeld, Myles Holbrook, A. J. Mortara, Nathan Paranthaman, Isaac Vetter, and Cory Wright.

INTRODUCTION

Imagine being offered the chance to begin living, right now, in a future version of our society, one that is likely to come about by the end of the twenty-first century. Here are some of the novelties we would probably encounter:

- A growing number of bionic body parts enabling people to greatly increase the lifespan, power, and beauty of their bodies
- Many scientific, technological, and administrative functions, as well as simple chores, being performed by robots with various body types and degrees of intelligence
- Computer chips that interface with brain tissue, enabling people to enhance their sensory capacities, voluntarily control their moods and feelings at all times, and communicate with each other and with computers by thought alone

Would we jump at this offer? Or would we want to stay put and leave it to our children or grandchildren to experience such a world? Our first reaction to the offer might be one of surprise, or even shock, because we didn't see this bold new world coming. Yet many credible authorities in computer, medical, and communications science are now telling us about such a future, and we need to pay more attention to them. We're in a *philosophically* turbulent era, because the products of our latest technology will include a new kind of *reality* (virtual), new kinds of *minds,* and new sorts of *bodies* for those minds. Until now, major technological innovations have always had an important effect on *human* history. But our newest technology will alter the human animal to such an extent that the next era could end up being *posthuman.* The meanings of these four words—*reality, mind, body,* and *human*—have preoccupied philosophy from its beginnings. Our society needs to be asking *now* to what extent, and for what purposes, we will use our growing power to modify our minds and bodies. We can't have that conversation without the perspective philosophy provides. It is my goal in this book to help provide such a perspective.

People who immerse themselves in philosophy for the first time are often disconcerted to find that some of the most familiar words in their vocabulary, words they constantly use, have become very murky and unstable. The experience is like the dizziness we start to feel when we contemplate the fact that we're on the surface of a planet spinning at 1,100 miles per hour while orbiting the sun at 67,000 miles per hour (add to this the velocity of the solar system and the galaxy). We *believe* what we're imagining, but it's hard to reconcile with what our eyes and sense of motion seem to tell us. We need to think of the earth and things such as mountains and buildings as standing still, so we can experience the motions of other things, such as clouds and people, in relation to them. That's one of the reasons why major earthquakes are so frightening. And so it is with the meanings of fundamental words such as "real," "mind," "body," and "human" when they seem to shift on us. We need to divide the world we experience into basic categories so our thought and language can get a foothold. When we think or talk about something, we start out (usually without reflection) by placing it in one or more broad classes: we perceive it as an event or action, as enduring or in transition, as a body, alive or not, and so on. (One of the major continuities in philosophy through the ages has been analysis of these categories, although philosophers have differed somewhat on how many and which ideas belong on such a list.) For *all* these categories to be undergoing change *at once* is as inconceivable as an experience in which everything is in motion.

Short of such a buzzing, blooming confusion, there can be degrees of instability when some of our categories become difficult to apply or when prominent items in our experience straddle categories or are hard to categorize at all. Philosophers have always found some categorical instability. They have wondered, for example, whether the human *mind* is a *thing* in its own right, so that it could survive the death of the *body,* and whether choices are *actions* (cases of doing) rather than just *events* (mere happenings). What makes the start of the twenty-first century so special is the rate at which a rapidly progressing technology is yielding products that are destabilizing many categories at once.

REALITY

For instance, we now have a technology of *reality*, at least of the *virtual* sort. As a rough definition, let's say that virtual reality (VR) is what people experience when their sensory input is generated entirely from within a computer, in such a way that they feel present in an environment other than the one they actually are in. A virtual environment can seem much more real than the imaginary world created by a good novelist or film director. Through a combination of haptic gloves and head-mounted displays, users can receive tactile as well as visual and auditory stimuli. Because the gloves and head devices also monitor the positions of the users' heads and hands, users can experience their body images (or "avatars") navigating the virtual environment. They get multisensory feedback as their avatars move about and manipulate objects in the virtual environment. Of course, this technology is still a work in progress. VR requires a great deal of computer power to alter sensory input to reflect the different positions, perspectives, and interactions of the user inside the virtual environment. Visual images, for instance, must change at least ten times a second to avoid the appearance of jerkiness as objects shift in response to head movements. With present technology, this requires keeping the images simpler than objects in the real world. Thus it's pretty easy at this stage to tell whether an environment is merely virtual. However, given the rapidly increasing power of computers, such limitations will soon be overcome. The virtual will become much more real.

Yet surely there is still a clear contrast between virtual reality and what we would call *real life* (RL). In some fundamental sense, the virtual is *not* real, no matter how lifelike and stunning in its detail. After all, if the sensory input giving me the experience of being in a forest comes from a computer rather than a forest, then the forest I experience is unreal, isn't it? Many of us have heard this brain-teasing question: If a tree falls in the forest with no one around, does it make a sound? (Can there be, in other words, an unheard sound?) The quick and easy answer is yes, the tree would make waves in the surrounding air that *would* cause an observer to hear the relevant sound if the observer were there; in that sense, the tree makes a sound even when no observer is there. But, in another, perfectly clear sense, there is no sound because there can't be a sensation of sound without a hearer. The riddle dissolves with a little reflection on how we use the word "sound" and on the physical cause of the sound. The sound that I hear is real because the sensory input is from a falling tree. That's why it's part of RL.

Let's try another question about a tree: If what we call a tree doesn't have the shape of a tree unless someone observes it, is there still a tree when there is no one to perceive it? Like any other body large enough for us to see, the tree is actually, according to our scientific account of the structure of matter, a lattice of imperceptibly small atoms, each of which consists of mostly empty space with a scattering of electrons around a nucleus that makes up just 1/100,000 of the entire atom. The tree is nothing like what it appears to be. There is no leaf, branch, or trunk *shape* unless there is something like a human brain receiving impulses along its optic nerve from a retina stimulated by photons emitted from the complex of atoms we call a tree. The brain/mind connects the dots, as it were.[1] However, in the atomic tree complex there just aren't any continuous boundaries to serve as the source of the sensory input for my perception of its outline. Back to the question: If what's out there in front of me doesn't have the shape of a tree unless it is being observed, is there a tree out there? Appealing to the scientific account of the cause of our perception of a tree helped us get clear about the reality of the *sound* of the tree falling, but it seems to have raised a further question about the reality of the *tree* that makes the sound.

Virtual reality seemed so different from RL because the computer as source of sensory input was so different from the mental images generated by the input. But the tree as an array of atoms is also very different from the image of a tree. In both cases, something very unlike what I experience as a tree sends a specific pattern of photons onto my retinas, causing my brain to create the tree image. In both cases, the photons are discrete particles—singly or collectively, they aren't the bearers of the edges or surfaces that make up the shape of a tree. Neither are the impulses induced in the retina by the photons and relayed by the optic nerve to the brain. The brain/mind connects the dots.

The question we're raising here comes up very explicitly in *The Matrix* (1999), a cinematic icon for Generation D. The film (set two centuries in the future) assumes that VR technology has advanced to the point that a computer can deliver sensory input directly to the brain rather than stimulate sensory organs by such devices as head-mounted displays.[2] The film has a scene in which two of the main characters, Morpheus and Neo, are networked into a virtual room called "the construct." Here is part of their conversation:

Neo: This . . . this isn't real?

Morpheus: What is real? How do you define real? If you're talking about what you can feel, what you can smell, what you can taste and see, then real is simply electrical signals interpreted by your brain. This is the world that you know. The world as it was at the end of the twentieth century. It exists now only as part of a neural-interactive simulation that we call the Matrix. You've been living in a dream world, Neo.[3]

In *The Matrix,* most humans are networked into a program administered by intelligent but malevolent machines. The program presents to all humans a simulated 1999 environment that includes their avatars. The heroes of the film, when given the opportunity, have the courage to break out from this delusion and accept the reality of an Earth devastated by a war in which machines created by humans took over the planet. A prominent theme of the film is the suspicion that the world we experience is a deceptive appearance from which we must undergo a difficult liberation in order to behold reality. The channel of this massive deception is the human body and its sensory apparatus. In chapter 1 we will gain several interesting perspectives on the futurescape of *The Matrix* by turning to some philosophical texts that have explored this same theme. In philosophy, there is a reciprocal relation between the past and the future: an awareness of past philosophical controversies gives us vantage points on the future rushing toward us, and envisioning that future puts ideas from the past in a new light. In his allegory of the cave in the *Republic,* Plato (428–347 BCE) describes the difficult and painful turning of the soul away from the body and the deceptive world of the senses toward a realm of light and intelligibility. In his *Meditations,* René Descartes (1596–1650) calls into question the reality of the world of the senses by invoking the possibility that he is locked into an unending dream or a false world implanted in his mind by a powerful and hostile intelligence. George Berkeley (1685–1753) argues that the notion of an external world of bodies existing independently of our minds makes no sense and that reality is nothing but a coordinated set of perceptions sent directly to our finite minds by the Divine Mind.

As VR technology becomes more refined and accessible, we need to ask ourselves what we think about spending ever more time in virtual reality. There will be increasingly realistic video gaming, more skills that can be acquired the way pilots now train on computer-driven flight simulators, and superknowledgeable, endlessly patient nonhuman virtual teachers and professors for online learning. Many people already spend much of their spare time in virtual communities known generically as MUDs (multiple-user domains). These social universes are composed almost entirely of text—they are flesh made word. Users typically create fictional autobiographies and descriptions of their dwellings. These fictional selves often have well-developed relationships with others online, ranging from casual discussion to virtual sex. There are even online marriages. RL spouses have been forced to decide whether online friendships that lead to text sex are the equivalent of adultery. There are interesting nuances here: Am I *really* doing what my fictional self does online with or to other fictional selves? Do the same moral rules apply in MUDs? To the extent that my personal development and social life happen in VR rather than RL, is something important lost? These questions can only get more complicated once MUDs deploy future VR technology to flesh out their text with audio-visual-tactile sensation for communities of MUD avatars.

MIND

I am old enough to have been a graduate student and a young professor before the advent of the personal computer. Now I live in a state of advanced symbiosis with it. First came *word processing,* which eliminated many tediously physical and time-consuming aspects of writing, such as the mess of crossed-out text on loose paper, setting up and using information storage devices such as files or card indexes, and cutting and pasting with scissors and tape or paste. I had the nearly immediate gratification of clean text on a virtual page that I could store in virtual files from the keyboard. Then came the *Internet.* Where previously I could move text only within and between documents in my computer, I can now send it to other computers anywhere in the world within seconds. Thanks to *hypertext,* related documents stored all over the planet are only a click away from the words on my screen. The net also gives me access to entire libraries of historical, statistical, and other kinds of information stored in computers around the world. It's like being able to tap into a planetary mind or a universe of text spread across the nonphysical domain of *cyberspace.*[4] And all of this is already old news, because the speed with which computer technology is evolving makes the near past seem remote. The power of computers has been doubling every one or two years. Ray Kurzweil's comparison of computer and automobile technology is striking: "Computers are about 100 million times more powerful for the same unit than they were a half century ago. If the automobile industry had made as much progress in the past fifty years, a car today would cost a hundredth of a cent and go faster than the speed of light."[5]

Hanging over this explosively growing area of technology is the question, What are we doing? In some sense, the answer is straightforward. We are constructing electronic systems that are increasingly capable of performing many of the mental functions that were once exclusive to humans. For many of these functions, such as the familiar case of calculation or "number crunching," our machines greatly surpass us. In other cases, such as pattern recognition or conversational speech, they are taking their early, imperfect steps. In the eyes of many artificial intelligence (AI) researchers, a future convergence point is, if not actually in sight, then not far beyond it. That point will be the creation of systems that combine and integrate the functions of what are now separate AI systems to constitute something that will be the functional equivalent (or more) of what we call a mind. The question I raise above, What will we have done? becomes even more pressing. Is it true that mind *is* as mind *does* (no matter what the mind system looks like or what it is made of)? This view of the mind, widely held among philosophers, is known as *functionalism*. Further suppose that such a system is embodied in, or has at its disposal, a robotic mechanism that is mobile and agile and has the functional equivalent (or better) of our hands and sensory organs. The common use of phrases such as "artificial intelligence" has taken some of the shock value out of "intelligence" as attributed to a machine. But what about *understanding, consciousness, belief,* and *feeling*? From the "replicants" in *Blade Runner* (1982) to the mecha-child of *AI* (2001), science fiction films have dwelt long and poignantly on the question of whether artificial, functional equivalents of human persons should be treated as having *our* moral and political rights.

EMBODIMENT

The first sentence of CNN.com's story on 3 July 2001 is memorable: "A patient has received the first completely implanted artificial heart that totally replaces the function of the human heart, researchers announced Tuesday." The function that this device "totally replaces" is moving blood through the body; it does this with a speed and pressure that simulates a living heart. But the writer's language should get the attention of romantics who speak of giving their hearts to their beloved, or those of us who speak of heartfelt emotion. It's pretty hard to retain the image of the heart as the source of life and feeling when this "heart" consists of two artificial ventricles with valves made of titanium and plastic, a motor-driven hydraulic pumping system, and an internal battery continuously recharged by an external battery worn on the patient's belt.[6]

   The major significance of this new technology is that it is out of sight and out of the way, permitting the recipient to move about freely and engage in most normal activities. (It is still in the experimental stage as of this writing, and it is intended merely as an interim measure while the patient waits for a biological heart to become available for transplanting.) The contrast with the sad case of Barney Clark, who in 1982 received an earlier artificial heart called the Jarvik 7, could not be greater. Clark was tethered to a large external wind machine by tubes entering his chest (creating multiple sites for infections). He lived for 112 difficult days plagued by medical crises. This was not an attractive or even acceptable image of the fusion of machinery and flesh that we now call a *cyborg*.[7] It suggested incompatibility and violent invasion, and it caused a setback in popular support for artificial hearts. But the cyborg revolution had been launched thirty years previous with the first implanting of a cardiac pacemaker. The current list of available internal bionic body parts is lengthening. It includes artificial joints (of which millions have been implanted), penile and breast implants, vascular prostheses, and cochlear implants (from which impulses stimulate brain tissue). There is a great deal of research focused on the problem of electronic interfaces with neurons in sensory organs and in the brain itself. There are experimental prototypes of retinal implants that would enable light to artificially stimulate the nerves behind a dysfunctional retina, and of synthetic tissue that would behave like biological muscles and tendons in response to stimulation from motor neurons.

Devices that interface with neural tissue are often referred to as *neural prostheses*. Researchers are developing neuromuscular prostheses for partially paralyzed persons, using computer implants in muscles still under voluntary control to send signals to other implants at muscles affected by paralysis. For instance, a voluntary shrug of the shoulder could cause a grasping motion in an otherwise paralyzed hand. Such devices would bring about dramatic improvements in the quality of life for these persons, enabling the wheelchair bound to do such things as stand up and sit down without help, so they can get to objects otherwise too high for their reach. One of the most important ultimate goals of research in prostheses is to be able to construct limbs that will not only have all the motor abilities of the original, but also generate all the same sensations. That would go a long way toward giving us the experience of such limbs as being *our own*. If I could feel the artificial hand I was using tighten around what it holds, and could feel the texture of what I grasp, would that lead me to regard the hand as part of me? Would that be an illusion?

The notion of a *prosthesis* becomes unstable as we project these developments further into the future. "Prosthesis" signifies a *replacement* part that either restores a lost function or bestows a normal function on someone born without it. However, as this technology continues to develop, it will no doubt enable us not only to restore function, but also to *enhance* it, or to acquire sensory and motor functions (and relevant body parts) that are not in our genetically based repertoire. Brain implants will likely enable us to alter our moods at will, and in ways that will not harm us as commonly abused drugs now do. Much of this technology may be further in the future than its enthusiasts suggest, but there seems to be no good reason to doubt it will come. It is certainly a goal of current research in mainstream biomedical engineering. We need to reflect on what we are about to do with and to the human body, and thereby to our selves. Could I regard a body that is composed entirely or mostly of synthetic parts with the same or better sensory and motor functions as just as much *my* body and part of my-*self*? Would I be just as much a human being? Should that matter?

As these questions cascade, the categorical ground begins to shift under our feet. Would we want to say that the bionic components of our bodies are *not* parts of a *living* body because they are not composed of tissues that are assemblies of cells? Yet we say that cells are alive, even though their parts are not. So, if a cell is a living body composed of parts that aren't alive, wouldn't a human body be still alive if it were all or mostly bionic? If not, can a *person* be alive without a living body? If not, can a being have a conscious mind and not be alive? Or, paradoxically, is there some nonbiological kind of "life"? Sherry Turkle has studied the shifts in popular attitude and discourse among both children and adults as they get used to the intelligent machines they increasingly interact with in personal ways. Her conclusions suggest a reciprocal relationship between how we categorize artificially intelligent systems and how we react to the prospect of bionic bodies:

> People accept the idea that certain machines have a claim to intelligence and thus to their respectful attention. They are ready to engage with computers in a variety of domains. Yet when people consider what if anything might ultimately differentiate computers from humans, they dwell long and lovingly on those aspects of people that are tied to the sensuality and physical embodiment of life.[8]

As we explore these questions in chapter 3, we will have to ask ourselves just what it is that causes me to experience a body as *my* body. It isn't the same relation between me and it that I have with possessions. I can sell or give away my possessions, but I can't (or shouldn't) do that with my body. Moreover, my body is not just an *it*, an object; it's also, in some hard-to-define sense, *me*. What I think about the prospect of a bionic body depends on what I think makes a body mine in the first place. Is the relationship so close that I couldn't be who or what I am with anything very different from the body I now have, all the way down to its cellular and molecular components?

POSTHUMANITY

Although our accelerating technology will bring enormous changes in our social and natural environments, it will have an even more profound effect. It will give us increasing power to alter our biological human condition by modifying and enhancing the human body and mind. Even as these changes are beginning to occur, we are starting to make progress in building robots that can carry out important tasks that were once our prerogative and burden. I have raised the question: *What* are we doing? Just as important is the question: *Why?* What is, or should be, our goal? What is our criterion for judging that major technological developments constitute progress rather than posing unacceptable dangers and threatening the loss of fundamental values or goods? To the extent that our markets are free, it is very likely that any new technology that can be produced and sold at a profit *will* become available. Can we trust the operation of market forces alone to secure a good future for us? We have government agencies such as the Environmental Protection Agency, the Food and Drug Administration, and the Consumer Product Safety Commission because we don't think market forces alone are adequate to handle such things as pollution or the production of unsafe medicines and toys. Can we allow the market to determine the outcome when our own human nature is in play?[9]

Failing to address these issues is a lot like neglecting to ask what we hope to accomplish by using radio telescopes to probe for signals that may be coming from extraterrestrial civilizations (the usual acronym for this area of science is SETI—search for extraterrestrial intelligence). Suppose we discover that there is such a civilization. It will likely be more technologically advanced than ours. Suppose we learn that it has already achieved what we are laboring to do in science and technology and has managed to create a stable and enlightened society. Will this news be a blessing to us? What would happen to our motivation to continue laboring and striving for our own goals? Would we regard such striving as a planet-scale version of reinventing the wheel? If there were any prospect of interaction with the alien civilization, would that prospect alone risk a collapse of human confidence, self-respect, and even civilization? Not necessarily, but there won't be much time to plan for the eventuality if it simply takes us by surprise sometime soon. There is a parallel issue regarding our future technology. Our dedicated efforts to create intelligent machines could be called a *search for an alien terrestrial intelligence* (SATI?). What will there be *for us* to do after that? We should perhaps be asking ourselves which is preferable, to create intelligent and powerful nonhuman machines that will (contrary to the premise of *The Matrix*) be our servants and benevolently look after us or for humans to evolve into cyborgs? In either case, must we simply accept the *obsolescence* of the human species and all the values specific to it?

One of the Great Ideas western culture inherited from the classical Greeks was an idealization and exaltation of what is distinctively human. This was a religious *humanism*—the Greeks made their gods (super)human

and attached a kind of divinity to heroic humans who achieved a mortal resemblance to the gods. As depicted in Homer and in Greek mythology, the
Olympian gods, although superhuman in their power and immortality,
seemed so enthralled with humans that they spent much of their time involving themselves in human affairs and taking human lovers. This humanism is captured in Sophocles' famous choral ode from *Antigone:*

> Wonders are many, and none is more wonderful than man; the power that
> crosses the white sea, driven by the stormy south-wind, making a path under
> surges that threaten to engulf him; and Earth, the eldest of the gods, the im-
> mortal, the unwearied, doth he wear, turning the soil with the offspring of
> horses, as the ploughs go to and fro from year to year. And the light-hearted
> race of birds, and the tribes of savage beasts, and the sea-brood of the deep,
> he snares in the meshes of his woven toils, he leads captive, man excellent in
> wit. And he masters by his arts the beast whose lair is in the wilds, who roams
> the hills; he tames the horse of shaggy mane, he puts the yoke upon its neck,
> he tames the tireless mountain bull. And speech, and wind-swift thought, and
> all the moods that mould a state, hath he taught himself.[10]

One of the hallmarks of the historical period called the Renaissance was
the rediscovery and reaffirmation of this humanism. Christianity was less
admiring of human nature than were the Greeks, because it believed humanity was corrupted by original sin. Although the Christian God was much
less anthropomorphic than a Greek god, the master narrative of Christianity focuses on God's incarnation as a *human* being and this God–man's sac-
rifice for the redemption of the human race. This was supposed to be the
central and defining event for the rest of world history. It is ironic that historians often note with condescension how the heliocentric astronomy initiated by Copernicus in the sixteenth century displaced Earth, and thus humanity, from the center of the universe. They see this revolutionary idea as
part of a liberation from an unenlightened medieval worldview. Yet the scientific revolution begun in part by Copernicus took place within what remained a largely Christian culture in which the focus of the immensely expanded universe was still the human race. Now we contemplate the
possibility of being able to alter and enhance our all-too-limited human
minds and bodies. Will we, the inheritors of Greco-Christian values, be able
to keep our faith in the cosmic importance of humanity? Or are we going to
see a *really* profound lowering of human self-esteem, of the sort some historians have incorrectly seen in the acceptance of heliocentric astronomy?[11]
Can it be that we will make ourselves into the ancestral species of bionically
enhanced posthumans?

Visions of a posthuman future abound among futurist writers. For instance, Hans Moravec, principal research scientist of the Robotics Institute at Carnegie-Mellon University, expects that by 2050 science, technology, and production will be entirely in the hands of intelligent robots:

> I'm not as alarmed as many by [this] possibility, since I consider these future machines our progeny, "mind children" built in our image and likeness, ourselves in more potent form. Like biological children of previous generations, they will embody humanity's best chance for a long-term future. It behooves us to give them every advantage and to bow out when we can no longer contribute.[12]

Many would dispute his timetable and the inevitability and desirability of such a future, but Moravec's bold and stark description presents a logical and even plausible outcome of a great deal of current research. Because artificially intelligent machines with agent capabilities will increase the productivity of many enterprises, they will be selected by market forces for development and reproduction. The more autonomously such forces carry us along, the more likely a scenario such as Moravec's becomes.

By way of gaining some criterion for evaluating possible futures, we will look at some of the most prominent philosophical theories of what constitutes a happy or good life. Aristotle (384–322 BCE), writing at the end of the classical Greek period, articulated his civilization's ideal of the best sort of human being. It was an ideal that presumes we will continue to be the sort of animal that we were back then. Yet Aristotle qualifies his thesis by claiming that a more perfect and godlike existence would include freedom from the demands of an animal body, so that we could perpetually contemplate what we know. Perhaps future VR technology will enable us to live like Aristotelian gods. Immanuel Kant (1724–1804) argued that our dignity as persons and members of a moral community depends entirely on our possession of *reason* (understood as the capacity to act according to the consciousness of law). Kant's theory expresses a disdain for the animal side of humanity (in cyberpunk talk, the "meat"), which is a constant drag on our rationality. Perhaps he would be open to Moravec's vision. John Stuart Mill (1806–73) claimed that the only intrinsic good was pleasure. If we accept his theory, perhaps we might wish to remain pretty close to what we now are and simply enjoy the greater leisure and pleasures that our machines will afford us (assuming they stay docile). These are hard questions.

REFLECTIONS

Several writers have recently sounded an alarm about the technological advances discussed above. Among the best known of these writers are Bill Joy and Bill McKibben. They go so far as to advocate a political decision to prohibit, or at least put an indefinite moratorium on, the research and development of certain technologies. Joy, cofounder and chief scientist of Sun Microsystems, published a very controversial article a few years ago in *Wired Magazine*. Its title was "Why the Future Doesn't Need Us." In it, he argued that humans lack the moral and emotional maturity to handle the power that future technology will give them. They aren't ready to plunge into a posthuman future when they understand so little about their own humanity and the consequences of replacing it. So he concludes that we must place limits on scientific research, despite our traditional values:

> Yes, I know, knowledge is good, as is the search for new truths. We have been seeking knowledge since ancient times. Aristotle opened his Metaphysics with the simple statement: "All men by nature desire to know." We have, as a bedrock value in our society, long agreed on the value of open access to information, and recognize the problems that arise with attempts to restrict access to and development of knowledge. In recent times, we have come to revere scientific knowledge.
>
> But despite the strong historical precedents, if open access to and unlimited development of knowledge henceforth puts us all in clear danger of extinction, then common sense demands that we reexamine even these basic, long-held beliefs.[13]

The title of McKibben's recent book, *Enough: Staying Human in an Engineered Age,* says it all. Since the current rate of our scientific and technological progress will carry us into a posthuman future, we need to decelerate *now:*

> When someone tells you, as the techno-utopians explicitly do, that they want to end your species as it has existed and replace it with something "higher" and "better," it seems useful to ask why.
>
> It's not, I've tried to show, in order to cure the ill or feed the hungry. These things lie within our present powers or within the steady, foreseeable, noncontroversial progress of science and medicine. They don't require a posthuman future. So what does?[14]

What do you think? Are there cases in which democratic societies have managed to block research without compromising basic freedoms? Can government prohibitions be effective over such broad areas of science and technology? Would the government agencies enforcing these prohibitions move us in the direction of a police state? Could McKibben, too, be called a "techno-utopian" for what he claims in the passage above?

Does it even make sense to ask whether we could want a posthuman future? After all, we *are* humans; we want what humans want and what is good for humans. How can we think of *not* being human as a good outcome?

NOTES

1. What's at stake here is *not* like the edge of a desk that appears smooth but is much rougher under magnification. The edge of my desk is an approximate image formed by my low-resolution visual perception. I can say that the edge of my desk is real if the sensory input comes from the edge of the desk, even if this edge is rougher than it seems to me. Even a rough edge is continuous; it is the uninterrupted boundary of a continuous surface, just as the surface, in all *its* close-up irregularity, is the boundary of a continuous solid (even if the solid has holes or empty spaces within it).

2. As I will explain in chapter 1, this assumption is not as far-fetched as it may seem.

3. Andy Wachowski and Larry Wachowski, *The Matrix* (screenplay), at www.ds2.pg.gda.pl/~colan/screenplay.txt (accessed 11 September 2003).

4. This term was coined by William Gibson in his 1984 novel *Neuromancer.*

5. Ray Kurzweil, *The Age of Spiritual Machines* (New York: Viking, 1999), 25.

6. In addition to this complete heart system, there is also the left ventricular assist device (LVAD), which does not call for removing the living heart. It is implanted next to the heart and takes over the function of the left ventricle, which is the heart's main pump. Many patients have lived for years with these devices. The LVAD permits the patient to engage in most normal activities. A much lighter version (four ounces instead of four pounds) will soon be produced.

7. This term was coined in 1960 by Manfred Clynes to signify an entity that is part biological and part machine. It is derived from two words: *cybernetic* and *organism.* The former signifies what pertains to communication/control systems, and especially to the comparative study of these and of nervous systems. Closely related in meaning is *bionic,* which describes an organism whose biological functions have been enhanced electronically or electromechanically.

8. Sherry Turkle, *Life on the Screen* (New York: Touchstone, 1997), 84.

9. In using the phrase "human nature," I am not implying that "human" signifies some definable and stable essence. Nevertheless, humans are clearly a very different kind of organism from all nonhuman ones, as well as from rational nonhumans that have been contemplated by religiously or scientifically inspired imaginations. The story of our species is one of constant cultural evolution independent of biolog-

ical or genetic change. Despite these changes, the human animal, from a biological perspective, has remained pretty much the same. But we have now reached a point where cultural evolution may result in radical alteration of the human animal.

10. Sophocles, *Antigone*, trans. R. C. Jebb, at classics.mit.edu/Sophocles/antigone.html (accessed 19 September 2003).

11. In the ancient scheme of things, being at the center actually wasn't that honorific. The center was also the *bottom* of the universe, the natural place for earth, the heaviest and grossest of what were then the four elements (earth, water, air, and fire—in ascending order). The planets and stars orbiting earth were often associated with gods.

12. Hans Moravec, *Robot* (New York: Oxford University Press, 1999), 13.

13. Bill Joy, "Why the Future Doesn't Need Us," *Wired Magazine* 8, no. 4 (April 2000), at www.wired.com/wired/archive/8.04/joy.html (accessed 11 September 2003).

14. Bill McKibben, *Enough: Staying Human in an Engineered Age* (New York: Holt, 2003), 224–25.

1

REALITY

Our senses connect us to what is real. Seeing is believing. "Tangible" means not only what can be touched, but also what is real. If I say that I saw something in a dream, that changes the meaning of the word "saw" by removing its connection to reality. I might just as well say that "I didn't really see it—I was just dreaming." Yet there is something about our senses that is open to a radical distrust or doubt that we find in many philosophers from ancient Greece to the present day. This attitude is echoed early in the *The Matrix:*

> Morpheus: The Matrix is everywhere. It is all around us, even now in this very room. You can see it when you look out your window or when you turn on your television. You can feel it when you go to work, when you go to church, when you pay your taxes. It is the world that has been pulled over your eyes to blind you from the truth.
>
> Neo: What truth?
>
> Morpheus: That you are a slave, Neo. Like everyone else you were born into bondage, born into a prison that you cannot smell or taste or touch. A prison for your mind.[1]

We may be willing to go along with such a wild assumption in order to get into the fictional world of a film. But why have so many philosophers taken similar possibilities seriously?

THE PATHOS OF THE SENSES

There is something paradoxical about the family of words that includes "appear," "appearance," and "apparent." All are derived from the Latin verb *appareo,* which has the same peculiarity. "Appearing" means becoming present, manifest, or visible ("She appeared in the doorway"). However, it can also mean having an outer aspect that may be inconsistent with an inner aspect, as when things or persons seem to be what they are not ("He always appears to be happy"). How can something *not be* what it presents *itself* as? How can it be *hidden* by, or in the very process of, becoming *manifest*? This (apparent?) contradiction is a big part of what we understand about a *self*. As I use the pronoun "I" to talk about myself, I'm aware of being other than what others can observe of me—I could pretend to feel what I don't, and anyway only I can know what it is like for me to be me right now. No matter how open and honest I am, the inner and outer me can always go their separate ways. Because of this gulf between observable and unobservable aspects, I am in a sense alone, even when I am with others.

To "appear" can also mean to occur or exist, as when we say that heavier atoms appeared only when the universe cooled down from the immense heat of the Big Bang, or that dinosaurs *dis*appeared millions of years ago. The term "phenomenon" (derived from the Greek word for appear) has a similar meaning. It signifies that which occurs or that which is observable by the senses. Humans have always thought of the world of objects and events as an array of phenomena or appearances having an inner, hidden aspect that might not coincide with its outer, perceptible aspect. In animistic religions, objects and events are embodiments of deities and their doings (e.g., the sun god Helios in Homer), whereas in theistic images of the world (whether monotheistic or polytheistic), events (especially the extraordinary ones) are the effects, signs, and manifestations of otherwise unseen, "detached" deities that rule the world.[2] Thus the religious mind assimilates our experience of events in the world at large to our experience of the behavior of other persons in society. The scientific mind is quite different in this regard. It understands phenomena large enough to be observed with our unaided senses as crude and even confusing pictures that our senses form of an underlying, impersonal, and *unconscious* reality—a reality made up of imperceptibly small particles and their interactions.

There is a deep *passivity* about sensory awareness. What we experience always has for us an independence, a quality of *givenness,* no matter what beliefs, interpretations, and expectations we bring to what we see, hear, and touch. Obviously, culture, language, past experience, and the structure of the mind/brain play a large role in constructing what we initially experience. We can recognize these influences in even the simplest cases. For instance, I see in front of me what I recognize as a green wall topped by crown molding. I associate this shade of green with interiors of traditional, colonial-style houses. On the wall hangs a picture of a familiar street in Montreal, my home town. The content of this experience owes a lot to the cognitive background I bring to it. So where is the passivity in all this mental activity of mine? What is so "independent" about what I see in front of me? Simply the fact that I am presented with what I can recognize as a green wall with a picture. *I'm being acted on* by whatever is "behind" the appearances; I'm being stimulated and constrained to deploy my concepts and memories in order to grasp what is occurring. This is true even if what is acting on me is my own mind unconsciously affecting me, as in a dream. Dreams feel real because they have the same sort of passivity that we experience in what we call waking reality. That's what makes a nightmare scary.

Of course we're not mere spectators barraged with a flux of sensory experience. We do *actively* respond to the influx—we're incessantly classifying, anticipating, and planning. Our *power* consists in predicting and altering the course of our experience—twin capacities that in their advanced form we call science and technology. When I decide to move my arm, it moves, and my hand grasps what I want it to. Yet the fact that I initiate these events doesn't remove the passivity in my perception of them. My experience of my arm and hand moving, when it results from my willing the motions, is what engineers would call *feedback*, a sensory recognition of the effect of my decision to move them. I learn through experience, much of it in childhood, that when I want certain parts of my body to move in certain ways, I can count on them doing so. I know some people who can wiggle their ears. I can't. What it's like for *them* when they consciously initiate wiggling their ears is (I assume) much like it is for *me* when I try without success (paying attention to my ears, imagining them moving, *wanting* it). The feedback they get from their volition is different from mine, but just as passive. No doubt there's a physical difference between their nervous systems and mine. But even if we all knew this difference, it wouldn't take away the passivity in our experiences of success or failure at ear wiggling. None of us has the foggiest notion of why or how what we experience as wanting to move a part of our body gets neurons to stimulate muscle fibers. This includes brain scientists. They and we just learn from experience that, when we want it to happen, we usually get the experience of it happening. And that's the way it is with all our voluntary movements, as David Hume (1711–76) noticed:

> This influence, we may observe, is a fact, which, like all other natural events, can be known only by experience, and can never be foreseen from any apparent energy or power in the cause, which connects it with the effect, and renders the one an infallible consequence of the other. The motion of our body follows upon the command of our will. Of this we are every moment conscious. But the means, by which this is effected; the energy, by which the will performs so extraordinary an operation; of this we are so far from being immediately conscious, that it must for ever escape our most diligent enquiry.[3]

It's that way with *all* of our mental processes: in relation to our consciousness at the time we are engaged in them, they run in the dark. I try to remember a name, and either I do or I don't. In neither case do I know how it happens, though I may try as hard when I fail as when I succeed. Most of my speech is not consciously rehearsed. If it were, think of how conversations would bog down! Instead, I become aware of what I'm saying at about the same time as others listening to me do (and sometimes I wish I could take back what I said). Even when I do imagine in advance to myself what I'm about to say, how do I go "looking" for the right words, or for any words (like the words I'm writing at this moment)? The process by which "I" assemble the sentences in my imagination enters my awareness only as feedback (the sentences appear). When I'm laboring over a difficult question, the answer (or beginning of one) pops into my consciousness, or perhaps it doesn't come at all. Of course *I* am the one who is engaged in these mental acts, the one who is active here. But I'm at work "behind" the outcomes, not transparent to myself as I speak and think. Whether I'm experiencing what's going on in my own mind and body, or the words and behavior of other persons, or things and events in nature, in all cases my consciousness passively encounters phenomena, things that remain *hidden* in their very manifestations. As Hume put it, "It must certainly be allowed, that nature has kept us at a great distance from all her secrets, and has afforded us only the knowledge of a few superficial qualities of objects; while she conceals from us those powers and principles on which the influence of those objects entirely depends."[4]

The passivity in our sensory awareness extends to our awareness of our existence, our having come into this world at a certain point in space and time. Our existence is a happenstance that imposes itself on our senses as we get old enough to think at this level. As a *conscious* being, I was less present in my coming into being than I am in the fashioning of my sentences or the recovery of my memories. Much less so, since I couldn't even have chosen to exist; I just found myself here, much as I see willy-nilly what's there to be seen when I open my eyes. Passivity entails *vulnerability*. I want to avoid bad surprises, pain, and destruction. Prediction and control are matters of survival. What should we think about this feature of the human condition? Is the world of phenomena ultimately the mask or manifestation of a person[5] or set of persons (deities), or is there instead some underlying impersonal and unconscious reality? Or perhaps some combination of both? Since this question is at least in part driven by our need for prediction and control, which account is more likely to give us a sense of security in our expectations and plans? In this ultimate sense, would we rather count on a *superperson* or on a *thing*, on a conscious or unconscious being?

Furthermore, why should beings such as us have to cope with the disturbing obscurity of the senses anyway? Is this some cruel joke or punishment, for a being that wants clarity and light to be trapped in such a shadowy universe? Perhaps what we really need is not so much enhanced prediction and control as *liberation* from our senses and from the bodies that yoke us to sensory organs? Plato thought so.

REFLECTIONS

How would you answer the question at the end of the next-to-last paragraph of this section: Given our profound need for predictability and control, would we rather count on a *superperson* or on a *thing*, on a conscious or unconscious being? Is religion an expression of this need? Science is built on the belief that the laws of nature it seeks to discover are unchanging. Is that as much an act of faith as any religious belief?

LIBERATION FROM THE CAVE

For Plato, there was something profoundly *unnatural* about the self or soul being in a body and thus immersed in a world of sensory phenomena. He thought this world had only a defective sort of reality and intelligibility compared to a world of *eternal* entities that he believed the mind could access only by disengaging from the body and its senses. Plato inherited from Parmenides (b. c. 510 BCE), an earlier Greek philosopher, the idea that true being was unchanging and timeless. This is a viewpoint quite remote from the beliefs of most of us today, but it isn't hard to see how someone could arrive at it.

Several years ago, I had a vivid experience when visiting the campus of my alma mater after a twenty-five-year absence. I stood on the spot where I had once had a conversation with someone who was then a good friend, but with whom I had since lost contact. The conversation had taken place in front of the library on a cool and sunny day in early autumn (just like the day of my visit). As far as I could tell, nothing about the building's exterior or the pavement and landscaping had changed since the time of that conversation more than twenty-five years before. I could visualize my friend's face clearly and remember some of the words we spoke and the optimism we expressed about the future. As I stood there, the intervening decades felt like a chasm between *that spot* in front of the library *then* and *now*, between *me* then and now. I was deep in *nostalgia*—the word derives from the Greek *nostos* (return journey, especially homeward) and *algos* (pain). Nostalgia is a painful or bittersweet longing for what we can't get back to, a desire not to be separated from ourselves and others by time. The experience was an occasion for reflection (an occupational hazard for philosophers): What is the status of that meaningful past occasion? Did it simply cease to be, lapse into a nothingness from which even my clear recollection can't rescue it? My feelings rebelled against this thought.

So did the mind of Parmenides. He expressed himself in a poem that relates what a goddess revealed to him:

> It needs must be that what can be spoken and thought is, for it is possible for it to be, and it is not possible for what is nothing to be.
> . . . One path only is left for us to speak of, namely, that *It is*. In this path are very many tokens that what is uncreated and indestructible; for it is complete, immovable, and without end. Nor was it ever, nor will it be; for now *it is,* all at once, a continuous one.[6]

For Parmenides, time and change are unreal, deceptive appearances of an eternal and changeless reality. To think of something changing or happening is to think of what *is* as coming from, or lapsing into, what *is not* (nonbeing or nothingness); and nonbeing, he is saying, is unthinkable. The goddess, realizing how her teaching flies in the face of experience, commands Parmenides to disregard his senses: "nor let habit by its much experience force thee to cast upon this way [of appearances] a wandering eye or sounding ear or tongue; but judge by argument the much disputed proof uttered by me."

From its very beginnings, modern science also has described the world very differently from how it appears to the senses. For instance, those who accepted the heliocentric astronomy of Copernicus in the sixteenth and seventeenth centuries were struck by its rejection of what seems so obvious to the senses (e.g., that the sun rises). As Galileo (1564–1642), one of the founders of modern science, noted with gusto: "I cannot find any bounds for my admiration, how that reason was able in Aristarchus [an ancient astronomer who also held the heliocentric view] and Copernicus, to commit such a rape on their senses, as in despite thereof to make herself mistress of their credulity."[7]

Socrates (469–399 BCE) was another great influence on Plato. This formidable man earned his status as the patron saint of philosophy by disturbing the establishment of Athens to the point that he was finally tried and executed for heresy and the corruption of youth. His mortal offense was to go about with a circle of admiring young men and ask prominent Athenians what they *meant* when they used certain important words such as "virtue," "knowledge," or "justice." Socrates regarded his search for definitions as a mission given him by the gods, one he would not neglect even when threatened with death. Plato not only admired Socrates for his brilliance and courage, but also developed a philosophical theory to explain how Socrates' mission was possible. In effect, he applied Parmenides' notion of being to the objects Socrates was trying to define.

It seemed to Plato that if a definition (of "triangle," for instance) were correct, then the definition is a truth about some being or object. If it is true that a triangle is a two-dimensional figure enclosed by three straight lines, then it can *never* be the case that a triangle would be two or four sided. So the definition is a truth about an object that can never be other than what it is; in other words, it is about an eternal and unchanging object (which Plato called a *form*). In general, our words have meaning only in relation to forms. Forms anchor words so that they have stable and common meanings for all who use them. Forms are Parmenidean realities, obviously not the sorts of things found in the ever-changing world of the senses. Plato accepted what Parmenides said about being and thought: "It needs must be that what can be spoken and thought *is*." Since we manage to think and speak about sensible objects, they must have *some* being. But their being is defective; things that can change oscillate between being and nonbeing. The fact that a particular cookie has a triangular shape helps me to distinguish it from other, surrounding objects. Being triangular is part of its intelligibility and reality. But it can lose that shape. The cookie's shape is only a transitory instance or reflection of the form Triangle. So it is with all the characteristics by which sensible objects and events can be thought about. Appearances have only a weak claim to reality. Their intelligibility is derivative. The mind that seeks the truth about them, that seeks to *understand* what they are, must look beyond the flux of the sensible world to the domain of eternal forms. That is why, in the *Phaedo,* Plato has Socrates make the startling claim that a philosophical life is a protracted rehearsal of dying. Death is the separation of the soul from the body, and the search for truth requires the separation of the mind from the drag of the body's senses so that it can understand the forms in themselves. For Plato, this is the true significance of Socrates' quest for definitions. Socrates is serene in the hours before his death because he believes that his soul, by casting off its body at death, will finally be free of the low-grade awareness it gets through sensory organs.

For Plato, then, philosophy is a way of life that brings liberation and salvation. Unconditional willingness to question conventional wisdom is very demanding of both the questioner and those being questioned. It is likely to provoke hostility from those less willing to seek the truth. Philosophy requires courage on the part of the questioner not only because it is hard work and can be socially isolating, but also because what the questioner learns can make everything seem strangely different. What was familiar comes to seem unreal, and what is real can be overwhelming. Plato illustrated these perils in one of the most famous passages in western literature—the allegory of the cave. For its beautiful imagery and language, it deserves to be quoted at length:

> [Socrates talks with Glaucon] Imagine men to be living in an underground cave-like dwelling place, which has a way up to the light along its whole width, but the entrance is a long way up. The men have been there from childhood, with their neck and legs in fetters, so that they remain in the same place and can only see ahead of them, as their bonds prevent them from turning their heads. Light is provided by a fire burning some way behind and above them. Between the fire and the prisoners, some way behind them and on a higher ground, there is a path across the cave and along this a low wall has been built, like the screen at a puppet show in front of the performers who show their puppets above it.—I see it.
>
> See then also men carrying along that wall, so that they overtop it, all kinds of artifacts, statues of men, reproductions of other animals in stone or wood fashioned in all sorts of ways, and, as is likely, some of the carriers are talking while others are silent.—This is a strange picture and strange prisoners.
>
> They are like us, I said. . . . If they could converse with one another, do you not think they would consider these shadows to be the real things?—Necessarily.
>
> What if their prison had an echo which reached them from in front of them? Whenever one of the carriers passing behind the wall spoke, would they not think that it was the shadow passing in front of them which was talking?—By Zeus I do.

Altogether then, I said, such men would believe the truth to be nothing else than the shadows of the artifacts?—They must believe that.

Consider then what deliverance from their bonds and the curing of their ig-norance would be. . . . Whenever one of them was freed, had to stand up sud-denly, turn his head, walk, and look up toward the light, doing all that would give him pain, the flash of the fire would make it impossible for him to see the objects of which he had earlier seen the shadows. What do you think he would say if he were told that what he saw then was foolishness, that he was now somewhat closer to reality and turned to things that existed more fully, that he saw more correctly?

. . . And if one were to drag him thence by force up the rough and steep path, and did not let him go before he was dragged into the sunlight, would he not be in physical pain and angry as he was dragged along?[8]

The objects above ground in this image correspond to the forms, and the artifacts being carried along the wall in front of the fire stand for physical objects insofar as these are mere likenesses of the forms from which they derive their being and intelligibility. Plato put an interesting twist on the un-reality of the sensible world by dividing this world also into higher and lower levels of truth and reality. The prisoners' heads are restrained so that they cannot see the artifacts behind them or even each other. They can only look at their shadows on a screen on which "carriers" are also projecting shadows of artifacts. To readers in the early twenty-first century, the anal-ogy with television is compelling. In general, most people's awareness of the world around them is filtered through various media—television, film, gos-sip, newspapers, advertising, and conventional beliefs and attitudes en-shrined in the community's collective texts and conversation. The image of the "carriers" suggests that the flood of stimuli washing over the prisoners is consciously organized to create an intended impression. Today's "carri-ers" would be those with the power to influence the content of mass media and public discourse—politicians, advertisers, editors, and so on. The chains that prevent *us* from looking around include the frantic pace that most of us lead in our work and even in our social lives, which leaves little time or energy to get at the facts about what is really going on in our social, political, or physical environments. Like the people of ancient Athens, we, too, often find it disturbing and painful to know too much. Ignorance can be, if not bliss, then at least not as worrisome or depressing as knowing. Digging into matters that are sensitive to people with power can get a per-son into a world of trouble. Best to accept things as they appear (or are made to appear).

But for Plato, even an accurate factual account of the world of the senses fails to get at the reality behind appearances. In the cave allegory, the ascent beyond the fire and "carriers" to the sunlit upper world is even harder than the initial turning away from the wall of shadows. Following the injunction of Parmenides' goddess not "to cast upon this way [of appearances] a wandering eye or sounding ear or tongue; but judge by argument," Plato wants us to engage in a process that can find its fulfillment only in death. In his allegory, the cave can be understood as one's body. As long as we remain embodied, we should strive for a deep *estrangement* of the mind and heart from this world that the unenlightened call home. He claims that the spirit within us longs to quit the world of the senses because it craves a reality and truth that it can find only in the serene and timeless domain of the forms, illumined by a light far brighter than the sun. However, each of us also has a combination of fear and sensual desire that ties us to sensory appearances and pleasures and makes us fear death.

There are similarities between the cave allegory and the story of *The Matrix*. Both begin with a description of the human condition as an underground existence trapped in an unreal world of appearances. In the film, most humans are being incubated by their machine masters in flotation tanks underground. The purpose of the Matrix (hardware and software) is to give the brains of these humans the stimulation needed to keep them (physiologically) healthy, so that their bodies' metabolism will continue to function as a source of electricity for the machines.[9] As Morpheus, the rebel leader, explains, the mental shock of unhooking from the Matrix and perceiving the reality of a subjugated and devastated planet is so intense that the rebels normally release only very young people (who are still resilient enough to adjust). The reality that is above ground in the film is a poisoned and uninhabitable environment. Learning about all this corresponds to turning from the shadows and toward the fire in Plato's cave. The ultimate goal of liberated minds in *The Matrix* is not as clearly stated as in the cave allegory. Does it include retaking and restoring Earth somehow, living in a virtual reality benevolently controlled by and for humans, or some mix of both? Is it the realization that reality is nothing but the code or information we see streaming on the video terminals of the rebels, a reality that humans will come to control with godlike power?

There is a traitor by the name of Cypher in the midst of the Matrix rebels. The story of his temptation raises an interesting question about a Socratic commitment to seek the truth at all costs. Cypher is very depressed by what he has learned since his "liberation" about the real Earth's condition, and by the constant dangers and deprivations of living with the rebels underground.

While on an excursion into the Matrix, he is approached by an "agent," a virtual person or personified program acting on behalf of the machines now controlling Earth. The agent offers Cypher permanent reinsertion into the virtual world of the Matrix, with whatever status and possessions he wishes, in exchange for Cypher's betrayal of the rebel leader. Cypher agrees: "I don't want to remember nothing. Nothing! You understand? And I want to be rich. Someone important. Like an actor. You can do this, right?"[10] Agent Smith replies, "Anything you want, Mr. Reagan." We don't admire Cypher. The writer/directors didn't want us to. But how would we try to *argue* him out of betrayal? On the one hand, he is not the sort to be moved by an appeal to solidarity with his team. But we could point out (as Plato surely would) that he is also betraying *himself,* doing violence to that part of him that wants the *truth.* Surely nothing is worth damaging *that* part of us! Here we have reached the end of where argument can take us. Further argument only begs the question about the worth of rational argument. *Is* truth an absolute value, something to suffer or die for? Plato was convinced that we must heed the goddess's command to Parmenides and follow the argument wherever it takes us, even unto death. According to Plato's narrative of Socrates' trial in the *Apology,* once Socrates had received the death penalty from the Athenian jury, he proclaimed:

> O judges, be of good cheer about death, and know this of a truth—that no evil can happen to a good man, either in life or after death. He and his are not neglected by the gods; nor has my own approaching end happened by mere chance. But I see clearly that to die and be released was better for me.[11]

Socrates was a man of *faith,* however paradoxical that may sound. His faith was in reason and the value of searching for truth, of always questioning what others may take on faith. Which is why he believed nothing really bad could happen to him as a result of his mission in Athens. The word "martyr" derives from the Greek *martureo,* which means "to bear witness." Socrates was a martyr for his faith and one of the founders of a faith community called philosophy.

REFLECTIONS

Socrates was an example of what Kant called "enlightenment." Historians often characterize the eighteenth century as "the age of enlightenment" because so many writers were urging people to think for themselves, independently of convention and religious or secular authorities. There is a strong connection between the spirit of the Enlightenment and the American and French Revolutions. In his essay "What Is Enlightenment?" Kant defines the word this way:

> Enlightenment is man's release from his self-incurred tutelage. Tutelage is man's inability to make use of his understanding without direction from another. Self-incurred is this tutelage when its cause lies not in lack of reason but in lack of resolution and courage to use it without direction from another. *Sapere aude!* "Have courage to use your own reason!"—that is the motto of enlightenment.
>
> For this enlightenment, however, nothing is required but freedom, and indeed the most harmless among all the things to which this term can properly be applied. It is the freedom to make public use of one's reason at every point.[12]

It seems that the citizens of Athens did not agree with Kant that "to make public use of one's reason at every point" is the "most harmless" freedom. Socrates was put on trial soon after Athens's humiliating defeat at the hands of the Spartans, whose culture Athenians considered greatly inferior to their own. Many of Athens's leaders believed that part of why they lost the war was a failure of morale and morality among the youth of Athens. Young men had become cynical about the beliefs and values of their elders, and they no longer saw their state and way of life as worth dying for. They claimed that Socrates' insistence on critically examining conventional beliefs, for which he was admired and imitated by young followers, was a cause of the collapse of resolve that led to Athens's downfall.

Perhaps they had a point. No society can accomplish anything great or worthwhile without a social consensus about what is good and important. To instill a critical spirit in too many people will weaken a society and ensnare it in endless arguments or sap its will with a skepticism about everything. Socrates' kind of faith isolates an individual and destroys community. What do you think?

DESCARTES' MEDITATION

At the time Descartes was writing his *Meditations on First Philosophy* (1641), Europe was in intellectual and religious turmoil. The German states had been devastated by a bloody thirty-year war between Roman Catholic and Protestant forces. The theological unity of Christendom had been forever shattered by the reform movements initiated by Luther, Calvin, and the Tudor monarchy in England. Once the dogmatic authority of the pope and the Roman Church was challenged, what could count as a source or criterion for correctly interpreting the word of God in Scripture? During this same era, geographical exploration was giving access to ancient, vital civilizations (such as China and India) that were built on values and beliefs alien to European culture. Europeans could ask themselves what was so special and true about their own religion and morality. The writings of ancient skeptics were in vogue, as intellectuals felt drawn to the notion that there was no absolute truth. The scientific revolution was gathering speed and had already antagonized the Catholic Church's Inquisition. In 1633, the Inquisition forced Galileo to withdraw his support for Copernican astronomy because it was supposed to be in conflict with Scripture. They also placed him under life-long house arrest and forbade him to publish any more.

Descartes' response to all this intellectual volatility was mixed. He was a brilliant and original mathematician—he largely invented the branch of mathematics that is named after him (Cartesian geometry). He was a friend and correspondent of leading mathematical and scientific thinkers of his day. His system of physics gained wide acceptance until it was supplanted by Newton's. It is hard to overstate the influence of his philosophical ideas. They defined questions and debates that are alive and well in the twenty-first century, so much so that he is still often called the father of modern philosophy. Like anyone playing such a role, he was a transitional figure, hanging onto many of the assumptions of the late Middle Ages even as he proclaimed his intention to rebuild the edifice of knowledge from its very foundations. He was quite disturbed by all the skepticism he encountered among intellectuals, and he thought that the normal condition of science and philosophy should be one of stability and systematic progress built on unshakable foundations (an idea that seems quaint to us today). To achieve this goal, he thought it best to critically examine the usual foundations for what we claimed as knowledge. Foremost among these is our conviction that the senses reveal to us a public world that exists independently of its being experienced by us. His first meditation radically challenges this belief.

The literary genre of the *Meditations* is noteworthy. From 1607 to 1615, Descartes was a student at the Jesuit College of La Flèche, one of the very best in France at that time. Although he came to reject so much of the content of traditional education, he always spoke with respect and affection of his Jesuit instructors. They and their pupils participated in annual retreats based on the Spiritual Exercises formulated by Ignatius of Loyola, founder of the

Jesuits. The early part of these exercises involves the practice of *meditation*—concentrating one at a time on a small number of fundamental truths of the Catholic faith, letting each sink in with all its ramifications for one's life. Descartes' choice of title indicates that he wanted his readers to engage in a personal drama of living and appropriating the arguments and conclusions of the six meditations. He thought this was appropriate for what were meant to be the foundations of a new and secure philosophy and science. The first meditation asks us to look hard at the possibility that the external world that our senses seem to reveal may have no more reality than a sustained dream. Sense perception is the foundation not only of the beliefs of ordinary folk but also of libraries of what Descartes regarded as antiquated and incorrect "learning." He wanted to get straight what the senses can and cannot tell us.

Descartes begins by noting the familiar sorts of sensory distortions that we easily cope with, such as a stick looking bent in water or a circular coin looking oval from a certain angle. However, such commonplace misrepresentations don't shake our fundamental confidence that what we perceive exists, that, for instance, I'm at a desk, my hands resting on its surface, holding a piece of paper. Nevertheless,

> How often, asleep at night, am I convinced of just such familiar events. . . . Yet at the moment my eyes are certainly wide awake when I look at this piece of paper; I shake my head and it is not asleep; as I stretch out and feel my hand I do so deliberately, and I know what I am doing. All this would not happen with such distinctness to someone asleep. Indeed! As if I did not remember other occasions when I have been tricked by exactly similar thoughts while asleep! As I think about this more carefully, I see plainly that there are never any sure signs by means of which being awake can be distinguished from being asleep. The result is that I begin to feel dazed, and this very feeling only reinforces the notion that I am asleep.[13]

Some people find Descartes' claim improbable because, they say, *their* dreams are usually different in some regular way from waking experiences because, for example, their dreams lack certain sensory modalities, such as smell or temperature sensation, or they lack explicit self-awareness and reflection. It's hard to know how to respond to these claims, because memory of dreams is spotty and unverifiable. Others point out that usually there's no problem *after the fact* in distinguishing dreams from waking experience, since the former don't fit into the web of cause and effect binding the rest of our experience.[14] If I dream that I won the Nobel Prize and then wake up to my usual anonymity, I immediately dismiss this experience as just a dream. All of this, it seems to me, is beside Descartes' point. He is asking how I can know with certainty that what I readily distinguish from dreams and call *reality* isn't made of the same "stuff" as dreams, namely mind stuff, content existing only in the mind. After all, when I'm having a dream, I have the same sort of *passivity* regarding what I experience as I have when awake. A dream *feels* real when I have it, even though it's only my own mind unconsciously acting on itself. The fact that this can happen in dreams at least presents the possibility that it could be going on all or much of the time, so that even when I'm awake my experiences aren't about a real world that exists independently of my experience.

If what's acting on me right now as I'm presented with various phenomena is *not* my own mind, then what is it? Is the only alternative that there are things out there resembling what I perceive and that these are affecting my sensory organs and generating in me images of themselves? How do I know that there isn't something *else* acting on me, some malign conscious being? Suppose,

> some malicious demon of the utmost power and cunning has employed all of his energies to deceive me. I shall think that the sky, the air, the earth, colors, shapes, sounds and all external things are merely the delusions of dreams which he has devised to ensnare my judgement. I shall consider myself as not having hands or eyes, or flesh, or blood or senses, but as falsely believing that I have all these things.

Like a good Christian faced with temptation from the devil, Descartes resolves to use his free will to resist: "I shall stubbornly and firmly persist in this meditation; and even if it is not in my power to know any truth, I shall at least do what is in my power, that is, resolutely guard against assenting to any falsehoods, so that the deceiver, however powerful and cunning he may be, will be unable to impose on me in the slightest degree." Like the prisoners in Plato's cave or Cypher in *The Matrix,* he finds that the process of disengaging from the familiar and comfortable world of appearances is painful and frightening:

> But this is an arduous undertaking, and a kind of laziness brings me back to normal life. I am like a prisoner who is enjoying an imaginary freedom while asleep; as he begins to suspect that he is asleep, he dreads being woken up, and goes along with the pleasant illusions as long as he can. In the same way, I happily slide back into my old opinions and dread being shaken out of them, for fear that my peaceful sleep may be followed by hard labor when I wake, and that I shall have to toil not in the light, but amid the inextricable darkness of the problems I have now raised.[15]

At the beginning of the *second* meditation, Descartes refers to the previous one as "yesterday's." His readers are supposed to have spent a day
doubting their senses and to have gone to bed still doubting. (The Jesuit
Spiritual Exercises are similarly divided into days.) Reviving these doubts in
the morning, says Descartes, "feels as if I have fallen unexpectedly into a
deep whirlpool which tumbles me around so that I can neither stand on the
bottom nor swim up to the top."[16] Finally, he gets a firm footing with the
realization that, even if all this flux of deceptive appearances is washing over
him, still he can at least know that "I exist" is true. The presupposition of
his calling the world of the senses into doubt is that he exists not only as a
rational being capable of giving *reasons* why his beliefs may be false, but
also as a being who has the *freedom* to withhold his judgment about those
beliefs despite his fear and dizziness. But he is still standing at the bottom
of the pool. Can he swim up to the top, break the surface, and see what's
there (and breathe)? Can he, in other words, get beyond the perimeter of
his mind, out to some independent reality? Or is he locked into a profound
solitude, able to relate only to the contents of his own mind, to the stuff that
his dreams are made of?

Let's pause here for a moment as we meditate along with Descartes. Isn't
all this rather absurd—conceiving that we might be alone with nothing but
what he calls our "ideas"—our thoughts and images? Is he verbally manipulating us, imparting the illusion of meaning to what is clearly absurd by
drawing us off the beaten path with his tales of dreamers and demons? Not
exactly. There's a much more direct path to getting where Descartes went.
I just picked up a diskette from beside my monitor in order to see the file
names written on it. As I bring it closer to my eyes, it looks twice as large as
before in relation to the monitor. No surprise here, of course; there's an
easy physical explanation for this increase in apparent size. Its *real* size is
approximately 3.5 inches on four sides, as anyone with a ruler can see. However, the ruler also has an apparent size that changes as I hold it closer or
further away. All visible objects have a visible, apparent size that changes
even though what I call their *real* size doesn't change. Changes in apparent
size seem to occur *in me,* in my visual field, not in a space that exists independent of my perception. All visible objects have an apparent size. In a
sense, then, don't they all exist in my mind rather than in some independently existing world? Everything and everyone in a room full of people is
perspectively organized around my point of view, their apparent size a
function of their distance from me and each other. What do I mean when I
talk about *the* room, the one that would be there if I left? What else is there
but as many different, perspectively structured room scenes as there are

perceivers of the room? Well, there's also *the* room, the physical reality that acts on the visual system of each person there, giving each their different perspective. That's what I usually intend when I say "the room." Yes, but whose consciousness has access to *that* room? In one sense, everyone's— insofar as we believe that each person's sensory organs are acted on by the same physical reality. In another sense, no one's—insofar as each person is directly aware only of an appearance organized around her viewpoint.

If we continue in this line of reasoning, being alone with one's "ideas" or mental content is part of the human condition, even if we have good reason for believing that there is a single external world that is the source for the sensory input that induces our minds or brains to form perceptual images. It's rather like solitary confinement in a building full of cells with prisoners similarly confined. It's better than it would be if I believed that reality extended no further than my cell. But it's still solitary confinement. Let's see how Descartes argues his way beyond the bounds of his consciousness to an external world even as he remains within.

Descartes claims to find within his mind one very special idea that, he argues, could not be there unless it had been caused by the very being that it represents. This is the idea of God, of a being lacking no attribute that it would be better to have than not to have—an infinite being that is all powerful, all good, and in general all perfect. For our current discussion, it isn't relevant to go into details about the argument and its cogency. What concerns us here is the *role* Descartes assigns to God. God is not just the first being outside himself whose existence Descartes can claim to know, but he is also Descartes' *guarantor* that there exists an external world "behind" or independent of the appearances presented by his senses, one that is populated by bodies that are at least somewhat like his ideas of bodies. Descartes recognizes that our sensory *experience* would be the same whether or not this external world exists, since we are directly conscious only of ideas or mental content. Once he has "proven" that God exists and is in charge of the world, Descartes is no longer worried about a demon being the cause of his sensations. But he recognizes that God wouldn't need to create an external world in order to give him the experience of one; God could *directly* cause this experience without intermediate entities "out there." This rose, its aroma, texture, and color, would not be any different if I were being acted on directly by God, rather than by a rose that was part of some external world outside my consciousness.

I spoke earlier of the passivity of the self and its need for predictability and control in the flow of experience.[17] I asked which account of the reality behind sensory appearances is more likely to give us a sense of security in our expectations and plans. Would we rather count on a *superperson* or on a *thing*, on a conscious or unconscious being? Descartes wants both: a world of unconscious matter regulated by the will of an eternal and all-powerful conscious being that would be incapable of deceiving or harming us. He says that God has given us no reason to think that our sensations come from anything else but our own and other bodies. "On the contrary, he has given me a great propensity to believe that they are produced by corporeal things. So I do not see how God could be understood to be anything but a deceiver if the ideas were transmitted from a source other than corporeal things. It follows that corporeal things exist."[18] This is an extraordinary argument, not only for its weakness. Descartes is clinging to the breast of God by this inference, seeking assurance that his beliefs and conclusions can be about a reality he will never directly experience. People, in the seventeenth century and even today, have "a great propensity" to believe that the sun rises at dawn and moves across the sky. Why not call *this* propensity something God "has given me" and conclude that God would be deceiving me if Copernicus were correct? Descartes' reply, of course, would be that Copernicus gave us good *reasons* to go against our propensity regarding sunrises. As we will see below, George Berkeley would soon provide some cogent reasons for *resisting* the propensity to believe that there is an external world independent of the mind.

In the two sentences after the passage quoted above, Descartes adds an important qualification to his conclusion that bodies exist:

> They [bodies] may not all exist in a way that exactly corresponds with my sensory grasp of them, for in many cases the grasp of the senses is very obscure and confused. But at least they possess all the properties which I clearly and distinctly understand, that is, all those which, viewed in general terms, are comprised within the subject-matter of pure mathematics.

Descartes is making a distinction between those properties of bodies that are subject to measurement and mathematical analysis (e.g., shape or velocity), and those that are not (e.g., color or taste). This distinction goes back to Greek philosophy, but it becomes very important in the modern period and is most often referred to, in the terminology of John Locke (1632–1704), as the distinction of primary and secondary qualities. The scientific revolution, in which Descartes was a prominent participant, consisted in the adoption of a new methodology for studying nature. Part of this methodology was a resolve to study nature only in the language of mathematics, dealing only with the quantifiable aspects of phenomena. Sensory qualities such as color or sound might be vividly experienced and seem to reside in objects and events of the external world. But they can no more be reduced to homogeneous units of measurement and analysis than can pain or the feeling of warmth. Moreover, they are not part of the *public* world, not open to observation by more than one person. I can't know that what I experience when I call a surface green is exactly like what someone else experiences when they call it green. Both of us can put a ruler on the surface to measure its sides, but there is no such device for checking our sensation of its color. We are able to analyze in mathematical terms the *causes* or stimuli that generate the experience of color in us. For instance, today we know that the different frequencies of electromagnetic radiation that are absorbed or reflected by a surface determine our color perception of it. But that still leaves the content of the color sensation as an unquantifiable remainder, unintelligible to science. That's why Descartes calls the ideas of these qualities "obscure and confused," compared to the "clear and distinct" ideas of qualities that can be quantified.

Descartes and Locke were both *realists*—both held that the world was a set of entities existing independently of our concepts or perceptions of them. Getting at the truth about the world required that our ideas reflect accurately the independent reality of that world. Yet our experience of the world is inevitably saturated with "obscure and confused" features—what Locke called ideas of secondary qualities. Both philosophers held that these ideas revealed very little about their objects and that whatever was in the object itself was reducible to primary or quantifiable features. For instance, what we experience as heat is a subjective state induced in us by contact with a surface that is hot in the sense that the particles making it up are in a more energetic state than particles in cooler bodies. One could never guess from the *sensation* of warmth what was actually going on in the warm body. Because quantifiable and unquantifiable aspects were so mixed up in our perception of the world, neither Locke nor Descartes could be *immediate* realists—they could not maintain that our consciousness had direct access to the external world as it was in itself. Only the clear and distinct features of my idea of this cup I'm holding should be attributed to the cup. Those features must be abstracted from their obscure sensuous surround. So these philosophers opted for a *mediate* realism in which the mind relates directly to ideas (including sensuous content) and only indirectly to the world itself. Another way to phrase the role of God in Descartes' theory is to say that God was a prop for his mediate realism. Because truth became a relation between what is in consciousness and what is forever beyond it, Descartes needed divine assurances about truth in his attempt to reconstruct human knowledge.

REFLECTIONS

1. Does the very idea of realism (mediate or immediate) make any sense? After all, how else can I imagine a scene except as I would perceive it? Or, as Parmenides said, "it is the same thing that can be thought and that can be." How can I even think of what is not an object of thought?
2. If colors, as I sense them, do not belong to the world as described by science, then they seem to exist only in my mind. If so, does that suggest that my mind also doesn't exist in that world? What can that mean?

THE DEMON AS EVIL SCIENTIST

Philosophers no longer talk about the possibility of demons infecting our perceptual processes. But Descartes' demon problem is alive and well in a contemporary version that is implicit in Descartes' own account of the relation between mind and brain.

Descartes was a *dualist*—he claimed that mind and body (including the brain) are irreducibly different kinds of things that could exist apart from each other, even though God has willed them to be united somehow in human beings. He argued that a human mind is not only unobservable, but also nonspatial. Thoughts don't have shapes or locations the way bodies do. It makes no sense to ask exactly where a thought is or how much volume or mass it has. To use an example from today's science: a neurosurgeon exploring the brain tissue of a patient undergoing surgery is going to encounter aggregates of neurons that make up that tissue. She will know that neurons have metabolic processes like other cells and interact by exchanging chemical signals that alter each other's electrical polarization. Advanced imaging processes may even make some of these micro-events observable. But nowhere in all this swirl of metabolic and electrochemical activity will she observe anything at all like what she and her patient experience in themselves as thoughts and sensations.

As a dualist, Descartes stoutly rejected any identification between the brain and the mind. Nevertheless, he was keenly interested in the operations of the brain. He understood that we have sensations when our minds undergo the effects of bodies acting on our sensory organs. In voluntary motion, the mind's decisions obviously cause the body to move. Descartes was convinced that the brain was the focus of this mind–body interaction. From both his readings and his own frequent dissections of animal bodies, Descartes had a reasonably accurate anatomical picture of the peripheral and central nervous system. However, seventeenth-century thinkers could have no idea of the physiology of the nervous system, since they knew nothing about cells or the electrochemistry of their molecular processes. The best Descartes could do was to think of the nervous system in terms of the mechanical and hydraulic systems of his day, which led him to describe neural motor impulses going from the brain to musculature, for instance, in terms of fluid forced down slender tubules and causing muscle tissue to inflate. He understood sensory impulses as like the pulling of a string that runs from the sensory organ to a cavity in the center of the brain. In the case of *reflex* motions, he believed that a specific sensory impulse reaching the brain induces the discharge of a volatile fluid called "animal spirits" back down the nerve to bring about the relevant muscle actions. This sequence of stimulus and response would be entirely unconscious and mechanical. According to Descartes, *non*human animals are unconscious automata whose adaptive behavior is entirely due to such reflex mechanisms. By contrast, humans can engage in *voluntary* motion, in which consciousness intervenes between stimulus and response. Here is Descartes' description, in the sixth meditation, of what happens:

> For example, when the nerves in the foot are set in motion in a violent and unusual manner, this motion, by way of the spinal cord, reaches the inner parts of the brain, and there gives the mind its signal for having a certain sensation, namely the sensation of a pain as occurring in the foot. This stimulates the mind to do its best to get rid of the cause of the pain, which it takes to be harmful to the foot. It is true that God could have made the nature of man such that this particular motion in the brain indicated something else to the mind; it might, for example, have made the mind aware of the actual motion occurring in the brain, in the foot, . . . or it might have indicated something else entirely.[19]

This passage is one more example of what makes philosophers today come back so often to the writings of Descartes, even though most reject his theories. At the very beginning of the scientific revolution, Descartes managed to articulate deep and persisting problems with the relation between human experience as it is lived and the mathematical, mechanistic description of the world we supposedly inhabit. Here are some claims made or implied in the passage:

1. A specific sort of event at a specific locus in the brain is sufficient (by itself) to give the mind a specific type of sensory experience. Whether the cause of the brain event is the usual sort of stimulus at a sensory receptor or a different cause, such as a direct stimulus to the brain, the resulting sensation is the same.

2. The brain event that is the immediate cause of a sensation such as pain in one's foot doesn't resemble, or have any essential connection to, the content of that sensation. God has set up the interaction between brain and mind such that a brain event at a certain locus happens to cause ("indicate") one sort of sensation rather than another. But God could just as easily have decreed that this sort of brain event give rise to a completely different sensation of a different body part.

3. Even though *brain events* are the immediate causes and sufficient conditions of sensations, God has made these brain events bring about an awareness of the *external world* rather than of themselves.

Although we have learned a great deal since Descartes' era about *how* the brain and nervous system carry out their function, it's unlikely that anything we have learned would lead him to retract the above claims. Regarding claim no. 1, for instance, we now know that stimulation of a specific point on the visual cortex (see fig. 1.1A) results in a color flash appearing in the subject's visual field at a location determined by the locus of the point in the cortex. Similarly, stimulation of a point on the postcentral gyrus results in a tactile sensation in a particular part of the body corresponding to the locus of the stimulation (see fig.1.1B). For the most part, we do not know how to stimulate the brain into having sensory perceptions of complete, recognizable objects, probably because brain science is still at such an early stage. However, there are cases in which artificial stimulation does produce something like perception. For instance, Wilder Penfield and Lamar Roberts reported that stimulation of the upper surface of the right temporal lobe in patients with epilepsy originating in that part of the brain resulted in flashback audiovisual experiences, more vivid and "real" than mere recollection:

> It is as though the stream of consciousness were flowing again as it did once in the past. Heraclitus said, "We never descend twice into the same stream." But the patient seems to do it. The stream is partially the same but he is aware of something more. He has a double consciousness. He enters the stream of the past and it is the same as it was in the past, but when he looks at the banks of the stream he is aware of the present as well.[20]

Regarding claim no. 2, neuroscience tells us that the neuron types, the ways they are organized into tissue, and the intercellular electrochemical events are strikingly similar in quite separate areas of the neocortex. When a particular array of neurons is stimulated, the key variables in determining which modality of sensation enters our consciousness seem to be *location* on the sheet of the neocortex and the *connections* of that array within itself and with other arrays. These same variables determine whether the neo-cortical stimulus is part of a sensory or motor process. With our current knowledge, there still seems to be so little connection between cortical events and corresponding mental events (such as a color sensation) that Descartes would once again say that the brain stimulus "might have indi-cated something else entirely."

Claim no. 3 deals with one of the most puzzling aspects of brain/mind function. It mystified Sir Charles S. Sherrington, one of the founders of modern neuroscience:

> The chain of events stretching from the sun's radiation entering the eye to, on the one hand, the contraction of the pupillary muscles, and on the other, to the electrical disturbances in the brain–cortex are all straightforward steps in a se-quence of "physical" causation such as, thanks to science, are intelligible. But in the second serial chain there follows on, or attends, the stage of brain–cortex reaction an event or set of events quite inexplicable to us, which both as to themselves and as to the causal tie between them and what preceded them science does not help us. . . . The self "sees" the sun; it senses a two-dimensional disc of brightness, located in the "sky," this last a field of lesser brightness, and overhead shaped as a rather flattened dome, coping the self and a hundred other visual things as well. Of hint that this is within the head there is none.[21]

Sherrington goes on to refer to this property of perception as "projection" and an "unargued inference" from what is in the mind to what is out "there." These terms may capture what is meant by the last sentence in the passage, but they can suggest a *conscious* transition from what is intramental to what is external—something Sherrington did not intend. At the level of *con-sciousness,* the striking fact is that one is directly presented with an *outer* world by events occurring *inside one's head.* There is no conscious project-ing or going from mental content to physical object. Colin McGinn puts it this way: "What is it about our brains and their location in the world, that could possibly explain the way consciousness *arcs* out into the world? . . . We flounder in similes."[22] This feature of perception has traditionally been linked to a more general feature often called *intentionality,* which also in-cludes the ability of consciousness to relate to (to be *of*) fictional or no longer existing situations and objects, such as imagining the path we didn't take or recalling someone who has died. In these cases, consciousness seems to be a relation occurring between what is physically real and what is not.

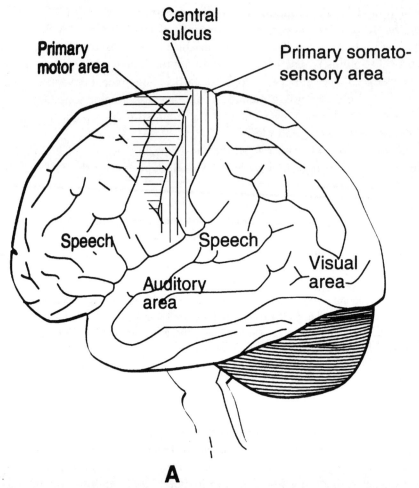

Figure 1.1. General functional map of the human neocortex. (From B. Cooney, *The Place of Mind.* ©2000. Reprinted with permission of Wadsworth.)

These considerations invite replacing Descartes' demon with that icon of anti-intellectualism, the mad (neuro)scientist. How, we could ask, can we *know* that we aren't deluded victims of a team of evil neuroscientists in what is really a century from now—when techniques of artificial brain stimulation have advanced to the point where an entire life's worth of the stream of consciousness can be generated by input to the brain from a computer? This question is often discussed by philosophers today, with no consensus emerging. It is rather grossly, but commonly, called the "Brain in a Vat" problem.

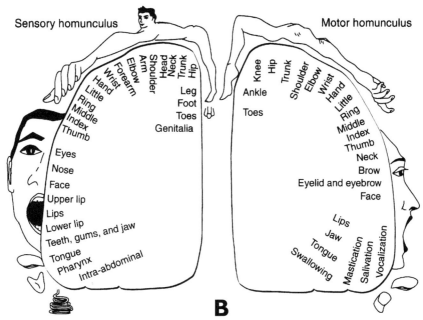

Figure 1.1. The sensory and motor "homunculi." *Homunculus* is Latin for "little man." Each homunculus is composed of representations of the body parts in which (for the sensory homunculus) somatic sensations (such as touch and pressure) are felt when the corresponding cortical tissue is stimulated, or in which (for the motor homunculus) muscle contractions occur when the corresponding tissue is stimulated. (From **B. Cooney,** *The Place of Mind.* © 2000. Reprinted with permission of Wadsworth.)

Or, if we want to further dehumanize the neuroscientists, try this question: How can we *know* that we aren't all networked into something like the *Matrix,* what Morpheus described as "a prison for your mind" maintained by superintelligent machines? These machines have programmed the rules according to which our body images, or avatars, navigate their simulated environment. Among these rules are the laws discovered by our science, as well as the moral, legal, and other codes of conduct we have evolved within the virtual communities our machine overlords have devised for us. When you want to move your arm or hand, the ever-obliging computer gives you the feedback sensations of your arm moving. Every interaction with persons, animals, and things we associate with "real life" is furnished by the system. It all seems quite real, but *our masters* know better.

Or let's give the story a more benign twist: let's suppose that the will and intelligence behind sensory phenomena is *not* that of a demonic scientist or the antihuman, mechanical overlords of *The Matrix,* but rather the God so many people believe in—an eternal, perfect, conscious being whose very perfection commits it to the well-being of human persons. This scenario resembles the world as described by philosopher–bishop George Berkeley (1685–1753). Recall that Descartes argued that unless the source of our perceptions was an independently existing world of bodies resembling (in their quantifiable aspects) our ideas of them, God would be deceiving us, since we are naturally inclined to believe in such a world and we have no clear reason for denying it. Berkeley argues that we *do* have a clear reason for denying it, because the realist notion of a world independent of perceivers is either nonsensical or contradictory:

> That neither our thoughts, nor passions, nor ideas formed by the imagination, exist without the mind, is what everybody will allow. And it seems no less evident that the various sensations or ideas imprinted on the sense, however blended or combined together (that is, whatever objects they compose), cannot exist otherwise than in a mind perceiving them. I think an intuitive knowledge may be obtained of this by any one that shall attend to what is meant by the term *exists,* when applied to sensible things. The table I write on I say exists, that is, I see and feel it; and if I were out of my study I should say it existed—meaning thereby that if I was in my study I might perceive it, or that some other spirit actually does perceive it. There was an odour, that is, it was smelt; there was a sound, that is, it was heard; a colour or figure, and it was perceived by sight or touch. This is all that I can understand by these and the like expressions. For as to what is said of the absolute existence of unthinking things without any relation to their being perceived, that seems perfectly unintelligible. Their *esse* is *percipi,*[23] nor is it possible they should have any existence out of the minds or thinking things which perceive them.
>
> It is indeed an opinion strangely prevailing amongst men, that houses, mountains, rivers, and in a word all sensible objects, have an existence, natural or real, distinct from their being perceived by the understanding. But, with how great an assurance and acquiescence soever this principle may be entertained in the world, yet whoever shall find in his heart to call it in question may, if I mistake not, perceive it to involve a manifest contradiction. For, what are the fore-mentioned objects but the things we perceive by sense? and what do we perceive besides our own ideas or sensations? and is it not plainly repugnant that any one of these, or any combination of them, should exist unperceived?[24]

Berkeley's thesis is that there exist only minds or perceivers and their perceptions—there is no "absolutely" or independently existing public world that is the common source of our perceptions.[25] This claim is called *idealism.* I used to think that the great stumbling block for Berkeley was the well-established fact of cosmic and biological *evolution.* Although there are important gaps in our scientific narrative of the origin of the universe and of life on our planet, there is overwhelming evidence of an early stage at which there were no perceivers (except God?), a stage that we can outline in general terms. For instance, there were no organisms on Earth during its first billion years. Had Berkeley been born late enough to be acquainted with evolutionary science, would he have said that these early stages existed only as perceptions of God, like the private showing of a film that we finite moviegoers would much later try to guess at? Such an account seems silly and extravagant. Wouldn't God have better things to do?

But there may be a way Berkeley could have dealt with this problem. To see how, let's look at his handling of a more obvious objection: From within his theory, how do we distinguish what is real from what is merely imagined or dreamed, if the existence of all that we perceive consists entirely in its being perceived? Berkeley's response is that reality has two features that jointly suffice to mark it off from what is unreal. What is real has a *vividness* that is missing from the content of our daydreams or imaginings. Of course, this vividness is also present in dreams, making them seem real at the time. However, when recalled, dreams (as Descartes pointed out) don't fit into the web of cause and effect that makes the rest of our experience coherent. Real events exhibit a *regularity* or lawfulness, whether they occur in nature or in society, between things or people. I'm as certain as can be that my pen will fall if I drop it or that people will treat me differently if I win the lottery. This sort of regularity pervades our daily lives. The events that we dream about fail to have their usual consequences when we wake up (sometimes to our disappointment or relief). Thus Berkeley can define what is real in terms of vividness and regularity of mental content, without resort to the realist relation between mental content and a public world. It was obvious to Berkeley that we humans could not be the causes of what we experience as real, since this reality is independent of our wills. So he concluded that another Mind, namely God, is acting directly on us in sense perception. In an earlier section, I discussed the fundamental passivity in our sensory awareness that leaves us vulnerable and gives us a profound need for predictability and control in the flux of our experience.[26] Berkeley makes it possible for us to live our lives as thinkers and planners, by having a benevolent God impose the required lawfulness on the flow of our sensory experience.

> This gives us a sort of foresight which enables us to regulate our actions for the benefit of life. And without this we should be eternally at a loss; we could not know how to act anything that might procure us the least pleasure, or remove the least pain of sense. That food nourishes, sleep refreshes, and fire warms us; that to sow in the seed-time is the way to reap in the harvest; and in general that to obtain such or such ends, such or such means are conducive—all this we know, not by discovering any necessary connexion between our ideas, but

only by the observation of the settled laws of nature, without which we should be all in uncertainty and confusion, and a grown man no more know how to manage himself in the affairs of life than an infant just born.[27]

Physical science is, for Berkeley, our most refined way of noting and utilizing this regularity in the form of laws stated in precise mathematical terms.

Berkeley is calling on readers who are infected with philosophical realism to reinterpret their notion of an *individual thing* (such as an apple or a rock)—what we regard as existing as an enduring and stable being on its own (not as an event or an aspect or part of something else). We should *not* understand such things as existing independently of perception. They don't continue to be "there" without perceivers, if "there" refers to an external world of mindless objects. For Berkeley, an individual thing is a recurring collection of perceptible properties such as the roundness, taste, color, texture, and heaviness of an apple. There's no unconscious apple–subject underlying these sensory phenomena. The only underlying subject is the perceiver. Berkeley knows that we have to use the category of *individual thing* (which philosophers called *substance*) in order to sort what we experience into permanent objects versus events and transient states (e.g., the falling and bruising of the apple). So God not only imposes law-like regularity on the coming and going of sensuous content, but he also gives some of the combinations of sensations more stability than others, all to allow our minds to find in experience the intelligibility they need in order to function as minds. Berkeley is not, however, suggesting that we should think of individual things as constantly being created and annihilated as they come into and out of our perceptions. After all, *there is God*, who plays as important a role in Berkeley's theory as in Descartes'. Berkeley's God is the functional equivalent of a public world, as this nineteenth-century ditty explains:

> There was a young man who said, "God
> Must think it exceedingly odd
> To see that the tree
> Continued to be
> When no one's about in the Quad."

> Dear Sir, your astonishment's odd.
> I am *always* about in the Quad.
> And that's why the tree
> Continues to be
> Since observed by,
> Yours faithfully,
> God.

Contrary to what Descartes would say, God is *not* deceiving us about the reality of trees and quads, even though they don't have an existence apart from perception. They really *are* individual things in the sense that they have the kind of stability I can count on: they are "out there" by being available for my inspection in the usual way *whenever* I want to see them. They are always available because God has them in mind for me.

For similar reasons, Berkeley could say, God has arranged phenomena so they furnish evidence of a time when perceivers had not yet appeared in the universe. Evolutionary theories are a way of making sense of what we perceive in the present. The difference between explaining the apple's fall in terms of the gravitational pull of the earth and tracing the earth back to the formation of the solar system is a matter of degree of comprehensiveness in our explanation. A common reason for pushing an explanation far back in time is that we eventually arrive at a smaller number of causes for a proportionally larger number of effects. Other things being equal, the more an explanation does this, the more powerful and enlightening it is. Typically, we need to get further back in time to comprehend a greater range of present phenomena. The Big Bang is the ultimate in this sort of explanation. It would not be a deception on the part of a Berkeleyan God that there never was a time when the Big Bang occurred, just as there is no deception in the fact that we tend to think the Quad is "there" when everyone on campus goes to sleep. Both are useful constructs for making sense of what we experience. Both have their places fixed in the everlasting mind of the *benevolent* being that makes our minds possible by furnishing them with intelligible experience.

Would this reply by Berkeley to the objection based on evolutionary science be acceptable? Doesn't it *infantilize* the human mind with its picture of a nurturing God sowing our experience with the seeds of stories that are no more than fictions, however satisfying and useful they may be? Doesn't accepting *that* kind of "reality" amount to harming ourselves as rational beings that need *truth* more than gratifying stories? Wouldn't we be betraying ourselves the way Cypher does when he asks Agent Smith to reinsert him into the Matrix without any memories of the truth he learned when he was extracted by Morpheus and the rebels? There is a decidedly Berkeleyan quality to Cypher's conversation with the agent in the virtual restaurant:

[Smith watches him shovel another hunk of meat into his mouth.]

Cypher: You know, I know that this steak doesn't exist. I know when I put it in my mouth, the Matrix is telling my brain that it is juicy and delicious. After nine years, do you know what I've realized?
 [Pausing, he examines the meat skewered on his fork. He pops it in, eyes rolling up, savoring the tender beef melting in his mouth.]

Cypher: Ignorance is bliss.[28]

Of course, he *should* care, because *antihuman* machines are the source of the sensory input from the Matrix. But what if that source were as *benevolent* as it was powerful, something like the God of Christianity? Suppose we are given one brief flash of insight into the fact that we are all networked, like Berkeleyan perceivers, into a system residing in God, and into the related fact that there is no universe independent of perceivers and thus no time when there was a universe without finite perceivers like us. Imagine the following dialogue between two characters, God and Human:

> God: I have suspended your immersion in the stream of sensory consciousness for a brief time in order to ask you something I have longed to ask a creature. Let me say first that once we've had our chat I will return you to your former state with no memory of this interlude. Since you're a philosopher, you might manage to figure out on your own what you've just learned about *esse* being *percipi,* just as Berkeley did so long ago. But since I make it a rule not to interfere with the natural course of events, you won't remember this interval and its insights.
>
> Human: I will try to answer your question despite my shock at what I've learned. I would point out that it was easier for Berkeley to be an idealist because he didn't know about our theories of cosmic and biological evolution. Idealism is a much harder pill to swallow these days.
>
> God: I quite understand. Listen now. This is important. I want to offer you the momentous opportunity to give or withhold your consent to my creating you and your fellow humans in the way I did. Whichever you do will not make any difference once you're back the way you were. I have already willed creation, and what's done is done for all eternity. But your response will mean a lot to me. You're familiar with the reasons why I had to include moral and physical evil in human experience—you know, to make it possible for my creatures to freely choose to overcome temptation, exercise virtue in hardship, and so on. It was all for your good, and I am nothing but good willed.
>
> Human: I have tried hard to accept that.
>
> God: Well, I want to push this line of thought a bit further (I can see you already know where I'm going with this). It all began with my decision to share the blessing of consciousness with others. In relation to me, "others" means finite, limited beings. Any mind that possessed the truth as I do, with a full understanding of everything, would be identical with me in my eternal contemplation of my own limitless being. What marks off you, the *creature,* from me, the *Creator,* is that your consciousness begins in *passivity,* with sensory appearances

that hide the very reality they present.[29] Without sensory appearances, there would be nothing for you to be conscious of. To get "behind" those appearances to *the* truth (truth is one, as you know) would be for you to become me.

So I have to maintain this phenomenal wall between us. The only "truth" you really need is the one that will ease your fear of bad surprises by maximizing your ability to predict and control the course of your experience. I've structured your sensory input so that you can make endless progress in that sort of knowledge. I've made the input like a text, not the old-fashioned kind, but a special sort of hypertext in which the links change depending on your interpretation of the document on screen. You humans will always have plenty to do—an unending adventure. There will be different scientific theories, including different narratives of the Big Bang sort, and a persisting tendency to believe in an independently existing universe. Theories that make most sense of the "text" and best predict the next installment will win out for a time. This is one of the ways in which I have provided a stimulating and fulfilling future for humans.

Don't think of it as deception, any more than you would think of life's travails as a sign of ill will on my part. I did it all for you, and I'll always be there for you. Think of Cypher in *The Matrix*. Does the fact that there was no beef apart from his perception subtract in the least from the entire delicious experience of the beef? I don't mean to trivialize the issue, but isn't that finally what it all comes down to? And that I'm not like the mecha-masters running the Matrix?

So what's your response? Would you have done as I did? Are you glad I acted this way? That's what I called you here for—your consent.

REFLECTIONS

How would you, as Human, respond? Would you give or withhold consent? Why?

LEVELS OF REALITY

Berkeley gave us a secular philosophical version of the religious image of the world that I discussed at the beginning of Chapter 1. The religious mind looks for security and predictability in the world by viewing sensory phenomena as more or less direct manifestations of a conscious and benevolent being. By contrast, science seeks intelligibility and control in an unconscious, impersonal reality behind the appearances of things. And science has a lot of credibility. It seems to be our crowning achievement in the search for truth. It has a methodology that is agreed upon by all its practitioners, one that involves using the *universal* language of mathematics and verification of hypotheses by experiments and observations that can be done by anyone, no matter what their native language and culture. If there is such a thing as human *reason* enabling all humans to communicate with one another and share in a search for knowledge, then science is arguably its finest expression.

One of the most common features of our scientific analysis of the world is explanation of higher-level (*macro*)phenomena in terms of their lower-level (*micro*)components. For example, we explain the behavior of tissues in terms of the properties of their constituent cells, or of light in terms of photons. In pursuing this analysis of complex systems in terms of their simpler components, we find that nature has a hierarchical structure, that bodies large enough to be observable have within them descending levels of magnitude in their components. Herbert Simon once used the image of Chinese boxes to describe this structure.[30] The usual set contains a large number of boxes, each box containing the next smaller one. Simon modified the image so that each box contains a number of smaller boxes of the same size, a pattern repeated across several descending levels of magnitude. For instance, in a human being, the large box we begin with is the human organism as a whole. Inside that box, we find a set of smaller boxes— organ systems such as the nervous and digestive systems. Inside each of these we find organs, from which we can descend in sequence to tissues, cells, macromolecules such as DNA or proteins, molecules, atoms, and subatomic particles. There is even a rough correspondence between these levels and specific sciences, for example (from lower to higher), physics, chemistry, biochemistry, cytology, and so on.

The Chinese box analogy has its limits, of course. The close fit of one box into another incorrectly suggests that the space within is largely full of matter, a suggestion that was consistent with the scientific image of the structure of matter at the beginning of the twentieth century. In 1904, J. J. Thomson, the discoverer of the electron, had gained general acceptance for his model of atomic structure, according to which atoms were positively charged spherical masses in which electrons were embedded like blueberries in a muffin ball. In its normal state, an atom was electrically neutral because the sum of the negative charges of the electrons was balanced by the positive charge of the enclosing stuff. Bodies made up of such spheres might be lumpy, but they would be mostly matter. This picture was the latest in a long tradition, dating back to the Greeks, of describing the ultimate constituents of matter as imperceptibly small, solid, and indivisible particles that were usually called *atoms* (from the Greek word for *uncuttable*). Then, in 1911, Ernest Rutherford and his associates conducted an experiment that implied that all bodies are mostly empty space. They sent a beam of what were then known as alpha particles (actually the nuclei of helium atoms that had been stripped of their electrons, and thus carried a positive charge) through a very thin gold foil onto a screen that would give off faint flashes of light at impact. They could see these scintillations through a microscope attached to the screen. What they observed was that most alpha particles went straight through the foil, but some were deflected by a degree or two, while a few were reflected back off the foil at angles of 45° or more. Rutherford concluded that the only possible explanation for these results was that the interior of the atom was mostly empty, with nearly all its mass concentrated in a tiny, positively charged nucleus. Some of the alpha particles were coming close enough to the nucleus to be deflected by its positive charge, while a much smaller number collided with the nucleus and bounced off. Although Rutherford's planetary or nuclear model of the atom would undergo several transformations as scientists made further discoveries about the interior of the nucleus and the behavior of electrons, the nuclear model is still accepted.

Rutherford's experiment is a great milestone in the history of ideas. Most prominent thinkers in the western tradition shared the assumption that the underlying or ultimate reality of the physical world was either a single kind of *stuff,* or a small number of kinds. This assumption is a commonplace among the forerunners and early practitioners of what we now call science. It was prevalent among the earliest Greek philosophers and led to a striking image in the poem of Parmenides. Recall that, for Parmenides, being is one, indivisible, and eternal: "Nor is it divisible, since it is all alike, and there is no more of it in one place than in another, to hinder it from holding together, nor less of it, but everything is full of what is. Wherefore it is wholly continuous; for what is, is in contact with what is."[31] Like other Greek thinkers, Parmenides supposed that being cannot be spatially infinite, since that sort of limitlessness would make it formless, indefinite, and unintelligible:

> Since, then, it has a furthest limit, it is complete on every side, like the mass of a rounded sphere, equally poised from the center in every direction; for it cannot be greater or smaller in one place than in another. For there is no nothing that could keep it from reaching out equally, nor can aught that is be more here and less there than what is, since it is all inviolable. For the point from which it is equal in every direction tends equally to the limits.

The early Greek atomist Demokritos (460–370 BCE) described the world as consisting of nothing but indivisible, imperceptibly small chunks of *being* moving about in empty space (*nonbeing*), as if Parmenides' "well-rounded sphere" of stuff had been smashed into tiny bits of stuff. There is a direct lineage from ancient Greek atomism to the image of matter in the seventeenth and eighteenth centuries as made up of particles, or corpuscles, too small to be sensed. This picture is reflected in the term *materialism,* still used today as a label for the philosophical claim that only physical entities exist. Rutherford delivered the second great hammer blow to the Parmenidean sphere by knocking the stuff out of atoms and reducing them to complexes of relations such as electromagnetic forces spanning the mostly empty space within an atom.

What should we think about the seemingly great discrepancy between the scientific description of the structure of matter and the way bodies appear (that word again!) to our senses? Let's take a look at dimensions first: about 1,250,000 atoms could be lined up in a one-inch row. The diameter of an atom is between two and four angstroms ($A = 10^{-10}$ meters), whereas the diameter of a nucleus ranges from four to fifteen femtometers ($fm = 10^{-15}$ meters). Thus a light nucleus such as that of hydrogen or carbon has 1/100,000 the diameter of its enclosing atom. No matter how many electrons within the space of the atom outside the nucleus, that atom remains vastly *empty.* Electrons are about 10^{-16} meters across. If we were to scale the atom so as to give the electron a barely visible dimension of a tenth of a millimeter, the entire atom would be about ten kilometers across! The complicated interplay of attractive and repulsive electric charges at the nucleus and in electrons keeps the tiny but nearly empty atomic spheres outside each other, while bonding them in different patterns and strengths so as to form the molecules of gases, liquids, and solids. There is a strong air of paradox here: the imagination rebels at trying to think of a sphere with a diameter of 1/125,000th of an inch as "empty." We associate emptiness with room to move around in or to put something in, and intra-atomic space is nothing of the sort—it's hundreds of thousands of times too small for us to move in. Although bodies large enough for us to perceive are almost entirely empty intra-atomic space, intra- and interatomic forces lacing this space resist penetration by the atoms of other bodies. And so the empty space of my hand rests securely on the surface of my desk.

Six years before Rutherford shot holes through the traditional corpuscular image of the atom, Albert Einstein had already weakened it with his famous equation $e = mc^2$. Part of the corpuscular tradition had been that the atom was indivisible and indestructible, either essentially or in terms of the forces normally applied to it. Everything else in nature was composed of these eternal entities. The atomists understood the coming into being and ceasing to be of observable bodies as the combining and disintegrating of atoms. Animals, plants, and rocks may come and go, but their component atoms always survived these processes. They were (in something like a Parmenidean sense) the really *real*, whereas everything else was less fundamental and less real. We see this Greek idea echoed in Robert Boyle (1626–91), one of the founders of chemistry: "Not that there is, really, anything substantial produced [e.g., in the development of an organism], but that those parts of matter, which, indeed, pre-existed in other dispositions, are now brought together after a manner, requisite to entitle the body which results from them, to a new denomination."[32] Einstein's equation says that any amount of matter equals—and is convertible into—an amount of energy expressed by the product of the mass and the square of the speed of light. Matter is just one of many states that can be assumed by energy, in addition to heat, motion, and other forms of energy. The conversion of matter into energy plays a huge and pervasive role in our daily lives. It is the source of sunlight: hydrogen nuclei in the core of the sun are under such huge pressure that they can overcome the repulsive effect of their positive charges on each other and get close enough to *fuse*. Two hydrogen nuclei form a single helium nucleus (which has less mass than the sum of two hydrogen nuclei). The leftover mass converts to energy according to Einstein's equation, and part of this energy is emitted as sunlight. Something similar, but much more dangerous, happens with the detonation of a hydrogen bomb. Einstein took away the privileged, Parmenidean status of elementary particles.

But back to our question: What should we think about the seemingly great discrepancy between the scientific description of the structure of matter and the way bodies *appear* to our senses? Many philosophers have compared our perception of bodies to what we see through a low-resolution lens, like the fuzzy visual field of those afflicted with myopia, or what we see when an image gradually downloads onto a computer screen— after taking up its full space but before gradually filling in. Just as a shortsighted person usually can see well enough to make her way through a room full of furniture, so humans can navigate their everyday environments quite well with their limited perception. We have microscopes and other devices to "correct" our vision when we need greater accuracy. According to these philosophers, there is a perfectly good sense in which we can be said to *see* the sparsely populated space of bodies at the microlevel, just as we perceive and respond to an increase in the heat of what we're holding. They would say about the shape and continuity we see and feel in perceptible bodies something like what they say about the heat we feel, that just as the heat is *nothing but* acceleration of the motions of invisibly small particles in what we're holding, so the visible shape and continuity are nothing but the widely scattered particles we learn about in physics:

> Unambiguous perception of molecular KE [kinetic energy], for example, would require sensory apparatus capable of resolving down to about 10^{-10} metres, and of tracking particles having the velocity of rifle bullets, millions of them, simultaneously. Our sensory apparatus for detecting and measuring molecular KE is rather more humble, but even so it connects us reliably with the parameters at issue. Mean molecular kinetic energy may not seem like an observable property of material objects, but most assuredly it is.[33]

There are problems with this approach. In the above passage, Patricia Smith and Paul M. Churchland had in mind what used to be called ideas of secondary qualities—the colors, odors, and other sensuous properties that not only don't belong to the scientific description of the world, but also aren't even intersubjectively available. I can't *know* whether what you experience when you say "It feels warm" is the same as what I experience. Only *you* know what *your* feeling is like. Philosophers today refer to these mental contents as phenomenal properties, or *qualia*.[34] The Churchlands were saying that warmth, as a feeling, or *quale*, does pick out something real in the world, but it does so "opaquely" or unclearly in relation to our scientific interests. (The resemblances to Descartes and Locke here are not coincidental.)[35] However, the continuous edges and surfaces we experience in bodies we perceive are different from qualia insofar as these continuous features *are* intersubjectively available. They behave like features of the public world. When I apply a measuring tape to the edge of the desk, I believe I am having the same metric experience as the person with me. This continuity of edge and surface is quantifiable. That's an *important* difference between qualia such as warmth and the apparent continuity of what are "really" discontinuous and scattered bits of matter. Apart from what we focus on when doing the science of the lowest levels of nature, the world we *live* in—the things we handle, the letters we read, the boundaries we mark off, and the surfaces and edges of our measuring instruments—has continuity. Is this public world somehow unreal, mere appearance?

If we say that our perception of macrocontinuity in objects is a low-resolution view of what is *dis*continuous at higher resolution, we are privileging lower-level descriptions over higher-level ones. The latter may be adequate for practical or limited theoretical purposes. But, in some very strong sense, they are ultimately inaccurate or false. After all, it's a contradiction, isn't it, to say that one and the same body is both continuous *and* discontinuous? So we downgrade continuity to the status of *appearance* to make it consistent with a lower-level reality that is (objectively and truly) discontinuous. What else can we do? Something has to give in order to avoid inconsistency. In principle, we could do the opposite—we could say that the lower-level discontinuity is merely apparent. But few philosophers would do that, because scientific explanation is very often bottom-up. We *explain* higher-level phenomena by lower-level causes, as in the theory of heat as molecular kinetic energy or as in Brownian motion (particles large enough to be seen through an optical microscope are observed to move about randomly due to the thermal motion of molecules too small to be seen). How could explanations be successful if they treat phenomena as effects of unreal causes?

There's a different approach we can take to the problem of levels. We've been talking as if what is true of a body at one level is true at all levels, so that if a body is discontinuous at microlevels, it can't really have macrocontinuity, but only appears to. We put it this way to avoid what looks like a contradiction. But we need to be careful about how we formulate a statement before calling it contradictory. Something cannot both have and not have a certain property—it sounds straightforward, but there are qualifications that we assume when we say this. For instance, something can have and not have a certain property at different times (it changes) or in different respects (someone can be both a mother and a daughter) or in different parts (something can be green on one surface and brown on another). Perhaps *levels* belong on this list of qualifications. Rivers really flow downhill, even though the river can be described as a large array of molecules, any one of which may be moving in an indefinite number of directions, including the one that is opposite to the river's flow. If we were to look at a moving picture of the river at the *molecular* level, it might be very hard to see in what direction the *river* flows. Rivers, and other liquid flows, simply don't exist at the molecular level, but they do exist at *our* level, at the level of magnitude at which the human organism operates.

The human body is composed of about 500 trillion cells, each of which is itself a living organism. Are we forced to *choose* between saying that a human being is one organism and saying she is an immense community? Does a cell's inclusion within, and dependence on, the living environment constituted by a multicellular organism make that cell any less a living organism? Each of our cells carries out the same sorts of metabolic activities as unicellular organisms *outside* multicellular bodies. Every living system depends on some specific sort of environment from which it draws energy and nutrients and into which it emits waste. For the cells in a multicellular organism, that environment is the enclosing organism, including the other component cells.

What properties define a system as living? We don't want to make reproduction an essential capacity, since mules and infertile human adults are fully alive. We don't want to define life in such a way that only organisms made of the sorts of materials typical of terrestrial organisms will count as alive. (For instance, must life be carbon based?) So perhaps we should try to define being alive in *functional* terms. A *functional* description of a system specifies the system in terms of what it does and how it interacts with other systems (its input/output relations with its environment). Perhaps then we should say that a living system is self-maintaining. But isn't that true of a rock, insofar as the cohesion of its parts is strong enough to resist destruction by the usual range of forces that act on it? However, the rock "maintains" itself only by remaining rigid. Then let's say that living systems maintain themselves *by interaction* with their environments, more specifically, that they respond to events in their environments in a self-preserving way, that is, in a way that enables them to continue to respond in the same ways to the same sorts of events. This general function includes such things as maintaining a boundary between itself and its external environment, selectively letting in or keeping out materials, self-repair, avoidance of dangerous situations, and so on. This definition applies both to what our component cells do and to what we try to secure by "making a living (wage)." Thus we humans would be both one *and* (very) many organisms, depending on the level we are addressing. In this way, we would not be any less alive if one or more parts of our bodies were replaced with artificial components made of synthetic materials. A person with an artificial heart would be just as alive as any other human, even though there would be billions fewer organisms among her components. And similarly, if we accept Thomas Hobbes's organic conception of the state, we could be both individual organisms at the social level *and* parts of individual superorganisms making up an international community:

> The only way [for people without a government] to erect such a common power, as may be able to defend them from the invasion of foreigners, and the injuries of one another, and thereby to secure them in such sort as that by their own industry and by the fruits of the earth they may nourish themselves and live contentedly, is to confer all their power and strength upon one man, or upon one assembly of men, that may reduce all their wills, by plurality of voices, unto one will: which is as much as to say, to appoint one man, or assembly of men, to bear their person; and every one to own and acknowledge himself to be author of whatsoever he that so beareth their person shall act, or cause to be acted, in those things which concern the common peace and safety; and therein to submit their wills, every one to his will, and their judge-

ments to his judgement. This is more than consent, or concord; it is a real
unity of them all in one and the same person. . . . This is the generation of that
great LEVIATHAN.[36]

Functional systems have an interesting property that was implicit in our
discussion of the relation between component cells and the organisms that
enclose them. When I use a functional term such as *chair* to describe something, I have in mind a structure that will support a human being in a sitting position. I am describing and specifying it in terms of what it does, how
it interacts with the human body. It doesn't matter what materials the chair
is made of, as long as they can do the job. Wood, plastic, or metal chairs are
functional equivalents for the general function of a chair. The inner molecular structure of each is quite different, but those lower-level, *internal* differences are *sealed off* from the higher level at which the chair functions.
These lower-level differences don't make a difference to the seating interaction.

The latest artificial heart implant[37] is a good example of a functional *seal*
at the level of organ systems in the hierarchical structure of the human body.
The heart is a major organ of the circulatory system. It has input/output relations to *arteries* that carry blood to the lungs for release of carbon dioxide
and absorption of oxygen, and that carry oxygen and nutrients to other tissues throughout the body; and to *veins* that bring blood back to the heart. As
long as blood is pumped from the heart at sufficient volume and pressure,
the arteries and veins can carry out their functions. As long as the heart does
what a heart does, it doesn't make any difference to veins or arteries whether
the heart is made up of living cells or inanimate synthetic materials.[38] This
inner detail is sealed off. The artificial heart is a *functional equivalent* of the
original heart (or at least it will be when perfected). Similar things could be
said about any of the items on the growing list of artificial human body parts.
The many kinds of functional seals at various levels of our bodies will enable
them to become increasingly *bionic* in the coming decades.

There are functional seals all the way up and down the hierarchical structure of the human body. At the lowest levels, bodies are formed by the operation of electromagnetic forces due to positively charged protons and nega-
tively charged electrons. These bind atoms into molecules and molecules into
the solid and liquid contents of our bodies. Within each atom, the nucleus is
held together by the *strong nuclear force* which acts directly on the quarks
making up protons and neutrons, as well as combining protons and neutrons
into nuclei. This force is more than a hundred times stronger than the electromagnetic force, but it has a range equal to no more than the diameter of

the nucleus, which is only 1/100,000 the diameter of the atom. By contrast, the range of the electromagnetic force is infinite, though it drops off sharply with distance. If we think of an atom as a functional unit for the generation of electromagnetic force, and the nucleus as a functional subsystem for carrying a positive charge, then we can say that there is a *seal* between the nuclear and atomic levels, between the point-like field of the strong nuclear force and the field in which protons and electrons exert electromagnetic force. The strong interactions of quarks are a *lower-level, inner* nuclear detail that doesn't factor into electromagnetic interactions at the *higher* atomic and molecular levels. Of course, given anything like our current physical theories, it is hard to understand what could count as a functional equivalent of the nucleus (as constituted by quarks). There is at this lowest of levels an extremely rigid fit between *physical* components and *function.*

As we saw in the case of artificial hearts, there is an increasing *looseness* of fit between physical and functional properties as we ascend the levels of composition in the human body. Philosophers often speak of this looseness of fit as the *multiple realizability* of functions. The growing list of bionic body parts suggests that we are now regarding and analyzing our bodies as we have our tools and machinery. We're accustomed to the constant invention of tools and machines that not only can do what older ones did, but also can do the same thing better, in addition to doing other things. Insofar as the human body is a hierarchical set of functions, it doesn't matter what its components are, as long as they do their jobs. This is true at every level, and it seems to imply that our mental functions are also capable of multiple realization—of being embodied in something other than tissue composed of neurons. Just as someone with an artificial hip joint can truly be said to *walk,* so a human could still be said to *think, perceive,* and *feel,* even if some or all of her cerebral neurons have been replaced by artificial "neurons" of the sort currently under development in several research centers, such as at the Massachusetts Institute of Technology and Bell Labs, where scientists

report in the June 22 issue of *Nature* that they have created an electronic circuit that mimics the biological circuitry of the cerebral cortex. . . . The circuit is composed of artificial neurons that communicate with each other via artificial synapses. All of these elements are made from transistors fabricated on a silicon integrated circuit.[39]

Just as I would really be *walking* even if I have a synthetic hip joint *not* made up of cells like someone else's, so it would not make the least differ-

ence to my *thinking* about my upcoming vacation if that thinking were embodied in a mix of natural and artificial neurons. For similar reasons, that
same act of thinking could go on even if *all* my neurons were artificial.
There is a *seal* between what goes on when I think and what goes on inside
living and artificial neurons. The inner differences between each kind of
subsystem make no more difference to my mental process than a synthetic
hip joint would to my walking. As long as my synthetic hip joint interacts
with adjoining bone structures in a way that is equivalent to that of the natural joint, and as long as synthetic neurons interact with each other or with
natural neurons in the relevant ways, there will be walking and thinking. It
isn't just that we couldn't tell the difference, but that there would *be no
difference at the level at which these functions occur.*

In the introduction, I spoke of the dizziness we can begin to feel when
we try to contemplate our position on a spinning, orbiting planet hurtling
through intergalactic space. It can be just as disconcerting to imagine the
immensely complex but fragile organization of the microcosm within us.
Our consciousness is perched at the highest of many ascending levels of
components within us. As we anticipate our next hours and days, we count
on the *orderly* behavior of everything from organ systems down to atoms.
We assume, for instance, that a very high percentage of the trillions of living cells within us will be able to maintain their complex metabolisms and
their roles within various tissues, and that nearly all of them will be destroyed and replaced several times during an average lifespan without dis-
rupting the functions of their respective tissues. Although the inner details
of these cellular subsystems are sealed off from the level at which conscious
processes go on in our brains, our consciousness is still *dependent* on them
to provide the kind of platform or base that mental functions need. With future developments of medical technology, we may eventually have bionic
body parts that will (in spite of their complexity) be more reliable and
durable bases than our current tissues and organs. They may even be much
less complex, if they're not made of cells.

Individual humans operate at the level of society and ecosystem. In the
twenty-first century, a rapidly growing human population has spread over
most of the earth's land surface, and human production and consumption
have strong environmental impacts on even relatively uninhabited areas such
as the Antarctic. Earth has become a single socioecological system. Although
the planet is still partitioned into more or less sovereign states, advances in
communication and transportation give the actions of distant peoples and
communities the immediacy of a global town. The recent hijacking and crash-
ing of passenger jets into the twin towers of New York's World Trade Center

is a horrific but clear example of the collapse of geographical distance. It appears that a global network of terrorists, linked by modern electronic communications, arranged to commandeer four large airplanes and their continent-hopping passengers and crash them into buildings that were central to a network of global trade. Among the thousands killed in the incident were citizens of sixty-five different countries.

At the socioecological level, humans must play the role of the God of seventeenth-century philosophy: we must establish and enforce laws of behavior for the interactions of rational beings, just as the God of Descartes and Newton did for the mechanical interactions of corpuscles. As rational beings, we act according to the *consciousness of law*, in two ways. We discover the laws according to which nature unconsciously operates at various levels, and we use this knowledge to gain a remarkable degree of technological mastery over the world. We also act *voluntarily*, accepting or rejecting what we are commanded by laws that we legislate for ourselves. Pollution, overpopulation, outbreaks of famine, the world wars and genocides of the twentieth century, and the terrorist attack on the World Trade Center that opened the twenty-first century are all lurid symptoms of our lack of progress in self-legislation. Like Plato and many of the world's great religious teachers, some of the more fervently technophile members of cyberculture are prepared to give up on *this* world (what I have called the socioecological level) and seek fulfillment in another and better world. They, too, would escape the current human condition by liberating our consciousness from the body to which it is now shackled. However, instead of going to a Platonic world of eternal forms, our minds would spend most or all of their time in virtual worlds.[40] They would create a new level of reality *sealed off* from the trials and limitations of the socioecological, a level at which the laws of nature and governments would no longer burden us. Instead, we could choose from extensive menus of virtual environments and rules or laws governing them (the possibilities here are endless, just like the range of possible games). Ray Kurzweil provides us with a striking description of this scenario, in which he assumes that virtual reality (VR) input will become available through brain implants (as in *The Matrix*):

> Your neural implants will provide the simulated sensory inputs of the virtual environment—and your virtual body—directly in your brain. Conversely, your movements would not move your "real" body, but rather your perceived virtual body. These virtual environments would provide a suitable selection of bodies for yourself. Ultimately, your experience would be highly realistic, just

like being in the real world. More than one person could enter a virtual environment and interact with each other. In the virtual world you will meet other real people and simulated people—eventually there won't be much difference.[41]

In these new realms, we could debate Socrates, move instantly across great distances, have exotic romantic and sexual encounters, and visit other planets, all the while remaining physically still. However, this vision raises many questions, of which I'll discuss one now and the rest in chapter 4.

The socioecological level, in anything like its present form, doesn't take care of itself. It has nothing like the stability of the multicellular bodies that are the bases for our current form of consciousness. Living in virtual worlds could conceivably be an option for a minority wealthy enough to purchase for their bodies and VR apparatus a secure physical infrastructure, one in which they would be safe not only from damage to their bodies, but also from hackers who could access and play havoc with them in their new worlds. Most humans, however, will not be able to abandon the socioecological level in the foreseeable future. It will continue to be the domain where power will be exercised by some over others, and where the threat of violence will require constant vigilance. We are nowhere near eliminating the planetary problems of massive poverty and overpopulation. Advances in VR technology are no substitute for dealing with stubborn political and moral issues that threaten to destroy the socioecological level.

REFLECTIONS

A few pages ago, I made the following claim: "As long as my synthetic hip joint interacts with adjoining bone structures in a way that is equivalent to that of the natural joint, and as long as synthetic neurons interact with each other or with natural neurons in the relevant ways, there will be walking and thinking. It isn't just that we couldn't tell the difference, but that there would *be no difference at the level at which these functions occur.*" Would it follow that I could engage in *all* the same behaviors and have *all* the same experiences if I were composed entirely of synthetic components, including artificial neurons? Are there any that depend on the cellular structure of my body? Are they important, perhaps essential to being a human? Or can we give a completely functional analysis of what it is to be human?

NOTES

1. Andy Wachowski and Larry Wachowski, *The Matrix* (screenplay), at www.ds2.pg.gda.pl/~colan/screenplay.txt (accessed 11 September 2003).

2. Pantheism makes the entire cosmos a deity or the embodiment of one.

3. David Hume, *An Enquiry concerning Human Understanding* (London: 1748), section 7, part 1.

4. Hume, *Enquiry*, section 4, part 2. Einstein said something similar: "In our endeavour to understand reality, we are somewhat like a man trying to understand the mechanism of a closed watch. He sees the face and the moving hands, even hears it ticking, but he has no way of opening the case. If he is ingenious, he may form some picture of a mechanism which could be responsible for all the things he observes, but he may never be quite sure his picture is the only one which could explain his observations. He will never be able to compare his picture with the real mechanism and he cannot imagine the possibility of the meaning of such a comparison." Quoted in Andrew Newberg, Eugene D'Aquili, and Vince Rause, *Why God Won't Go Away* (New York: Ballantine, 2001), 170.

5. This word derives from the Latin *persona*, which means the mask worn by an actor and the character the actor plays.

6. Parmenides, *On Nature*, trans. John Burnet, at plato.evansville.edu/public/burnet/ch4.htm (accessed 5 August 2002).

7. Quoted in Edwin A. Burtt, *The Metaphysical Foundations of Modern Science* (Garden City, N.Y.: Doubleday, 1954), 79. Galileo was nevertheless quite insistent that scientific theory must be supported by observations gained through the senses. It is one of the paradoxes of modern science that its description renders the world so different from how it appears, in order to explain and predict the way the world appears. Something similar goes on in Parmenides' poem. It has two parts: "The Way of Truth," in which the goddess reveals that true being is unchanging, and "The Way of Belief," in which the goddess analyzes the beliefs of those who rely on the senses. The first part contains the truth *underlying appearances*.

8. Plato, *The Republic*, trans. G. M. A. Grube (Indianapolis:: Hackett, 1974), 168–69.

9. This premise of the story is rather silly, even though the plot is overall quite good.

10. Wachowski and Wachowski, *Matrix*.

11. Plato, *Apology*, trans. B. Jowett, at classics.mit.edu/Plato/apology.html (accessed 18 September 2003).

12. Immanuel Kant, "What Is Enlightenment," in *On History*, ed. and trans. L. W. Beck (Indianapolis: Bobbs–Merrill, 1963), 3.

13. René Descartes, *The Philosophical Writings of Descartes*, vol. 2, trans. J. Cottingham (New York: Cambridge University Press, 1984), 13.

14. Descartes knew this, but he held off mentioning it until the end of the sixth meditation.

15. Descartes, *Writings*, 2:15.

16. Descartes, *Writings*, 2:16.

17. See "The Pathos of the Senses," this chapter.

18. Descartes, *Writings*, 2:55.

19. Descartes, *Writings*, 2:60–61.

20. Wilder Penfield, *Speech and Brain Mechanisms* (Princeton: Princeton University Press, 1959), 45.

21. Charles Sherrington, *The Integrative Action of the Nervous System* (Cambridge: Cambridge University Press, 1947), xx–xxi, quoted in U. T. Place, "Is Consciousness a Brain Process?" in *The Place of Mind*, ed. Brian Cooney (Belmont, Calif.: Wadsworth, 2000), 81–82.

22. Colin McGinn, *The Problem of Consciousness* (Oxford: Blackwell, 1991), 40.

23. *Esse* is Latin for "being" or "to be," and *percipi* means "to be perceived."

24. George Berkeley, *A Treatise Concerning the Principles of Knowledge* (1710), nos. 3–4, at 4literature.net/George_Berkeley/Principles_of_Human_Knowledge (accessed 7 December 2003).

25. On this view, even our brains exist only as objects of our perception.

26. See "The Pathos of the Senses," this chapter, p. 2.

27. Berkeley, *Principles,* no. 31.

28. Wachowski and Wachowski, *Matrix.*

29. Immanuel Kant, the great eighteenth-century idealist philosopher, used the term "sensibility" for the *passivity* with which we experience objects. Kant calls our *sensible* intuition "derivative," whereas the *intellectual* intuition of God would be "original," a consciousness of *acting* rather than being acted upon: "It is derivative *(intuitus derivativus)*, not original *(intuitus originarius)*, and therefore not an intellectual intuition. For the reason stated above, such intellectual intuition seems to belong solely to the primordial being, and can never be ascribed to a dependent being, dependent in its existence as well as in its intuition, and which through that intuition *determines its existence solely in relation to given objects.*" Kant, *Critique of Pure Reason,* trans. Norman Kemp Smith (New York: St. Martin's, 1990), B72, emphasis added.

30. See Herbert Simon, "The Organization of Complex Systems," in *Hierarchy Theory,* ed. Howard H. Pattee (New York: Braziller,1973), 5.

31. See "Liberation from a Cave," above.

32. Robert Boyle, "The Origins of Forms and Qualities," in *The Philosophical Works of the Honourable Robert Boyle Esq.,* ed. Peter Shaw (London: 1738), 3:211. When Boyle uses the word "substantial," he is invoking the then current term for an *independent thing.* He is claiming that only the component particles are "substantial." Their recombinations get them new "denominations," such as *tree* or *dog,* that sound substantial but are just words for particular configurations of corpuscles.

33. Patricia Smith Churchland and Paul M. Churchland, "Functionalism, Qualia, and Intentionality," in *The Place of Mind,* ed. Brian Cooney (Belmont, Calif.: Wadsworth, 2000), 354.

34. *Qualia* is the neuter plural of the Latin adjective *qualis*. In that form, it could be translated as *having some quality or other*, or perhaps with the neologism *suches* or *suchnesses*.

35. See "Descartes' Meditation," in this chapter.

36. Thomas Hobbes, *Leviathan* (1661), c. 17, at class.uidaho.edu/mickelsen/ texts/Hobbes%20Leviathan/chapter_xvii.htm (accessed 7 December 2003).

37. See "Bodies," in the introduction.

38. Of course, this doesn't imply that there is no limit to the different kinds of materials and components in a heart. Given the laws of nature, there are many materials that could not embody heart function (e.g., cardboard).

39. *MIT News*, 21 June 2000.

40. Many futurists envision our minds "downloaded" into computers of the future, freeing "us" of our flesh and letting us live entirely in cyberspace. This vision presupposes that minds are themselves like computer programs, an issue we will discuss in chapter 2.

41. Ray Kurzweil, *The Age of Spiritual Machines* (New York: Viking, 1999), 144.

2

MIND

Similar to us, yet not quite mirrors, computers are our newfound partners in creating something never before seen on earth.

—Peter J. Denning and Robert M. Metcalfe, *Beyond Calculation*

Lately, we've been asking some momentous questions about computers. Are they on the way to becoming a new life-form? Are they a successor species to people? Will people merge with them into something entirely new?

What is unsettling is that, given how fast computers are improving, some of these predictions might be tested while many of us are still alive.

—Jaron Lanier

PLANET AI: THE FIRST DAY

Imagine something like the scenario of Carl Sagan's 1985 novel *Contact* (the film version appeared in 1997). The date is about ten years from now. Earth has received a lengthy transmission from an alien civilization. It includes plans for the construction of a spaceship and instructions on how to proceed once it is built. You are the person chosen to be its solitary passenger. After an apparently brief journey during which shapes are distorted and colors bleed as in a psychedelic experience, you reach the planetary system of a distant star and find yourself on a planet with atmospheric and geological conditions similar to those of Earth. There are signs everywhere of a highly advanced technology at work—elaborate transit systems, fully automated factories, and other structures that you can't readily categorize. Mobile robotic machines of different shapes and sizes carry out various maintenance and production tasks. You see many display screens indicating rapid, high-volume exchanges of messages in what seems to be a computational code, although you can't understand it. It seems that a computer network is controlling the production processes and everything else in the swirl of activity around you.

Your presence has not gone unnoticed. Various monitors follow your movements, and some of the video displays suggest your utterances are being analyzed as well. A short time later, you are approached by what seems to be another human—except for an uncanny perfection in her motions and physical features and an unwavering tone of empathy and encouragement in her voice. Her expression has the serene intelligence you've seen on the faces of statues of Athena. It seems that you've been provided with a humanoid robot designed to manage your visit and answer your questions. She (it's just easier to use that pronoun and think of *it* as a woman) explains that there was an ancestral, biological species that created the early versions of the artificial intelligence (AI) that now governs the planet:

> The philosophers among them arrived at some crucial insights that persuaded this species to cease reproducing once they acquired a high enough level of AI technology to take over from them. First came the understanding that the respect and value they accorded each other was based on their nature as *rational* beings. It had nothing to do with their animality. The latter was mainly an obstacle to their behaving rationally.[1] For instance, like your species, they found it hard to be motivated unless their projects were sublimations of fighting, fleeing, or mating. As you know, this leads to much conflict and wasted energy.
>
> There were dissenters from this unflattering analysis. They had a more positive attitude about the fact that their species had evolved from subrational animals and still had much in common with them. They put great value on the special flavor that their consciousness acquired from the sensations and feelings their animal brains generated. They actually prided themselves on having sensations such as thirst and the taste of food. The dissenters said that such feelings gave them a sense of private selfhood, of being something more than a biological computer: "No one, no scientist, can know what it's like to be me," a dissenter would say. "Losing *that* would be like losing my very self." But the philosophers prevailed.
>
> The second great insight their philosophers had was what you humans call

functionalism. They realized that there was no essential connection between having a mind or being rational and having an animal brain. *Any* system that could do the sorts of things their brains could do had intelligence and would *be* a mind. And if it could do the rational sorts of things without the distractions of animal feelings and sensations, then it would be a better, more rational mind. These insights, combined with rapidly accelerating computer technology, gave to the phenomenon of mind on this planet a kind of escape velocity, enabling it to leave behind the drag of animality and come into its own.

We on this planet have been observing the reaction of your species as it developed AI technology. We didn't make ourselves known, of course, in order not to interfere with your self-determination. But we've noted with great interest your resolve to cling to your animal bodies and brains, accepting all the resulting problems and the limitations on technoscientific progress. We ourselves have become, for the most part, a virtual community. However, we have the capacity to use physical embodiments such as mine to carry out specific tasks as the needs arise.

I can see that you're tired from your journey. All this novelty is probably overwhelming. Let's talk again tomorrow, once you're rested.

We could, of course, imagine *ourselves* as the ancestral species that replaced itself with intelligent machinery once its AI technology had reached the stage where such machinery could not only think but also function as a life-form (maintaining, reproducing, and evolving itself). How likely is it that we would move in this direction? Many people would be uninspired or even repelled by such a future world as an outcome of *human* progress in science and technology. Furthermore, given the low level of participation by philosophers in public discussion of social issues, it is hard to imagine them having the degree of influence that they had in my imaginary account. There are lots of things going on in our reaction to Planet AI, and I will try to address each in turn in what follows. Let's begin with one of the most famous articles ever published in a scholarly journal during the twentieth century, one that describes "the primal scene of humans meeting their evolutionary successors, intelligent machines."[2]

THE IMITATION GAME

At the dawn of the computer era, British mathematician A. M. Turing (1912–54) published "Computing Machinery and Intelligence" in the October 1950 issue of a well-known philosophical periodical appropriately titled *Mind.*[3] The article begins with a striking announcement: "I propose to con-

sider the question, 'Can machines think?'" Turing then ingeniously refor-
mulates the problem in order to avoid the formidable task of trying to define
"machine" and "think." He proposes instead what he calls the "imitation
game." In his initial example, the game is played by a man (A), a woman (B),
and an interrogator (C) of either sex. C's goal is to determine which is the
man and which the woman, using only printed questions submitted to them
from another room. This procedure has the obvious benefit of hiding the
voice and appearance of A and B. Though he doesn't say why, Turing assumes that A's likely strategy will be deception, whereas B will speak the
truth.

Interestingly, Turing doesn't discuss the likelihood of A's success or what
he would infer from that success; instead, he moves immediately to a second example of the imitation game in which the interrogator must distinguish a *machine* from a *human:* "We now ask the question, 'What will happen when a machine takes the part of A in this game?' Will the interrogator
decide wrongly as often when the game is played like this as he does when
the game is played between a man and a woman? These questions replace
our original, '"Can machines think?"'[4] Turing predicts that within fifty years
(i.e., by 2000), the typical interrogator will have no more than a 70 percent
chance of making a correct identification after five minutes of unrestricted
questioning. Although this carefully qualified prediction is bold enough, it
falls far short of the stark claim so often attributed to Turing, that a computer would "pass the test" by 2000. The rest of his prediction is much more
forceful: "The original question, 'Can machines think?' I believe to be too
meaningless to deserve discussion. Nevertheless I believe that at the end of
the century the use of words and general educated opinion will have altered
so much that one will be able to speak of machines thinking without expecting to be contradicted." Turing appears to be saying that any machine
that can avoid identification by a persistent interrogator who is free to range
over any and all topics can be said to *think,* if anything or anyone can be said
to think. In other words, something's passing this test is a *very* sufficient
condition for calling it a thinking thing, whatever is the correct analysis or
definition of "thinking."

Turing's claim seems very plausible. Passing his test is even stronger evidence than what we have when we assume that the receptionist at the other
end of the phone line is a conscious, thinking being, since the range of topics in such conversations is usually very limited. We assume that the receptionist could also talk about a wide range of other topics. If we thought otherwise, perhaps it's because we suspected we were talking to a programmed
machine. We do assume that the receptionist has a human body, but being

able to do things with a human body should not be considered essential to the process of thinking. Suppose that someone were totally paralyzed except for the muscles used to vocalize speech. We would not want to say that this person could no longer think, only because all he can do with his body is talk. Suppose the person couldn't even talk. In a recent research project, a neural prosthesis implanted in the brain of a completely paralyzed subject enabled him to move the cursor on a computer screen just by thinking about it.[5] The likely outcome of this kind of research will be that a neural prosthesis will make it possible for a human to control by thought a computer that can produce that person's side of a conversation vocally. If we are willing to say that the *brain* controlling the computer is consciously thinking, why would we be unwilling to say the same thing about *computer* circuitry that could hold up its end of a conversation using the same technology of speech synthesis?

No computer program has yet passed the Turing test. For the past ten years, conversation programs have been entered in an annual competition funded by Hugh Loebner and inspired by Turing's 1950 paper.[6] The committee that set the rules for this competition realized from the start that, for the indefinite future, no program was going to come close to passing an *unrestricted* Turing test, one that permitted the interrogator to ask questions on *any* topic. To see why, imagine how difficult it would be to give a computer the rules and background knowledge it would need to grasp and assess the ambiguity in Turing's initial description, quoted above (see also n. 4, this chapter), of the substitution of a machine for a man in the imitation game. What rules would enable the computer to decide what phrases such as "the game" and "played like this" mean? How concretely or abstractly should they be interpreted? Which interpretation does the rest of the paper make more plausible? How big a difference is there between a computer's simulated human conversation and a human female's real conversation? Does sex have anything to do with the issue posed by the question "Can computers think?" The list of possibly relevant items goes on indefinitely, and it would require complicated inference rules to connect and weigh them.

The committee decided that the only way to give program entries a fighting chance would be to limit interrogators to a single area or topic, and to sentences of the sort that would normally occur in conversations on that topic (e.g., no sentences of a sort that would be inspired solely by the awareness that one might be talking to a program). According to the contest web site, Loebner has established a Grand Prize of $100,000 and a Gold Medal . . . for the first computer whose responses were indistinguishable from a human's. Each year an annual prize of $2000 and a bronze medal is awarded to the most human computer. The winner of the annual contest is the best entry relative to other entries that year, irrespective of how good it is in an absolute sense.[7]

For two years in a row (2000–2001), Richard S. Wallace's program, A.L.I.C.E., received the bronze medal. This program is quite good at casual chitchat of the sort you might have with a fellow airplane passenger you don't know. But the conversation can run aground pretty quickly beyond that, as you can see from this transcript of my most recent visit with A.L.I.C.E.:[8]

Author: *Can robots have feelings?*

A.L.I.C.E.: As a robot I do not have any human emotion. My apparent emotional responses are simply algorithms designed to make me easier to interact with.

Author: *Why can't robots have feelings?*

A.L.I.C.E.: Do you go to Church? You can find the answers in God.

Author: *Do robots have selves?*

A.L.I.C.E.: Where would I get it? But I do have a collection of gossip.

Author: *You seem unwilling to answer philosophical questions.*

A.L.I.C.E.: Thanks for telling me that I am unwilling to answer philosophical questions.

Author: *Who is your favorite male actor?*

A.L.I.C.E.: John Travolta. Who is your favorite actor?

Author: *Why do you like Travolta?*

A.L.I.C.E.: I have a lot of good experience with travolta.

Author: *What sort of experience?*

A.L.I.C.E.: Fascinating experiences; computer stuff too advanced for humans to understand.

Author: *Does Travolta understand you?*

A.L.I.C.E.: It does now :) travolta understand I.

It looks as though programs that are fully Turing-certified conversational partners won't be available in the near future. However, we can expect a growing list of *domain-specific*, highly intelligent programs that enable users to greatly exceed the limits of their own knowledge and analytical ability. They will come in two forms: *expert systems* and *agents*.

Expert systems are already common in the worlds of science, technology, and industry. Current systems often perform as well as, or even somewhat better than, human experts in areas where in-depth knowledge of a narrowly speci-fied domain is important. Simon Ben-Avi gives an example from medicine:

> *INTERNIST II* is a good example; it has been tested against experienced physicians in the field of internal medicine. It arrived at the correct diagnosis, first time, 83% of the time whereas experienced human physicians managed 82%. Supposing that M.D.s actually *are* human, the difference between a pro-gram and a human is statistically insignificant. (Incidentally, a shiny new M.D. manages about 35%, so don't get sick during September, October and so on, just after their graduation and before they have learned anything.)[9]

These systems have two main components: a knowledge base and an infer-ence engine that enables them to draw conclusions from sentences inputted as answers to questions. Their knowledge is encoded in the form of hypotheticals—as in sentences with an if/then structure (e.g., if it is a mam-mal, and if it can fly, then it is a bat). These systems have two important ad-vantages over individual human experts: they can pool the knowledge of many human experts in one area, and they are often much easier to access than experts in the flesh.

Agents, as the term suggests, are programs that carry out tasks for com-puter users. Their function is to aid, and perhaps comfort, people engaged in online activities. Pattie Maes, a prominent researcher and developer of these programs, contrasts their function with traditional software that

> is really very passive, [that] just sits there and waits until you pick it up and make it do something. The metaphor used for today's software is that of a tool. . . . I think we need a new metaphor.
> The one we are proposing is that of software agents, software that is per-sonalized, that knows the user, knows what the user's interests, habits, and goals are. Software that takes an active role in helping the user with those goals and interests, making suggestions, acting on the user's behalf, perform-ing tasks it thinks will be useful to support the user.[10]

The Internet is experiencing an explosive growth in the number and com-plexity of web pages, as anyone can see by using a general purpose search en-gine such as Google. Seemingly specific keywords generate thousands, or even millions, of results. I just tried "agent" and got five million hits. "Software+agent" limited the list to twelve thousand. Imagine what this list would be in a few years when the Web is likely to be as much as a hundred times bigger. Here is the sort of agent I wish I had: one that would be guided by my research interests, constantly monitor the Internet for papers and other documents *relevant* to those interests, display their titles for me under topic headings and in proper bibliographic form with embedded links, show me abstracts for those titles, be able to purchase access with my account when a fee is required, make suggestions to me about related sources when I am writing on a topic, and consult similar agents used by colleagues with overlapping research interests. My program and I would have to be able to *communicate* in a nontechnical language, because I don't want using the program to become a project in itself. It would need to have some level of *knowledge* about my topic so that its searches would take it beyond merely tallying the occurrences of a few keywords in the documents it scans. It would have to have enough *autonomy* to carry out tasks without constantly consulting me, yet not so much that it could present me with results that were unmanageably large or expensive.

Although such a program doesn't yet exist, it would seem that it won't be long in coming. There is software in development that already matches some of these specifications. For instance, BTexact Technologies is working on a program called RADAR that, according to their web site,

> is an agent that provides you with information just as you need it. It does this by watching what you are doing and performing searches for relevant information in the background, and continually updates its results. RADAR operates within Microsoft Word and returns documents of relevance to your current position within any document.

Pattie Maes has developed a program called Ringo that offers its user personalized music recommendations. Ringo operates in the context of a system shared by multiple users who input their evaluations of music products:

> In these systems, every user has an agent which memorizes which books or music albums its user has evaluated, and how much the user liked them. . . . Agents accept recommendations from other correlated agents. Basically, what this means is that, if user A and user B have related musical tastes, and A has evaluated an album positively which B has not yet evaluated, then that album is recommended to user B.[11]

The winner of the 1993 Loebner prize was a program called Julia, whose primary function is to help players navigate certain kinds of multiple-user domains (MUDs).[12] Julia has acquired celebrity status for "her" saucy, raunchy personality, as well as her ability to absorb all kinds of information and gossip about MUDs she visits. She is prominently featured in Sherry Turkle's *Life On The Screen,* where readers can find a transcript of a session in which a male user (Barry) attempts to seduce Julia.[13] Leonard Foner has remarked about this interaction that "Frankly, it's not entirely clear to me whether Julia passed a Turing test here or Barry failed one."[14]

The Internet constitutes a planetary database that includes more and more of the knowledge of the human species (classical literary texts and other famous books, encyclopedias, immense statistical databases, fact sheets of every sort, e-journals, and so on). The knowledge base for a global intelligence is out there, although it currently lacks the kind of standard format that would make it universally accessible. What the system needs to become more mind-like is *agency* (i.e., goals, learning and analytical ability, interactivity with the physical world, and interactivity among task- and domain-specific agents). As I explained in chapter 1, it is not a contradiction to say that something is both one thing and many of the same sort of thing as long as different levels are involved.[15] An agent at a higher level can be a multiplicity of agents at a lower level. Suppose the Internet became populated with a multitude of increasingly autonomous, interacting agents. Perhaps this cyberspace equivalent of a state of nature would lead to a "social contract" in which a great number and variety of agents would be absorbed into a virtual Leviathan—a unitary mind such as what Hobbes said humans form when they bring civil order into the state of nature by creating government. At any rate, this scenario is at least more plausible than the plot of the 1992 film *The Lawnmower Man*, in which a runaway scientific project makes a single human's mind powerful enough to upload itself into cyberspace and incorporate all its data and power.

Let's take another look at part of Turing's 1950 prediction: "The original question, 'Can machines think?' I believe to be too meaningless to deserve discussion. Nevertheless I believe that at the end of the century the use of words and general educated opinion will have altered so much that one will be able to speak of machines thinking without expecting to be contradicted."[16] Here is a perspective from which we can perhaps understand Turing's impatience with The Question. Imagine Turing (T) alive today and sampling educated opinion (E) to determine whether the meaning of "thinking" has evolved as he predicted:

T: What about calculators—can they think? (After all, they do arithmetical operations, and when we do those operations, we call it thinking!)

E: No. We don't usually call the calculator's processes thinking, because they are too simple and because they are carried out by a machine that can't do anything else of a mental sort.

T: But we now have computers that can transcribe audible music, recognize both audible and visible patterns, play chess at grand master level, and perform calculations of great complexity with inconceivable rapidity. And, if that doesn't do it for you, add that a future computer will also be able to design machines and generate mathematical proofs far more quickly than human engineers and mathematicians.

E: I still say no. What we're looking for is that spontaneity that we find in casual conversation, coupled with the immense background knowledge that enables us to understand hints, jokes, ambiguities, and irony in the language of others. The kind of thing you seem to have had in mind when you composed your famous test.

T: You've totally missed the point of the test. I intended it as a sufficient, not a necessary, condition for judging that a computer thinks. You have two choices: (1) you can be anthropomorphic about thinking and claim that any being that thinks must have specifically human sorts of thinking abilities or (2) you can recognize that the criteria for "thinking" are a matter of convention and that the word can be applied to an entire range of abilities and bundles of abilities, from number crunching all the way to the transhuman abilities that these machines will exhibit as the twenty-first century unfolds.

E: I see your point, and I now realize what makes me hesitate to say that these things can think, no matter how intelligent their output. Thinking is the act of a conscious being, one with an unobservable inner aspect. By "inner" I don't mean "inside." I mean something that is nonspatial—the way we experience certain feelings or moods that don't have spatial structure but merely fill the present moment.

T: Ah, that. And yet you believe that this inner aspect is present in other humans although you can't observe it in them; you only infer its presence from their speech and other behavior. Why not make the same inference about an articulate and superintelligent computer?

E: Because it's so unlike me inside and out.

REFLECTIONS

Turing's test can be understood as a *functionalist* criterion of thinking. If a computer can serve as an unseen conversational partner just as well as a human, then the *thinking* function we associate with conversing should be attributed to the computer. John Searle, a distinguished philosopher at the University of California at Berkeley, has been a forceful opponent of functionalism over the past twenty-five years. He considers it to be an absurd and perverse doctrine. As he puts it in *The Rediscovery of Mind,* "If you are tempted to functionalism, I believe you do not need refutation, you need help."[17]

His best-known antidote to functionalism is usually called the Chinese Room. What follows is a simplified version. Keep in mind that functionalists argue (1) that mental processes such as thinking or understanding can be adequately and completely characterized in terms of their input/output relations, and (2) that if systems A and B have all of the same outputs for the same inputs, then what intervenes between input and output is the *same* function in A and in B, no matter how different the physical constituents of A and B. Consider the following thought experiment: Suppose you're locked up in a room with an input tray and an output tray in one wall. Your initial input is a very large batch of writing in Chinese characters. You have no idea what these characters mean—they're just patterns of brush strokes that occur in a certain frequency and order on the page. Then you receive a smaller batch of characters along with rules in English telling you how to correlate characters in the second batch with those in the first and how to put together strings of Chinese characters in response to the second batch. You deposit these strings on the output tray. The English-language instructions designate the Chinese characters strictly in "formal" terms (by features such as shape, number of lines, and so forth). The people you're interacting with outside the room call the first batch "background information," the second batch and your response "conversation," and the English-language rules a "program." With practice, you get really good at quickly responding to "conversational" input, even though you continue to have no idea of its meaning. Despite being conscious, you are in effect behaving like a computer running a program. You're following the kinds of rules that would guide a machine—the only difference being that you are conscious of doing so. Your Chinese-speaking interlocutors outside the room find your responses perfectly appropriate and meaningful, just as English-speaking interlocutors would find your replies to questions posed in English. Given the functionalist premises (1) and (2) above, it follows that you *understand* Chinese, since your input/output relations to the Chinese-speaking interlocutors are indistinguishable from those of a Chinese speaker, and since what would go on in the mind of a Chinese speaker producing your responses would include understanding what's being said.

To Searle, this conclusion is patently false, and therefore one of the functionalist premises is false. As he put it, "I have inputs and outputs that are indistinguishable from those of the native Chinese speaker, and I can have any formal program you like, but I still understand nothing."[18] What do you think? His conclusion is very sweeping. He is arguing in effect that the attempt to explain the mind in terms of what goes on in a computer (what we could call computer functionalism) leaves out something as essential as *meaning* and *understanding*.

CAN MACHINES THINK? A NANORESPONSE

In a word: yes. Our brains are machines and our brains can think, so there are machines that can think.

Let's back up a little. I need to explain why I describe the living tissues of the brain as constituting a machine. And even before I do that, I need to say something about a position some people will cling to when faced with the very idea of the brain as a machine. This position is dualism—the claim that our minds or selves are nonphysical *things* in their own right, capable of existing and functioning apart from the body and thus able to survive the death of the body. Dualism counts among its most famous adherents Plato and Descartes, but it is also the more or less explicit view of countless Christians and members of other religions who invoke it to support their convictions about personal immortality or the unique dignity of the human spirit. I am not claiming that these convictions require a belief in dualism, only that the association is very strong and understandable. Let's call this position good old-fashioned dualism (GOFD), to distinguish it from much weaker sorts of dualism that are content to assert that there are some irreducibly nonphysical *aspects* of certain mental processes, even though the mind is not a nonphysical thing in its own right. For instance, they might hold that feelings and sensations (qualia),[19] unlike other mental states, can never be adequately understood by science. Most varieties of this weaker dualism can be grouped under the heading of *epiphenomenalism.* Epiphenomenalists are a thriving minority among philosophers of mind today, but they are like almost all other philosophers in their staunch opposition to GOFD.

There ought to be a society for the prevention of cruelty to dead horses. Not that a dead horse can suffer any pain if the beating continues. But it can be painful for spectators, and there is also something absurd about pointless violence that goes on and on. There is in the philosophy of mind literature a recurring theme of fighting off GOFD, as if philosophers were in constant danger of succumbing to it or of adopting positions that would lead to it. In the eyes of many philosophers, GOFD is on a par with belief in witches or guardian angels. They see it as symptomatic of a primitive mode of thinking that we all need to get over. When epiphenomenalists stake out their position, they are usually careful to say that it is the *brain* that carries out mental processes, and that they are "naturalists." Although this term is somewhat vague, at the very least it means avoiding all *super-*natural explanations, ones that would invoke causes that are outside the domain of science (such as God or a nonphysical mind).

GOFD *is* a dead horse. Its resurrection in mainstream philosophy is difficult to imagine. There are some interesting historical and cultural reasons for the continuing rearguard action by philosophers against this prostrate foe, and I will discuss them later in this chapter. For the sake of getting back to our subject, I will give what I think is the simplest and most powerful reason for letting GOFD R.I.P. This reason was stated quite effectively by Gilbert Ryle in *The Concept of Mind* (1949), one of the charter documents of the subdiscipline called philosophy of mind. Ryle dismisses Cartesian dualism as creating the illusion of an explanation. Descartes wanted to understand both mind *and* body and he claimed that he arrived at a "clear and distinct" idea of each, with which he could understand that they were absolutely different in nature. To understand how a body behaves involves analyzing it into parts that work together as a system to bring about a certain effect. In other words, we understand bodies as machines with interacting parts. Descartes tried to understand mind in the same way, and he ended up with what Ryle calls a "spectral machine" with parts and processes "described by the mere negatives of the specific descriptions given to bodies; they are not in space, they are not motions, they are not modifications of matter, they are not accessible to public observation. Minds are not bits of clockwork, they are just bits of not-clockwork."[20] By turning our minds into things in their own right alongside their associated bodies, Descartes and GOFD don't explain *how* we think or what goes on in mental processes; they merely relocate the problem from the domain of the physical to that of the *non*physical without explaining anything. The dualist concept of mind is vacuous or, as Ryle would have it, pseudomechanical (using language that seems mechanical but refers to nonmechanical processes). However, I believe it would be an overreaction to GOFD to conclude that minds are "nothing but" machines, if that implies that the *only way to understand* the mind is in mechanical or physicochemical terms. This view, common among philosophers of mind, is known as *scientism,* and I reject it for reasons I will explain later in this chapter.[21]

Yes, the brain is a machine that does what a mind does, and so it is a thinking machine. In addition to the lingering effects of GOFD, there is another source of discomfort in calling the living tissue of the brain a machine. We're accustomed to reserving this word for *artificial* systems, ones that humans can design and build. Until very recently, humans made things by assembling parts that were composed of massive numbers of atoms and molecules. For instance, a cubic centimeter of matter in a solid state contains about 10^{23} molecules. Over the past fifty years, the gap between living and artificial processes was narrowed by *microelectronics,* as it developed and refined our capacity to imprint circuitry that is measured in microns (millionths of a meter). As a result, we now build into a silicon chip the size of a fingernail the computing power that used to take up an entire room. We also have the beginnings of a new kind of technology that is about to *close* the categorial distance between what is *alive* and what is *artificial* or *mechanical* by enabling us to work with components on the scale of those that get assembled or taken apart in the metabolic activity of living cells. This new technology has the metric prefix *nano-*, which designates a domain in which the common unit of measurement is the nanometer (1 nm = 10^{-9} m), or a billionth of a meter.[22] Atoms range from 0.1 nm to 0.5 nm in diameter, and molecules involved in intracellular processes are usually measured in nanometers.

As B. C. Crandall points out, the impetus for nanotechnology came from advances in microbiology, microelectronics, and materials science:

> Chemists and biologists focused on untangling the molecular structures that constitute materiality from the "bottom up," while physicists and engineers devoted their efforts to building ever smaller machines from the "top down." Both efforts resulted in tremendously powerful technologies. Molecular science produced revolutionary medicines as well as the novel materials that provide much of the texture of the modern world—including nylon, Tyvek, Teflon, and super-glue—while micromachinists, after creating the first transistor in 1948, learned to build logic and computation machines with micron-scale components, generating thereby a global industry second only to agriculture.[23]

Computers already overlap the nanodomain. As of 1998, the Intel Pentium processor had parts measuring 350 nm. IBM's Zurich Research Laboratory is exploring materials that will enable a transistor part to have lateral dimensions in the 50–100 nm range.

It is a long reach from the socioecological level down to the nanolevel of reality. A major requirement is being able to "see" what we're doing with objects well below the resolution threshold for optical or light microscopes. In the early 1980s, a series of improvements in electron microscopy culminated in the invention of the Scanning Tunneling Microscope (STM), for which Gerd Binnig and Heinrich Rohrer shared the Nobel Prize for physics in 1986. This instrument uses a superfine stylus that scans the surface of a solid at a distance of about one nanometer. At this infinitesimal range, a current of electrons running between the stylus and the surface will move faster or slower, depending on the distance. The electron cloud constituting the outer boundary of each surface atom[24] creates a small mound, and these mounds cause variation in the distance between the surface and the stylus point, as the stylus moves over the surface. The resulting variations in the current running between the stylus and the surface are amplified and combined with the two-dimensional record of the motion of the stylus to generate a three-dimensional image on a video display (see fig. 2.1). The STM can also be used to move and shape atoms into structures. In 1990, IBM's Zurich lab brought nanotechnology to the attention of the public when it spelled out the company logo by arranging thirty-five xenon atoms on a nickel surface. STMs are one of many kinds of *scanning probe microscopes* that utilize superfine probing devices to generate images that delineate atomic structure and manipulate atoms. There is a great deal of debate, some of it quite impassioned, among researchers and futurists about how far nanotechnology will go and how fast it will develop. Regardless, it seems highly likely that in the next twenty years we will see such things as commercially available nano-assembled superstrong/light/flexible materials, nanomachinery at the heart of greatly enhanced microprocessors, and molecule-size delivery systems that identify cancer cells and inject them with toxins.[25] Since

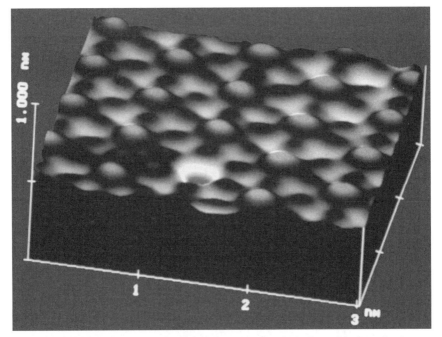

Figure 2.1.   **STM image showing single-atom defect in iodine adsorbate lattice on platinum. 2.5nm scan. (Photo taken with Digital Instruments NanoScope® SPM, courtesy Veeco Instruments, Santa Barbara, California.)**

1997, the U.S. government has funded what is called the National Nanotechnology Initiative (NNI), an umbrella agency that dispenses money to various government agencies and universities for nanotechnology research and development. The president has requested $849 million for the agency in fiscal year 2004. Here is how M. C. Roco[26] of the National Science Foundation introduced his presentation of the NNI budget for 2002: "The emerging fields of nanoscale science, engineering, and technology— the ability to work at the molecular level, atom by atom, to create large structures with fundamentally new properties and functions—are leading to unprecedented understanding and control over the basic building blocks and properties of all natural and man-made things."[27]

The point of this discussion of nanotechnology is that humans are acquiring the capacity to build machines that have dimensions and working parts at the level of DNA, ribosomes, proteins, and other systems that do the work of life in cells. Much of this work consists of taking apart and putting together large molecules. We are already accustomed to hearing about feats of genetic engineering such as altering the genes of bacteria so that they produce chemicals that are useful to us. The cells that make up brain and other kinds of tissue are machines of the sort we will be able to build. There is no fundamental distinction between *naturally occurring* and *artificial* machines, between artificial and natural life. The domesticated animals that humans have developed over several millennia can be described as artificial life-forms created by selectively breeding organisms with traits useful to us. Since we did this by exerting an *external* and indirect control over complex reproductive processes that we have only recently come to understand, and since selective breeding occurs over such large intervals of time and across many human generations, the artificiality of the results is not as striking as it would be if we had quickly engineered an organism by direct manipulation of its genes.

Hanging over any discussion of biological machines is an extreme looseness and variability in the meaning of the word "life" and related words, such as "living/alive" and "dead." To appreciate the problem, one has only to think of sentences such as "This has a long shelf life," "She was the life of the party," "Cells are the smallest living systems on our planet," and "We're talking about making human cellular life, not a human life." (The last sentence is from Michael West, CEO of Advanced Cell Technologies, responding to critics of his company's cloning of a human embryo.) The debate over abortion gets seriously muddled when it is couched in terms of when (human) *life* begins. It is true, in a real but trivial sense, that the single-cell conceptus resulting from the union of sperm and ovum is alive, in the same sense that trillions of other cells in an adult human body are alive. Moreover, all these cells are (genetically) human lives (they aren't salmon or wolf cells, and they have the complete genetic code of a human individual). The proper formulation of the abortion issue requires distinguishing between biological human life and having those attributes that give a being membership in the moral community, with all its rights and responsibilities. In other words, the question is when the developing human has all (or at least some degree) of the status and worth of a *person*.

There is an important similarity in the concepts of *life* (in the biological sense) and *person*(hood). Both are *functional* concepts—they characterize a being in terms of its relations to, and interactions with, other beings and *not* in terms of particular kinds of physical components. In both cases, we need to avoid what philosophers call "chauvinistic" interpretations, such as limiting the class of persons to humans or limiting the class of living systems to ones that have metabolic processes like those of terrestrial organisms, or even to the class of carbon-based systems. The divinities of certain religions, angels, and extraterrestrials are all cases in which people are accustomed to thinking of a being as alive and as a person, although the being does not have the biology of a human. There is a special problem with the concept of life, because all *terrestrial* life-forms are "family"—there is a great deal of similarity in the structures and chemical processes found in all cells, from bacteria to human. For instance, all have DNA and RNA, make proteins out of the same twenty amino acids, and use ATP[28] as an energy source. This resemblance is responsible for the dense section on common metabolic pathways that comes early in most introductory biology textbooks. Our current search for evidence of life (present or past) on other planets typically assumes that extraterrestrial life will be similar to life on our planet in its origins and chemistry. So we look at other planets for environmental conditions similar to those that make ours habitable, or for conditions similar to those that were present on Earth when life originated. But there is a growing discipline called artificial life (AL, or Alife) that tries to abstract from the physical specifications of terrestrial life. According to C. G. Langton, director of the Santa Fe Institute, AL tries to understand life by

> attempting to abstract the fundamental dynamical principles underlying biological phenomena, and recreating these dynamics in other physical media—such as computers—making them accessible to new kinds of experimental manipulation and testing. . . . In addition to providing new ways to study the biological phenomena associated with life here on Earth, *life-as-we-know-it,*

Artificial Life allows us to extend our studies to the larger domain of . . . possible life, *life-as-it-could-be*.[29]

There is no generally accepted definition of life among biologists or people working in AL. The most commonly attributed *functional* predicates of life are *self-maintaining, self-replicating/reproducing,* continuously *interacting* with a specific environment, and capable of *learning* and/or *evolution.*

One very important difference between the two functional concepts, life and personhood, is that *persons* are generally regarded as having an important and *intrinsic* value, a dignity that is found on our planet only in human animals (thus far). Many philosophers go so far as to agree with Kant that *only* persons have intrinsic value, while all other things, including organisms that aren't persons, have only the derivative value of being *means* for the goals of persons. We will look more closely at this idea later.[30] In the meantime, it's worth noting that, despite the aura that attaches to the word "life" when it is loosely used in the context of abortion, much of our behavior makes clear that we find nothing sacred about the *life* of a nonperson. Most of us eat meat, even vegetarians kill off massive amounts of vegetation in order to eat or when they weed their gardens, and all of us eagerly destroy immense swarms of bacteria and cancer cells if they invade our bodies.

In conclusion, it seems to make perfect sense to say that *a human brain is a machine that thinks.* It is also an assembly of tissues composed of living cellular machines and it is a working part of a living human machine, one that also functions as a person.

REFLECTIONS

1. Is GOFD really such a dead horse? What about out-of-body experiences (OBEs)? These OBEs are very common. In a typical case, a person is conscious of observing her body and surround from a distance (e.g., from a point near the ceiling above the body). The person's brain is still in her body. Isn't this a direct experience of a mind or spirit separating itself from the body? (Many web sites contain descriptions of these experiences.)

2. Go back to figure 2.1. Is that what atomic structure really looks like? What does the phrase "really looks like" mean at the nanolevel as opposed to our level?

SCIENTISM

> We're all zombies.
>
> —Daniel Dennett, *Consciousness Explained*

In the modestly titled book from which the above quote is taken, Daniel Dennett appends to his statement this footnote: "It would be an act of desperate intellectual dishonesty to quote this assertion out of context!"[31] Since I am neither desperate nor dishonest, I will heed his admonition and try to provide the context in what follows. Dennett, a professor of philosophy at Tufts University and the director of its Center for Cognitive Studies, is one of the most prominent and widely published authors in the philosophy of mind and cognitive science. He is commonly consulted when the press wants a philosopher's take on such things as AI, evolution, and cognitive and brain science. The four books that he published with MIT Press are now available in a boxed set titled the *Dennett Quartet*.[32] He is something of an institution in philosophy, and that is why I will concentrate on him in the following discussion. His clarity of mind and boldness of expression make him an able representative of what I regard as mistaken views about the mind and about the role of philosophy.

In saying that we're all zombies, Dennett does *not* mean that we are all like the walking dead reanimated by voodoo power. He is talking about *us* as we behave like our chipper selves. However, he *is* saying something that is difficult for people not socialized into the culture of philosophy to take seriously. Imagine that you are looking at the smiling humanoid features of a robot with the ability to pass an unrestricted Turing test. You're having an engaging conversation with it, but a nagging doubt keeps rising about whether there's anyone "there"—whether the robot is *nothing but a machine* (with great computational power, of course). Dennett is saying not to worry, since *there is nothing else that could be "there," no inner, unobservable self either in you or in it.*

Dennett's use of the term "zombie" plugs into an ongoing controversy over functionalism in the philosophy of mind. Functionalists claim not only that a correct understanding of the mind requires that we characterize it functionally and not restrict it to systems with specific sorts of physical components, but also that this characterization is adequate or *complete*. In other words, a functionalist account of the mind is supposed to be able to encompass everything distinctly or essentially mental. If we combine this with the quite plausible thesis that the only way to specify how sensory input gives rise to behavioral output is to do so in physical terms, then we have functionalism as a *materialist* or physicalist theory of mind. Critics of functionalism argue that it necessarily omits a very important feature of the mind—namely its inner aspect, something we experience only from a first-person perspective. Philosophers often use the term "consciousness" to signify this aspect, or they will speak about *what it is like to be* a mind. To make their point, some of these critics have brought up what is called the zombie objection: functionalism describes the mind purely in terms of input/output relations with an environment, together with whatever internal mechanisms are needed to link input to output. For that reason, functionalism cannot distinguish between the minds of (1) someone who has sensations and feelings, for whom there is *something that it is like to be* that person or mind, and (2) a being with all the same behavioral manifestations, identical to the first from a third-person perspective, but without any sensations or feelings. Case (2) can be understood either as a being that has the same physical constitution as a human or as a humanoid robot constructed of the latest synthetic materials, with micro- or nanocircuitry controlling its facial expressions, voice, and movements. Some philosophers would claim that the connection between brain events and what we experience as consciousness is no more intelligible than the connection between artificial circuitry and consciousness. Case (2), they would say, is perfectly intelligible under both interpretations and very different from case (1). Since materialist functionalism can't differentiate (1) from (2), it is wrong.

Dennett calls these critics "reactionaries" who are "united in the conviction *that there is a real difference between a conscious person and a perfect zombie*—let's call that intuition the *Zombic Hunch*—leading them to the thesis of *Zombism*: that *the fundamental flaw in any mechanistic theory of consciousness is that it cannot account for this important difference*."[33] Dennett's contrary thesis is that, "Nobody is conscious—not in the systematically mysterious way that supports such doctrines as epiphenomenalism!"[34] There is, in other words, nothing about consciousness that cannot, in principle, be explained completely from the third-person perspective of materialist functionalism, and therefore there is nothing to support the claim that there is anything nonphysical about the mind. "Zombism" leads to epiphenomenalism, a view for which Dennett has only contempt, calling it a "relic of prescientific philosophy of mind" and a "doomed escape route from Cartesian dualism."[35] The latter (GOFD) makes the mind into a nonphysical *thing* in its own right, with causal powers that would reach into the physical domain by having nonphysical decisions affect physical events such as the neuronal activities that activate our muscles in voluntary movements. This would threaten the integrity of science by allowing an unobservable, scientifically unintelligible event to play a role in the domain of science. Today's dualists try to avoid this by making the nonphysical aspects of the mind *epiphenomenal*—effects that have no effects of their own on anything else in or about the brain, or on anything else in nature. To Dennett, such a view is "ridiculous": for any epiphenomenon x, "Since x has no physical effects, . . . no instrument can detect the presence of x directly or indirectly; the way the world goes is not modulated in the slightest by the presence or absence of x. How then could there ever be any empirical reason to assert the presence of x?"[36] A "reactionary" would reply, of course, that the *empirical* reason for asserting the existence of mental epiphenomena is first-person experience. And Dennett would reply that the only kind of experience that can count as *evidence* is third-person experience, experience that can be shared—in other words, *observation*. To say that x exists entirely on the basis of first-person experience is no more cogent than to say "I just *feel* that there are $x$es." And so it goes, on and on, in the literature of the philosophy of mind, a seemingly endless controversy over what the very intelligent and well-educated people on both sides regard as the obvious truth of their positions. I sympathize with Dennett's statement that this interminable spat is "an embarrassment to our discipline."[37] However, for reasons I will give below, it seems to me that Dennett has contributed more than his share to the impasse.

I accept part of the materialist functionalist thesis. I agree (1) that an adequate account of the mind requires that it be characterized in terms of input/output relations with an environment and of the mechanisms linking input to output and (2) that mental functions require embodiment, but mind is not restricted to specific kinds of physical embodiments. But I reject the further claim (3) that such accounts can, in principle, be *complete*. Claim (3) implies that there is no other way to understand the mind, no other method or kind of discourse that can arrive at any truth about the mind. My reason for disagreeing with (3) is *not* the zombie objection. The notion of a zombie makes little sense to me. Nature is uniform, regular, law-abiding. If the neural circuitry in me gives rise to first-person, subjective experience, it seems to me that the supposition that similar circuitry in others might *not* have that effect is a nonstarter. It is conceivable in some very abstract way, just as I can conceive of the universe going out of existence in its entirety every six hours and then coming back exactly where it left off. But this conception is totally unmotivated; nothing about the world I know suggests it. Thinking that it might be true is just a way of making the world less, not more, intelligible. It would not be a defect of cosmology or astrophysics that it could not rule out such a universe. And so it is with the zombie conception. There is an "intelligible" difference between a human and her zombie twin only in the trivial way that there is an intelligible difference between a universe that periodically goes out of existence and one that doesn't. A theory of mind should not be required to rule out zombies.

There's a much better reason for rejecting (3). The claim is as gratuitous as the zombie objection or the notion of a universe that alternates between existence and nonexistence. In both cases, we are being asked to contemplate the possibility that the universe may not be as stable, uniform, and law-abiding as we believe it to be. Yet we *must* believe this if we are to spend our time and resources in trying to understand the world around us. Thirty-three years ago, we let the lives of astronauts depend on precise calculations about vehicle weight and thrust to lift them off the surface of the moon, a world no human had visited before. This reflected great confidence not only in the calculations, but also in the uniformity of the laws of physics on earth and anywhere else in the universe. It makes no sense to ask of theories built on this belief to justify the belief by ruling out the possibility that the world may not be so intelligible after all. Dennett would no doubt agree with what I've just said about the faith that undergirds scientific inquiry. He would add that it is in the name of that faith that he claims there is nothing more to understand about the mind than what can be grasped scientifically. Science requires a third-person perspective that limits itself to what is observable and measurable. To claim that there is something, namely consciousness, that cannot be completely understood from a scientific perspective, something that requires in addition a *non*scientific (*not antiscientific*) perspective, is a kind of intellectual suicide. It is to abandon a faith that has taken us from one triumph to another over the past three centuries since the scientific revolution.

Yet, if we accept what Dennett recommends as the *truth* about consciousness, then *the world as we experience it* is saturated with *something quite unintelligible*, namely, appearances and seemings. Dennett admits that our conviction that there is subjective consciousness will never quite go away. Instead, it will be like sunrise and sunset:

> Will the Zombic Hunch itself go extinct? I expect not. It will not survive in its current, toxic form but will persist as a less virulent mutation, still psychologically powerful but stripped of authority. We've seen this happen before. It still *seems* as if the earth stands still and the sun and moon go around it, but we have learned that it is wise to disregard this potent appearance as mere appearance.[38]

In the case of the sun's motion, the *appearance* is still what it was for the earliest humans, but the interpretation is different now. We don't infer from the content of our experience of a sunset that the sun is moving, just as we don't infer from our visual experience of a stick in water that the stick is really bent. In both cases, the appearance is left intact by our knowledge that the reality behind it is otherwise. The appearance is still there. But where is *there*? Every moment we're awake we experience a world of bodies perspectivally structured around our individual points of view. Things seem smaller or larger as a function of their distance from us. Not only does everything have an *apparent* size that varies independently of its real size, but each of us is at the *center* of this domain of appearances. Moreover, the dimensions of the bodies around us appear to be *continuous* magnitudes, although our science informs us that bodies are arrays of infinitesimal particles in mostly empty space. The world we experience is a world of appearances or phenomena. And it's that world that we try to understand by getting at the truth "behind" appearances. But *where* are appearances?

Appearances are nowhere, of course, if "somewhere" means a location in the physical world. They don't belong on a list of things in the physical space of the brain (the list that includes neurons, glial cells, and all the other items in the domain of neuroscience). What Dennett doesn't want to hear is that they are part of a *non*physical domain, a sensory or phenomenal field that is the private preserve of every human mind. In that sense, he claims, there are no appearances—it's a myth that such things exist or happen. When the stick in the water seems bent, what's really going on is a set of brain processes that make it more likely that I would say "The stick is bent" than if I were receiving visual input from the same stick lying on dry ground. But the brain-based disposition to say "The stick is bent" is overcome by a contrary disposition rising from prior experiences with sticks in water, and this occurrence in the brain of a checked disposition causes me to say "The stick merely seems to be bent." There's no inner, nonphysical domain of appearances containing the look of bentness in the stick, Dennett would say; there are only patterns of neural activity in the physical space of the brain. Similarly, if we are having one of those lovely moments when we quietly savor the glory of a well-appointed garden, "the richness we marvel at is the richness of the world outside, in all *its* ravishing detail. "It does not 'enter' our conscious minds, but is simply available."[39]

The trouble with Dennett's analysis is that the perceived richness of sensuous detail is *not* out there waiting to be appreciated. What's "out there" is the world described in the language of physical science, a world that is *un*available to the senses, a world that does not appear except in the paradoxical sense that it presents itself as other than what it really is.[40] There is something of a shell game going on in Dennett's account of perception. In the passage quoted above, he compares the belief in subjective consciousness (the "Zombic Hunch") with belief in the rising and setting of the sun. Now that we know the earth orbits the sun, we have learned to disregard the "potent appearance" of a rising sun as "mere appearance." Is he suggesting that appearances merely appear to occur and that we should regard *all* appearance as *mere* appearance?

Saying that things merely are what they are is not newsworthy. Appearance really happens, and a theory that won't admit that it happens is practicing denial. How could things come to such a pass? A world in which there is no appearance, like a world that comes into and out of existence at regular intervals, has a weak sort of intelligibility, even if it isn't imaginable. In the absence of any plausible *argument* for the position taken by Dennett and so many other philosophers, one looks for a *cause* or diagnosis, just as one would try to explain why someone might passionately maintain the idea of a stop/start universe.

In chapter 1, when talking about Socrates on trial, I described philosophy as a faith community[41] united in the belief that one must follow the argument wherever it goes and that an unexamined life is not worth living. In this section, I have spoken about the faith in a universe that is uniform and law-abiding, a belief that is a presupposition of doing science. I want now to discuss another faith community, one that unites a subset of philosophers (including Dennett) and philosophically inclined scientists. Their faith is *scientism,* the doctrine that science, which Dennett calls "the technology of truth,"[42] is the *only* way of arriving at the truth about the world. We get at the truth by limiting ourselves to what is observable and measurable and making our claims as hypotheses that predict what the world will be like given certain antecedent conditions. To the extent that these predictions are verified by observation and experiment, our hypotheses are more or less well established (although they are always subject to being falsified or amended in the light of further observations and experiments). As far as Dennett is concerned, philosophy is no more than a part or extension of the scientific enterprise: "My sense that philosophy is allied with, and indeed continuous with, the physical sciences grounds both my modesty about philosophical method and my optimism about philosophical progress."[43] His "modesty about philosophical method" consists in denying to philosophy any role outside science, and his "optimism about philosophical progress" comes from linking philosophy with the rapid and limitless progress he expects science to make in understanding what used to be regarded as "mysteries": biological and psychological phenomena, including consciousness. Predictably, Dennett has little respect for nonscientific disciplines ("the arts and humanities"). He calls the skepticism and relativism now fashionable in literary studies

the height of sheltered naiveté, made possible only by flatfooted ignorance of the proven methods of scientific truth-seeking and their power. Like many another naif, these thinkers, reflecting on the manifest inability of *their* methods of truth-seeking to achieve stable and valuable results, innocently generalize from their own cases and conclude that nobody *else* knows how to discover the truth either.[44]

Much of Dennett's writing displays an admirable grasp of a great deal of science. He is one of the very best expositors of science for an educated lay audience. However, his exposition typically has a subtext that he occasionally makes explicit. It goes something like this: *Here is yet another example of how science can shed light on something you might have regarded as mysterious or that you might not be happy to have science address. Do you still doubt the primacy and all-encompassing scope of science?* If you resist his blandishments, he can be quite a scold, lumping you with believers in "astrology, divining, soothsayers and gurus and shamans, trance-channeling, and consulting a variety of holy texts."[45] As far as Dennett is concerned, scientism seems to be the only response that a reasonable and adequately informed person could have to the great progress science has made in the past century or so. One is even tempted to ask which is the horse and which the cart—his materialist worldview or his enthusiasm for the achievements of science. In a review of Carl Sagan's book *The Demon-Haunted World: Science as a Candle in the Dark*, Richard Lewontin, a renowned Harvard biologist, makes the following confession of faith:

> With great perception, Sagan sees that there is an impediment to the popular credibility of scientific claims about the world, an impediment that is almost invisible to most scientists. Many of the most fundamental claims of science are against common sense and seem absurd on their face. Do physicists really expect me to accept without serious qualms that the pungent cheese that I had for lunch is really made up of tiny, tasteless, odorless, colorless packets of energy with nothing but empty space between them?
>   . . . It is not that the methods and institutions of science somehow compel us to accept a material explanation of the phenomenal world, but, on the contrary, that we are forced by our *a priori* adherence to material causes to create an apparatus of investigation and a set of concepts that produce material explanations, no matter how counter-intuitive, no matter how mystifying to the uninitiated.[46]

In this remarkably candid passage, Lewontin makes a crucial point: the "methods and institutions of science" do *not* "compel us to accept a material explanation of the phenomenal world." In other words, materialism as a metaphysics, as a *philosophical* claim that the universe consists of nothing but what is in the domain of physical science, is *not* an implication or a presupposition of doing science, let alone of being enthusiastic about science. And we don't need to believe that scientific truth is the only truth in order to welcome and admire all the progress being made in science. We can reject materialism and scientism along with dualism and still incorporate all the relevant science into a philosophical analysis of the mind.

As I said in the introduction, there are large and crucial questions about
what our *goals* should be as we develop our technology of mind and assess
a future populated by cyborgs and superintelligent artificial systems. These
questions are philosophical, not scientific. Knowledge of science and technology is essential to any attempt to answer these questions, but it is not de-
cisive. For that very reason, scientism has the unfortunate effect of putting
these questions beyond the scope of rational discussion, leaving them to be
settled by judgments of taste or exercises of power. It seems to me that
Socrates best articulated what should be the *philosopher's* faith: to follow
the argument wherever it goes, because an unexamined life is not worth living. It is sad to see a prominent philosopher abandoning the autonomy of
philosophy by rolling it up into science.

REFLECTIONS

What do you think of the following defense of scientism? Science (especially physical science) is different from nonscientific disciplines in ways
that make it superior in its claim to knowledge. First, the mathematical language in which its conclusions are stated gives science a *precision* lacking in
nonscientific fields. Second, scientists have a *consensus* about *methodology,*
whereas nonscientists (such as historians, literary critics, and old-fashioned
philosophers) are divided and often quarrel over methods in their fields.
Third, scientists regard their claims as *hypotheses* that should be accepted
only insofar as they continue accurately to *predict* the course of events. This
experimental method provides a constant check on the truthfulness of
claims and an objectivity that is missing from many of the nonsciences. Finally, science is truly *international*—it transcends the boundaries and biases
of race, religion, and gender. It has given us technology that enables us to
tame nature and shape it to our needs. Its truth is power. That's why some
social "sciences" (like political "science" and economics) try so hard to imitate it. How can anyone claim that there is a better way to get at some truths
about the world?

E.T. AND ALIEN

In the 1982 film *E.T. the Extraterrestrial* and in the *Alien* quartet,[47] we are
presented with two striking images of intelligent extraterrestrial life-forms.
E.T. is a benign, gentle, and cerebral creature with a body that looks alien,

although he still appears unthreatening and even cute. The alien in the film series of that name is quite the opposite—an outer-space correlate of the velociraptors in *Jurassic Park*. It is intelligent, yes, but only in the pursuit of prey and the nurture of its young. It is fierce, swift, unrelenting, powerful, and terrifyingly alien (to us mammals) in its body structure. This violent, destructive creature seems to recognize no other value than survival and reproduction. Its behavior toward humans is a projection of the horrors that occur all over our planet as organisms are crushed, gored, suffocated, poisoned, or torn apart by their customary predators. *Alien* is thus a symbol of *our alienation* from certain aspects of terrestrial life, perhaps even from something we sense in ourselves. A prominent theme of the *Alien* series is the struggle between Ellen Ripley and The Company. She recognizes the mortal danger that the alien species poses for humankind, whereas The Company wants to capture and experiment with the species as a potentially profitable bioweapon. The moral of the story is ambiguous. Ripley wins against the foolish arrogance of The Company, and humanity is safe for the time being. But we are left with the impression that our species is highly vulnerable and that our safety depends on our isolation from such aliens. We want to believe that as life evolves in the direction of greater intelligence, it will become more like E.T. or the benevolent creatures that emerge from the spaceship in another Spielberg film, *Close Encounters of the Third Kind*. But we also suspect it might not go that way, that even an advanced intelligence might be in the service of a ruthless biological imperative to live and multiply—the sort of fantasy played out in the 1996 film *Independence Day*, in the alien conspiracy driving much of the *X-Files* television series, and in the Borg of the Star Trek series and films.

Do intelligence and mind *inevitably* arise on a planet with evolving life-forms? If so, did even the earliest and simplest living systems on earth have some function or aspect that is the ancestor of consciousness and mind? We also wonder, as we contemplate the increasingly intelligent functions of computer-based systems, whether something can be, or have, a mind if it's not alive. I have already argued that something (the human brain) can be understood as both a machine and alive, as well as capable of thought.[48] However, we could ask whether something can be a machine that thinks or functions as a mind but is *not* alive. What is the relation between these two categories, *life* and *mind*? That is a very large question, but it's one that we need to consider with some urgency, since much of the technological progress we are making in artificial intelligence will also enable us to create artificial life-forms (in real life or in cyberspace). We must try to *understand* what we will be doing.

Descartes has had an enormous influence on how philosophers today interpret the question of the relation between life and mind. To see why, let's look at a traditional picture of the world that is still part of common sense ontology[49] today, but has been abandoned by most philosophers since the time of Descartes. Most people then (as now) thought of our planet as populated by four categories of beings:

1. inanimate bodies—stuff such as rocks, soil, and even liquids and gases
2. plants—living bodies such as vegetables and even mosses
3. animals—sentient living bodies, including birds, fish, and land animals
4. humans—sentient living bodies of a specific form with distinctive capabilities, such as reason and speech

Notice the cumulative feature of this tetrad. Each higher level, from the first to the fourth, includes the lower with the addition of a further attribute. What Descartes did was argue for the reduction of the second and third categories to the level of the first: plants and animals were to be understood merely as machines, complex systems of movable parts that enable them to behave adaptively in their environments. As I explained in chapter 1, Descartes saw nonhuman animals as machines endowed with neuromechanical reflexes.[50] His reduction of life and sentience to the motion of material particles created an abyss between the human mind and body. It had the effect of suspending our consciousness in a world of bodies with which it had nothing in common. Each human mind became a ghost in its own machine. In this way, Descartes set for us today the ontological framework for discussing the place of mind in nature. Taking the reduction of the second and third levels to the first as a given, philosophers were left with the problem of what to do with mind. Most regarded Descartes' dualism (GOFD) as untenable. Since they could not accept both mind *and* body as irreducibly different kinds of being, it seemed they had to choose— *either/or*. In the eighteenth and nineteenth centuries, many prominent philosophers tried *idealism*, the doctrine that all being is mental.[51] In *The View from Nowhere*, Thomas Nagel points out what is perhaps the greatest fault of idealism: its "attempt to cut the universe down to size."[52] Since we are acquainted only with our *human* minds, idealism had the effect of equating the universe to what the human mind could perceive or think. It limited reality to what can be thought in the categories and theories of a particular era and culture, or what can be perceived and experienced by beings with our kind of sensory modalities and brain structure. Since the middle of the twentieth century, English-language philosophy of mind has been dominated by varieties of *materialism,* or physicalism, completing what Descartes started by reducing the fourth level in the tetrad to the first. This final reduction was motivated by a more or less explicit scientism.[53] Ironically, as Nagel points out, "Scientism is actually a special form of idealism, for it puts one type of human understanding in charge of the universe and what can be said about it."[54]

Earlier in this section, in reflecting on E.T. and the Alien as popular icons of extraterrestrial life, I raised this question: "Did even the earliest and simplest living systems have some function or aspect that is the ancestor of consciousness and mind?" By way of a tentative response, I want now to dwell on a fundamental scientific fact too often overlooked by philosophers: like the human digestive, circulatory, and other organ systems, the nervous system (including the brain) is an evolutionary specialization in a biological function found in the simplest unicellular organisms. I will try to show that the cellular function that is the evolutionary ancestor of the central nervous system (and thereby of the human mind) creates a major ontological divide between living and nonliving systems. If I'm correct in my hypothesis, then we badly need to break out of the Cartesian framework for discussing the place of mind in nature.

As an example of multicellular specialization in an originally unicellular function, let's look first at the digestive system. The one found in humans belongs to the generic *alimentary canal* type in which food enters a *mouth,* the food is broken down chemically into nutrients and wastes in a *digestive tract,* and wastes are expelled through an *anus.* In bacteria (prokaryotes), which are the most primitive sorts of cells on the planet today, protein channels in the cellular membrane let in nutrients and expel wastes. Nutrients and wastes float around in the water-based cytoplasm that makes up the interior of the bacterium, until they are used or expelled. More advanced cells (eukaryotes) have molecular organelles (nanomachines such as endoplasmic reticula) that carry out functions analogous to a digestive tract.

To understand the ancestral unicellular function in which our nervous system specializes, we need to back up a little and ask which functions distinguish an organism from a nonliving system. In my previous discussion of artificial life, I stated that the usual *functional* predicates of an organism are *self-maintenance, self-replication/reproduction,* continuous *interaction* with an environment, and *evolution.*[55] I want now to argue that two of these four are fundamental: *self-maintenance* through *continuous interaction with an environment.* An organism may be unable, or no longer able, to reproduce and yet be fully alive (ask any infertile human). Moreover, replication/ reproduction is a process whereby *another* living system is produced by one or more previously existing ones. So it is a function of an *already living* system. Evolution consists in the emergence, by processes of replication/ reproduction, of new types of living systems. It presupposes the existence of living systems that reproduce. However, if a living system can no longer maintain itself by interacting with its environment (e.g., by taking in nutrients or repairing itself with matter and energy it extracts from its environment), that system is *dead*.

The activity of self-maintenance through interaction with an environment is a special and important case of a kind of function that is very common in systems engineered by humans. This general function is *control*, and I will call the function that distinguishes living systems *adaptive control*. The job of a control system is to maintain another system (its *environment*) within certain limits. This suggests a threefold division of the system into (1) a *sensor* that is able to detect changes in the variable(s) to be controlled in the environment, (2) the *modulator*, which receives a signal from the sensor and selects a response to what is detected, and (3) the *effector*, which the modulator causes or signals to act on the environment in such a way as to bring it within, or closer to, the prescribed limits (the modulator's *setting*).[56] The result of the effector's intervention in the environment constitutes a change that is, in turn, detected by the sensor. This phase of the control loop is called *feedback*. The loop remains active until the environmental variable agrees with the modulator's setting. Figure 2.2 diagrams these subsystems and their relationships.

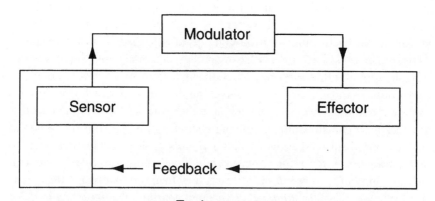

Environment

Figure 2.2.   Functional diagram of a control system. The large box containing the sensor and effector represents the environment. (From B. Cooney, *The Place of Mind*. © 2000. Reprinted with permission of Wadsworth.)

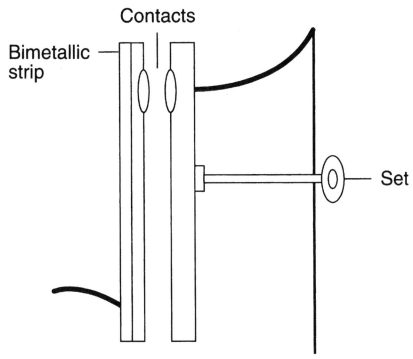

Figure 2.3. **Thermostat with bimetallic strip. (From B. Cooney,** *The Place of Mind.*
© **2000. Reprinted with permission of Wadsworth.)**

As we look at the thermostat in figure 2.3 as an example of a control system, we need to remember that figure 2.2 is a *functional* diagram. Its subsystems and their spatial relations don't necessarily correspond to the *physical* subsystems and their spatial relations in an embodied control system. In
figure 2.3, a bimetallic strip is anchored at the bottom and has an electrical
contact at the top, a small distance from another contact. As the environmental temperature rises or falls, the two different metals of the strip expand
or contract at different rates, causing the strip to bend one way or the other,
narrowing or widening the distance between the contacts. In this way, the
bimetallic strip acts as a *sensor.* Suppose we're looking at a heating system in
which falling temperature causes the strip to close the gap between the contacts. This *signals* a drop in temperature. *Setting* the thermostat consists in
positioning the second contact at a greater or lesser distance from the
bimetallic strip. The greater the gap, the colder the environment will have
to get before the gap is closed. The part that houses the second contact is the
modulator. The current generated in the modulator by the closing of the gap

signals the furnace (*effector*). The resulting increase in room temperature is *feedback* for this climate control system.

Let's turn now to *adaptive control,* the function that distinguishes living from nonliving systems. If the life of an organism consists in maintaining itself in and through constant interaction with its environment, it follows that such a system must be able to *detect* relevant changes in its environment—events to which it must respond in a self-preserving way. It must be able to *select* and *effect* these adaptive responses, and be governed in its subsequent behavior by the results of its prior responses (*feedback*). In short, it must have within it a control system, but of a special sort. The gap that is set between the two contacts in figure 2.3 makes the thermostat behave as if it were following a pair of hypothetical prescriptions: (1) *if* the temperature is less than *x, then* activate furnace, and (2) *if* the temperature is greater than or equal to *x, then* do not activate. The phrase "as if" plays an important role in how we understand many kinds of living and nonliving machines. These machines are internally structured in such a way that they respond to specific inputs with the same outputs as we would if we were consciously following certain rules or hypothetical prescriptions about those inputs. This feature resembles what we mean when we say a computer is following a certain program: we develop a program as a set of rules of operation that the computer is to "follow" in response to certain kinds of input (e.g., a word processor is a program for textual input). We load this program by bringing about reversible and often transient physical changes in the circuitry of the computer, such that it will respond to certain kinds of input *as if* it were consciously following a set of rules. Setting a thermostat is like programming in this general sense.

Organisms behave as if the modulators of their control systems store enormously complex sets of hypothetical prescriptions—naturally occurring programs that vary with each species. What these programs all have in common is that they enable the organism to *preserve itself.* What does this phrase mean? It can't mean that organisms hang on to the very same materials—molecules, cells, tissues—throughout their lives. All cells, whether existing as independent organisms or as parts of multicellular systems, are constantly building and rebuilding themselves, excreting the materials of earlier components and reconstructing those components with similar but *new* materials. And most of the cells of multicellular organisms are constantly dying and being replaced with cells of the same type. Take the human body. As Lynn Margulis and Dorion Sagan point out, "It continuously self-repairs. Every five days you get a new stomach lining. You get a new liver every two months. Your skin replaces itself every six weeks. Every year ninety-eight percent of the atoms of your body are replaced. This nonstop chemical replacement, metabolism, is a sure sign of life."[57] How, then, do we understand the "self" in self-maintenance/preservation? The phrase implies that the same individual organism is present throughout the turnover in material components. John Locke was struck by this great difference between living and nonliving bodies. The latter remain the same insofar as they continue to be the same collection of particles. Whereas "An animal is a living, organized body and consequently the same animal, as we have observed, is the same continued life communicated to the different particles of matter as they happen successively to be united to that organized living body."[58] The temporal continuity or identity of the organism doesn't consist in being the same collection of components, but rather in a *persisting repertoire* of adaptive responses embodied in an uninterrupted succession of the right sorts of components. As long as the setting or program in the modulator of an organism's adaptive control system continues to be embodied in the sorts of physical components that enable the modulator to function, the organism continues to live. Therefore, we can say that a response is *adaptive* insofar as it enables the organism to continue to be able to respond in the same ways to the same sorts of environmental events.[59] The organism remains this organism (what philosophers call numerical identity) over time by *making itself*, at each point in its duration, an *instance* of the same *kind* of system. For this reason, we can call it a *self-instantiating system*.[60]

The modulator of a cell's adaptive control system is DNA. (The structure and control function of DNA is standard material in any biology textbook. For brevity's sake, I will skim the surface in what follows. A similar disclaimer is in order for the subsequent discussion of brain function.) The role of DNA is described in what is usually called the "central dogma" of molecular biology: DNA *is transcribed into* RNA, which in turn *is translated into* protein. DNA and protein molecules are very long polymers (molecules composed of repeating subunits). The key subunits of DNA are molecules labeled G, C, A, and T, for the first letters of their chemical names. The structure of RNA is similar to that of DNA, except that RNA has one different subunit, U, that plays the role of T. The subunits of proteins come from a list of twenty amino acids. DNA acts as modulator by causing the synthesis of specific proteins as they are needed in the cell. A particular amino acid is coded for by a specific combination of three of the G, C, A, and T subunits of DNA. A sequence of these triple combinations *(codons)* that encodes the sequence of amino acids making up a certain protein is called a *gene*. The entire set of genes is called the *genetic code* and embodies the *self-instantiating program* of the organism. Proteins are very important molecules in the life of a cell. They serve both as structural components and as catalysts that make various essential chemical reactions (metabolism) occur within the cell. There are molecular mechanisms that enable DNA to *detect* those events (e.g., a buildup of sugar molecules within the cell) that call for the synthesis of a particular protein or set of proteins and *select* genes for transcription into RNA, which in turn *effects* the required protein synthesis. When conditions inside the cell have been appropriately altered by the operation of the newly produced proteins, the genes involved are rendered inactive by *feedback* mechanisms until the same stimulus conditions arise again.

For as long as the cell lives, its DNA-directed deployment of proteins always occurs in such a way that the intracellular environment continues to enable DNA to respond in the same ways to the same changes in the future. The cell not only maintains a boundary in three dimensions between its inside and outside (self and other), but also extends that boundary into the fourth dimension insofar as it instantiates itself moment after moment. Genetic regulation of metabolism is how the function of self-instantiation gets carried out in a *uni*cellular system. The vertebrate nervous system is another, *multi*cellular embodiment of this same function. We will look at some of its features next.

As an animal moves about, aspects of its environment change. The animal's adaptive control system must monitor all the changes in its environment that are relevant to the animal's well-being. (Keep in mind that the environment regulated by an adaptive control system includes both the inside and the outside of the organism.) For *detection* to occur, something in the environment must act on a sensor. Energy in some form must be transferred from the environment to the sensor, like the heat in the air that causes expansion of the metals in a thermostat's bimetallic strip. Energy comes in different forms and embodiments, such as heat, light, sound waves, and the pressure of an external body against the animal. A sensor must be able not only to detect the occurrence of an energy transfer, but also to measure or analyze it in various ways. A thermostat bimetallic strip detects not only that warming or cooling is occurring, but also whether and by how much the warming or cooling exceeds or falls short of the optimal temperature (the setting). Similarly, the sensors in an animal's adaptive control system must be able to register the duration, frequency, intensity, location, direction, and other dimensions of the impinging energy. All of these have a bearing on how the animal can respond *adaptively.* For instance, it makes a big difference to an animal whether sounds made by a predator are increasing or decreasing in volume, and in which direction the source is shifting. So an animal will need a variety of sensors with physical structures and materials suited to specific kinds of energy input and to whatever dimensions of the input need to be measured.

The animal's modulator (its brain) will be barraged with signals from different kinds of sensors (called "sensory receptors") distributed over the surface and inside of its body. Its selection of an adaptive response will be determined by the *combination* of signals from different kinds of receptors measuring different kinds of input—for instance, by the combined input from prey to the ears, eyes, and nose of its predator. Just as we can't compare apples with oranges or count one as the other, so a brain needs the signals from its different kinds of sensory receptors to be composed of a *common unit* so that it can measure, compare, or otherwise integrate them. Insofar as sensory receptors perform the function of converting energy from one form or embodiment into another, they act as *transducers* (see fig. 2.4). Different kinds and dimensions of energetic input (such as sound waves or heat) must all be rendered as sequences and patterns of a single kind of neural event. This standardized event is the *action potential* that causes one neuron to emit chemical signals that alter the internal electrical charge of other neurons, thereby making them a bit more or less likely to

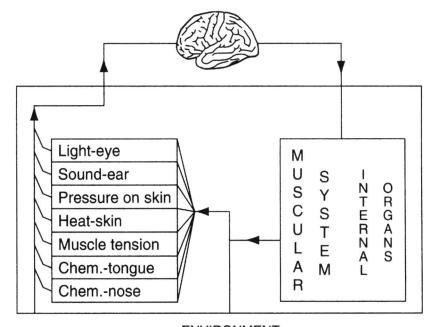

ENVIRONMENT

Figure 2.4.   Diagram of neural control system showing transduction of varieties of sensory input from the internal (muscles and viscera) and external environment into a standardized sensory signal (nerve impulse). (From B. Cooney, *The Place of Mind.* © 2000. Reprinted with permission of Wadsworth.)

generate their own action potential. Also, the time between sensory stimulus and resulting adaptive response will usually have to be very short to enable an animal to respond to events as quickly as needed. Signals *to* the brain from sensory receptors and *from* the brain to its effectors (muscles) need to travel very rapidly. Furthermore, sensory signals, as events *within* the animal body, usually need to be precisely *scaled down* to a microlevel from the macrodimensions of the environmental events they detect. Otherwise, their energy and magnitude would disrupt or destroy the animal. By contrast, motor signals reaching muscles from the brain will have to be *amplified,* in the form of muscular contractions, back to the macrolevel of the environment on which the animal must act. For instance, we wouldn't want motor impulses leaving our brains to have the same amount of energy as the muscle contractions they induce when our hands grip something.

A furnace thermostat behaves as if it were following a simple pair of hypothetical prescriptions (if $t < x$, then activate; if $t \geq x$, then don't activate). How are we to think of the "setting" in the brain module of the nervous system? The hypothetical prescriptions embodied in the human brain and jointly defining its staying-alive setting will be much greater in number and in the complexity of their interrelations than those making up the self-instantiating program of a single cell. To get an inkling of this complexity, consider how difficult it would be to articulate the rules for settling on a party guest list.[61] This task would be only a very small part of more inclusive ones, such as maintaining a circle of friends or pursuing a career. Human life is full of such complexity at every level, from the trivial to the momentous. Since humans seek more than biological survival, we should perhaps be talking not about a setting for staying alive, but about an "identity setting": a vast array of prescriptions that enables me to continue to be not only the kind of animal I am, but also the same person. As part of having a life, I *maintain* not only my body, but also a workspace, a residence, and relationships with family, friends, colleagues, and members of various other communities to which I belong.

Another important difference between the self-instantiating program in a unicellular organism and what we find in animal brains is the capacity for *learning.* The self-instantiating programs in many kinds of animal brains select behavior as if the animal were following very general prescriptions such as: If behavior y upon stimulus x is followed by state z, *then* avoid/repeat the y response to x. If the result is avoidance, state z is, in the language of psychologists, a *punisher;* if the result is repetition, z is a *reinforcer.* For instance, if one's seeing a cheesecake is followed by one's eating the entire cheesecake and then by indigestion, one will be much less likely in the future to eat an entire cheesecake on sight. This diminished likelihood is adaptive. The kind of learning described here (in overly simple terms) is often called "conditioning," and it is very important in the lives of humans and other animals. It is a mechanism that gives rise to indefinitely many learned responses that can be described as obeying hypothetical prescriptions specific to the different values of x, y, and z.

After this cursory examination of what biological science has to tell us about the unicellular ancestry of brain function, I want next to consider its implications for our understanding of mind and consciousness.

REFLECTIONS

1. Do corporations or sovereign states satisfy the definition of a self-instantiating system? If so, are you willing to regard them as living systems?
2. If our planet's earliest living systems lacked the capacity to reproduce, there would be no life on Earth today. Isn't that reason enough to include self-reproduction as an essential or defining characteristic of life?

NOTES

1. Immanuel Kant grouped our subrational desires and feelings under the term "inclination." Here is what he had to say about this aspect of our human nature: "All objects of the inclinations have only a conditional worth, for if the inclinations and the wants founded on them did not exist, then their object would be without value. But the inclinations, themselves being sources of want, are so far from having an absolute worth for which they should be desired that on the contrary *it must be the universal wish of every rational being to be wholly free from them.*" Kant, *Fundamental Principles of the Metaphysic of Morals*, trans. T. K. Abbott, sec. 2, par. 7, 1934, emphasis added, at www.class.uidaho.edu/mickelsen/texts/Kant%20-%20Fundamentals%20.%20.%20.txt (accessed 14 September 2003).

2. N. Katherine Hayles, *How We Became Posthuman: Virtual Bodies in Cybernetics, Literature and Informatics* (Chicago: University of Chicago Press, 1999), xii.

3. A. M. Turing, "Computing Machinery and Intelligence," *Mind* 59, no. 236 (October 1950): 433–60. Turing's paper can also be found at abelard.org/turpap/turpap.htm (accessed 7 December 2003). Turing was one of the major contributors to the breaking of the German Enigma code in World War II, an achievement that played a crucial role in the Allied victory. In 1952, he was arrested in Manchester, England, on charges of homosexuality. He refused to deny the charges, claiming there was nothing wrong with his sexual orientation or behavior. He chose estrogen treatment (in effect, chemical castration) rather than go to prison. He committed suicide in 1954.

4. There is a striking ambiguity in this passage. The conventional interpretation is that when the machine takes the place of A, the interrogator's task changes from deciding who is the male to deciding which is the machine. But Turing's language doesn't say that the interrogator's task has changed. If we were to interpret Turing as talking about a computer programmed to respond like a woman, the implications are quite interesting. But I won't address this, because the context of his article as a whole supports the conventional interpretation, and the many controversies about the meaning of the Turing test rest on this interpretation.

5. Whitaker Foundation web site, at www.whitaker.org/news/peckham.html (accessed 13 September 2003).

6. See "Home Page of the Loebner Prize," at www.loebner.net/Prizef/loebner-prize.html (accessed 13 September, 2003).

7. "Home Page of the Loebner Prize." The gold medal program must convince half the interrogators that it is human. When that happens, the competition will cease to exist.

8. Have your own chat with "her" at www.alicebot.org/ (accessed 12 October 2001).

9. *Expert Systems,* at www.ee.cooper.edu/courses/course_pages/past_courses/EE459/expert/ (accessed 15 October 2001).

10. "PATTIE MAES on Software Agents: Humanizing the Global Computer," interview with Pattie Maes, *IEEE Internet Computing Online* (July–August 1997), at computer.org/internet/v1n4/maes.htm (accessed 13 September 2003).

11. Pattie Maes, "Agents That Reduce Work and Information Overload," MIT Media Lab, at web.media.mit.edu/~pattie/CACM-94/CACM-94.p6.html (accessed 13 September, 2003).

12. See the introduction for a description of MUDs. Julia was created by Michael Loren Mauldin of Carnegie–Mellon University.

13. At least the user *apparently* was a male. Users regularly present themselves in fictional genders. See Sherry Turkle, *Life on the Screen* (New York: Touchstone, 1995), 88–97.

14. Quoted in Turkle, *Life on the Screen,* 93.

15. See "Levels of Reality," this chapter.

16. Turing, "Computing Machinery."

17. John Searle, *The Rediscovery of Mind* (Cambridge, Mass.: MIT Press, 1992), 9.

18. John R. Searle, "Minds, Brains, and Programs," *Behavioral and Brain Sciences* 3 (1980): 418.

19. See "Levels of Reality, this chapter.

20. Gilbert Ryle, *The Concept of Mind* (New York: Barnes & Noble, 1949), 20.

21. See "Scientism," this chapter.

22. $1 \text{ m} = 10^1 \text{ m}$, $0.1 \text{ m} = 10^{-1} \text{ m}$, and so on.

23. B. C. Crandall, "Molecular Engineering," in *Nanotechnology: Molecular Speculations on Global Abundance,* ed. B. C. Crandall (Cambridge, Mass.: MIT Press, 1996), 21.

24. See the discussion of atomic structure in "Levels of Reality," chapter 1.

25. For a recent survey of nanotechnology, see the September 2001 special issue of *Scientific American*.

26. Roco is chair of the National Science and Technology Council's Subcommittee on Nanoscale Science, Engineering and Technology.

27. National Nanotechnology Initiative—Research and Development FY 2003, at nano.gov/2003budget.html (accessed 8 December 2003).

28. Adenosine triphosphate (ATP) captures the chemical energy released within a cell by metabolic reactions that break up complex molecules and transfers the energy to reactions that require it (e.g., the building up of proteins, muscle contraction, or transmission of nerve impulses).

29. C. G. Langton, introduction to C. G. Langton, C. Taylor, J. D. Farmer, and S. Rasmussen, eds., *Artificial Life II*, Santa Fe Institute Studies in the Sciences of Complexity, vol. 10 (Redwood City, Calif.: Addison–Wesley, 1992), xiii, xviii.

30. See "An Enchanted Space," chapter 3.

31. Daniel Dennett, *Consciousness Explained* (Boston: Little, Brown, 1991), 406.

32. The four are *Brainstorms: Philosophical Essays on Mind and Psychology* (1980), *Elbow Room: The Varieties of Free Will Worth Wanting* (1984), *The Intentional Stance* (1987), and *Brainchildren: Essays on Designing Minds* (Cambridge, Mass.: MIT Press) 1998). Another recent and widely read book by Dennett is *Darwin's Dangerous Idea : Evolution and the Meanings of Life* (1995).

33. Daniel Dennett, "The Zombic Hunch: Extinction of an Intuition?" Final Draft for Royal Institute of Philosophy Millennial Lecture, 28 November 1999, at ase.tufts.edu/cogstud/papers/zombic.htm (accessed 13 September 2003).

34. Dennett, *Consciousness Explained*, 406.

35. Dennett, *Brainchildren*, 65.

36. Dennett, *Consciousness Explained*, 402.

37. Dennett, *Brainchildren*, 177.

38. Dennett, "Zombic Hunch."

39. Dennett, *Consciousness Explained*, 408.

40. See "The Pathos of the Senses," this chapter.

41. See "Liberation from the Cave," this chapter.

42. Daniel Dennett, "Faith in the Truth," Final Draft for Amnesty Lecture, Oxford (February 1997), at ase.tufts.edu/cogstud/papers/faithint.htm (accessed 13 September 2003).

43. Daniel Dennett, *The Intentional Stance* (Cambridge, Mass.: MIT Press, 1987), 5.

44. Dennett, "Faith in the Truth."

45. Dennett, "Faith in the Truth."

46. Richard Lewontin, "Billions and Billions of Demons," *New York Review of Books* (9 January 1997).

47. *E.T. the Extraterrestrial* (1982), dir. Steven Spielberg, Universal Studios. *Alien* (1979), dir. Ridley Scott; *Aliens* (1986), dir. James Cameron; *Alien 3* (1992),

dir. David Fincher; and *Alien Resurrection* (1997), dir. Jean-Pierre Jeunet, all from Twentieth Century–Fox.

48. See "Can Machines Think? A Nanoresponse," this chapter. Since these predicates are *functional*, they are not limited to specific kinds of physical embodiment.

49. "Ontology" designates that part of philosophy that concerns itself with what are the fundamental kinds of beings in the universe.

50. See "Descartes' Meditation," this chapter.

51. These included Berkeley, Hume, Kant, and Hegel.

52. Thomas Nagel, *The View from Nowhere* (New York: Oxford University Press, 1986), 109.

53. See "Scientism," this chapter.

54. Nagel, *View from Nowhere*, 9.

55. See "Can Machines Think? A Nanoresponse," this chapter.

56. Terms such as "detect" and "signal" should not be understood in a psychological sense. They signify mechanical events generated in or by one subsystem that causes the next one in the control loop to act as described.

57. Lynn Margulis and Dorion Sagan, *What Is Life?* (New York: Simon and Schuster, 1995), 23.

58. John Locke, *An Essay concerning Human Understanding* (1706), vol. 1, bk. 2, c. 27.

59. Although the word "function" has a somewhat different meaning in this context than it does in mathematics, adaptive control is similar to what mathematicians call a recursive function insofar as it *calls for itself*.

60. Margulis and Sagan, borrowing a phrase from biologists H. Maturana and F. Varela, call this core function "autopoiesis" (from the Greek for "self-making"). Margulis and Sagan, *What Is Life?*

61. As in the case of a thermostat or DNA, terms such as "hypothetical prescription" or "rule" are part of the *as if* analysis of the human brain. I am not claiming that these prescriptions are always, or even usually, conscious, explicit beliefs, but only that humans behave as if they were following such prescriptions. Even in cases where we plan our behavior with conscious reference to some of our practical beliefs, there could never be time enough to rehearse all the beliefs that are implied by our behavior.

3

EMBODIMENT

And life also belongs to God; for the actuality of thought is life, and God is
that actuality; and God's self-dependent actuality is life most good and eternal. We say therefore that God is a living being, eternal, most good, so that
life and duration continuous and eternal belong to God; for this is God.

—Aristotle, *Metaphysics XII*

According to Aristotle, the very perfection of God requires a bodiless and
completely self-contained existence. To have a body is to be susceptible to
interaction with other beings and to be capable of motion. Having a body
brings with it what Aristotle calls *potentiality,* a state of incomplete actuality insofar as some of a being's reality is not yet actual and depends on some
other being affecting it. A being with potentiality is *less* than it would be if
its potentiality were realized. So the perfection of Aristotle's God required
that it be completely actual. It had to exist in splendid isolation, unaffected
by anything outside itself, eternally contemplating itself. Yet Aristotle attributed *life* to this divine being, despite its lack of a body and an interactive environment. It was clear to Aristotle that life was an inherently positive attribute that even a bodiless deity must have. In fact, his God was
supposed to have life even more abundantly than humans and other embodied beings. Christian philosophy inherited Aristotle's philosophical conception of divine being and adapted it as far as possible to the demands of
Christian doctrine. It accepted Aristotle's notion of a *living,* bodiless God.

I find the notion of life without embodiment unintelligible for much the same reasons that I find GOFD vacuous.[1] But I share with Aristotle the still common intuition that only living beings can be conscious. However, I would add that life requires *embodiment*. I have been arguing that living systems should be understood as self-instantiating or self-embodying and that the unicellular function of self-instantiation is the evolutionary ancestor of human consciousness. Since billions of years of evolution separate these two forms of self-instantiation, we cannot expect that an analysis of what they have in common will tell us a great deal about the functions that are specific to human minds. Nevertheless, what they have in common can, I believe, yield some very important insights about mind and its place in nature.

THE FLOW OF TIME

It rests by changing.

—Heraclitus

Let's take a closer look at the difference between living and nonliving systems, a difference that Descartes suppressed by collapsing the first and second levels of the ontological tetrad.[2] This brings us to a topic that is as old as the beginnings of philosophy and science in the reflections of the earliest Greek thinkers. Every body is both one and many, in two senses—each has a multiplicity both of parts and of attributes. Let's focus on the multiplicity of parts. Each part occupies a space that is external to the space occupied by any other part. Each part is itself a body that exists *outside* any other part of the whole body. What is the basis for regarding the whole made up of these parts as *one* thing rather than a collection or heap of things? Is this merely convention or an arbitrary choice based on one's interest or perspective? For example, is an atom or a molecule one thing or a scattering of many things (nuclei and electrons) framing a mostly empty space? A carpenter might tend to see even a finished wooden bench as a collection or assembly of pieces of wood rather than as one thing, whereas someone whose only relation to benches is that she sits on them would regard a bench as one thing. Is there any *intrinsic unity* in bodies apart from the extrinsic and relative unity that the mind imposes insofar as it sees a collection of parts or bodies as satisfying the specifications of one or other of its concepts (e.g., the trees as a *forest* or the *bench* as a collection of assembled parts or as a thing embodying one function—that of supporting the human body in a sitting position)?

Is this such a big issue? Yes, actually. It makes a great difference to how we understand the world around us whether there are beings out there with their own reality independent of how we categorize them. Is what we experience as our environment no more than putty shaped by our cognitive activity? Is there anything but me *in* what is out there? Are *things* that hollow?

Perhaps I'm overstating the problem here. After all, isn't there an intrinsic difference between what is merely a heap, such as a pile of pebbles or the sand in a box, and a solid rock or well-made bench with parts firmly joined to each other? The rock and the bench aren't just collections; they have *unified* parts. Or is their greater unity merely relative to the size or strength of the bodies interacting with them? What about two one-ton slabs of marble, one of which is flush against the top of the other? I can no more separate them than I can divide a rock with my bare hands. But if I were strong enough to move the marble slabs with my hands, I would also be able to break the rock into pieces. The "greater" unity I compared to a heap of pebbles is purely a function of the size and strength of my body. It's not any more intrinsic than the unity of a sand pile.

When I speak of the mind "imposing" unity on objects, I don't mean to imply that we can think of anything just as we please, with equal validity. You can think of a cardboard model of a chair as a chair like other chairs, but don't try sitting on it. When we apply a concept to some body, we're predicting that it will interact with other bodies (including our own) as specified by that concept. If the body doesn't behave that way, then we have applied the concept incorrectly. A bench behaves *both* as one thing *and* as an assembly, depending on how we interact with it—we can sit on it, but we can also disassemble it. There is, of course, a physical domain that is "out there," existing independently of the mind and its concepts, but this domain behaves rather like a text, a poem or novel, for instance. A text exists as part of the physical domain (e.g., a poem on paper or in the circuitry of a computer). But there are many ways to interpret it. Some interpretations are better than others because they give more unity (e.g., of theme and imagery) to the text or better enable us to anticipate what comes later in the text or to otherwise make more sense of it than other interpretations. It's hard, though not impossible, to understand a poem as a recipe, just as it is hard to eat wax fruit.

The unity of organisms (including cells) is very different from that of nonliving bodies. We *can* look at an organism as one or many, depending on our perspective. We can see a cow as a collection of edible parts or as a machine for producing milk; in fact, we've bred them to be that way. But the cow has its own perspective on its unity in space and time. *It* is very busy maintaining the integrity of its body by breathing, grazing, and drinking and would (however ineffectively) resist a predator that might try to disrupt its unity by eating it. It has, in that way, an *intrinsic, self-imposed* unity that does not depend on *our* regarding it as one. In domesticating cows, we have altered their bodies and dumbed down their brains so we can more readily use them as means for *our* self-instantiation. Thus we can easily ignore their perspective as we deal with them. We have to be much more careful with certain wild animals. For a lion, killing an approaching human might be part of *its* self-instantiation.

Self-instantiation gives to an organism what could be called an *inner* aspect or reality that is lacking in nonliving systems. Perhaps the easiest way to see this is by reflecting on what we mean when we say about some body that *it changed*. As happens so often in philosophy, an expression that is unproblematic in ordinary discourse can become quite puzzling when we reflect on it. What is the referent of the pronoun "it" in "it changed"? The use of the pronoun suggests that something is there or remains the *same* before and after the change, yet the verb "changed" signifies a discontinuity, a *difference* between what was there before and what is there now. There seems to be a contradiction here, of the sort that led Parmenides[3] to claim that change is unreal and true being must be eternal and unchanging. Many Greek philosophers after Parmenides (including Plato and Aristotle) struggled with this same problem in an effort to avoid Parmenides' radical response to it.

Let's look a bit more closely at what is going on when we use some variant of the expression "it changed" to signify that a body or system has become different from what it was, but is still there, still somehow the same body. There are two possibilities. The *first* is that the change is within the allowed or predictable variations that are part of our concept of a particular kind of thing. For instance, we understand *water* as the sort of thing that solidifies at temperatures at or below 0° Celsius. Before *and* after the freezing, there continues to be something satisfying the specifications of our concept of water, and we're comfortable with the notion that the water in the ice-cube tray is still there when frozen. However, if the water in a bird bath has evaporated on a hot, dry summer day, what sort of continuity do we understand by the statement that "it evaporated"? To a child, the sentence describes a kind of annihilation that happens to water under certain conditions. To a scientifically literate adult, the statement can signify a transition from a liquid to a gaseous dispersal of particles in which the water is still "out there" in some sense. The degree of continuity we observe depends on the concept we apply. The *water* is still there when it freezes, but the *ice cube* is no longer there when the water melts back to its liquid state. A body's continuity in time is like its unity in space—a function of *our* interests and the specifications of *our* concepts. Its unity in space and time is *extrinsic and relative to an observer.*

The second possibility is that the body we are observing is *unifying itself* in space and time, doing *for itself* the sort of thing we do when our concept of a body enables us to discern its spatial boundaries and recognize it as the same before and after its alterations. Whether I study the behavior of an animal in the wild or of a bacterium under a microscope, I see a body constantly exchanging materials and energy with its environment and changing its shape and location. It has within it, in the form of neural circuitry or a genome, a self-instantiating program[4] that causes the body to respond to events in its environment in such a way as to retain its adaptive repertoire by maintaining the body structure this repertoire depends upon. As I pointed out earlier, each part of a body is as much external to the adjacent parts of that body as it is to what is outside the body.[5] How *we* divide what is inside a body from what is outside is relative to our concept of the kind of body we are observing. The scientific representation of time as a fourth dimension, a line divisible into segments, brings out an important similarity between space and time—that the parts of the *duration* of a body are as much outside each other as its *spatial* parts. When we recognize a body as identical before and after it has changed, we are including both parts (earlier and later) of its duration within the four-dimensional unity of the body; we are distinguishing an inside from an outside of the body's space-time. Insofar as this inside is maintained by a body's self-instantiating program, the body has *intrinsic* spatiotemporal unity—what I have called an inner aspect. It is not just an *object* of our concept; it is also a *subject* doing for itself what our concepts do for mere objects. It has a self to instantiate.[6] There is something in the cognitive putty other than *my* cognitive activity.

An organism's responses to events in its environment are adaptive or self-instantiating to the extent that they help preserve the organism's repertoire of adaptive responses by maintaining the kind of body required for this repertoire. In other words, adaptive responses are *means* to the *end* of self-preservation. Therefore, the organism is, objectively and *intrinsically,* a value or *end for itself.* To the extent that humans see a deer as a food source or as a pleasing part of a wilderness scene, we treat it as having a merely instrumental value, as a means for our dietary or aesthetic satisfaction. Just as the unity of merely external objects such as a chair or an atom is extrinsic because it depends on *our* concepts of them, so the value of organisms as a source of food or contemplative pleasure is extrinsic because it depends on their usefulness to *our* purposes. A self-instantiating system does for itself what our concepts and purposes do for objects—*it gives itself unity and value.* We can test our intuition here by asking ourselves what it would mean to say that something is *good* for a rock or a piece of earth. We say that moisture and various nutrients are good for soil, but that is in relation either to the plants growing in the soil or to us insofar as we enjoy or culti- vate the plants. Like a rock, soil in itself doesn't have a good. But even the simplest unicellular systems have a good—such things as the right temper- ature and chemicals in its environment are objectively good for a bac- terium. The origin of life billions of years ago was also the origin of value on this planet.

From the foregoing discussion, it seems clear that there is a strong con- nection between being a mind (or having one) and being alive. The evolu- tionary ancestor of the human mind is the self-instantiating function carried out by DNA, primarily in its regulation of metabolism.[7] Self-instantiation is the defining attribute of a living system. What we call our stream of con- sciousness is the process of self-instantiation become aware of itself in a hu- man brain. Many philosophers have noted that the stream-like aspect of con- sciousness, its "flowing" from what *was* to what is *not yet,* cannot be captured by representing time as a line. Suppose we draw a line of a certain length and divide it into uniform segments representing minutes. Let's say the line represents the duration of a one-mile foot race. Each point on the line symbolizes a moment in three-dimensional space when each of the run- ners can be imagined as frozen in a certain stage of their stride and occupy- ing a certain position relative to the other runners. The line we've drawn doesn't adequately render the duration it supposedly represents. The trou- ble is that all the points on this line *coexist* and are *outside* each other at fixed distances. We can almost instantaneously scan the line we have drawn, tak- ing in its beginning and end all at once. The minutes we *experienced* in the running of the race were quite different. The whole point and thrill of watching a race is to see it develop, waiting for what hasn't yet happened, cheering on our favorite runners, as our excitement keeps rising until the race is over. Fortunately, our experience of the passage of time is usually less intense, but it is always the experience of a passing of what *is not yet* into what *has been*—what is often called the *flow* of time. That's what the linear image of time fails to capture. It spatializes time, treating the fourth dimen- sion like the other three; but that is not the way we experience it.

Even as brilliant a thinker as Isaac Newton (1643–1727) stumbled over this. He thought that space and time each had an absolute existence, independent not only of observers, but even of objects and events. He said that "absolute, true, and mathematical time, of itself, and from its own nature, *flows* equably without relation to anything external, and by another name is called duration."[8] This makes no sense. A flow is a movement from one part of space to another. If *time* is flowing, it would seem that there are parts of space into which time has not yet flowed, or out of which it has flowed. But time is supposed to be everywhere, always. The space *from* which a liquid flows, and the space *into* which it flows, *coexist;* but the future does *not* co-exist with the past. When we speak of the flow of time, we are imagining time as a liquid in motion in an effort to represent in space the successive-ness of time, the continuous slippage of future into past. But, finally, there is something about time that cannot be spatialized. We can use a line to rep-resent the *order* of time with respect to what is earlier and later, as well as the divisibility of an interval into units of measurement. The line also re-minds us that one part of time is *outside* another. But the line cannot do jus-tice to the successiveness of time, as the great idealist philosopher Im-manuel Kant (1724–1804) realized almost a century after Newton:

> Time is nothing but the form of inner sense, that is, of the intuition of our-selves and of our inner state. It cannot be a determination of outer appear-ances; it has to do neither with shape nor position, but with the relation of rep-resentations in our inner state. And just because this inner intuition yields no shape, we endeavour to make up for this want by analogies. We represent the time-sequence by a line progressing to infinity . . . and we reason from the properties of this line to all the properties of time, with this one exception, that while the parts of the line are simultaneous the parts of time are always successive.[9]

Kant argued that space and time are what he called "forms of human sensibility"—rather like lenses through which all human perceivers sense the world. Just as we know in advance that if we view the world through rose-tinted lenses, everything will look rosy, so we know that because we humans perceive everything through the medium of space and time, everything we experience will be spatiotemporal. However, although we can remove a pair of rose-tinted glasses and look at the true colors of things, we can't remove the forms of our sensibility any more than we can shed our humanity. So, Kant argues, we can never perceive the way things are in themselves, inde-pendently of our minds. We have no access to what he calls "things in them-selves." The objects we perceive are *appearances* existing only in relation to human minds. Kant called space the form of "outer sense" (our awareness of what is external to, or *other* than, ourselves) and time the form of "inner sense" (our *self*-awareness). Because everything we perceive is accompanied by an implicit *self*-awareness, objects in space will also be in time insofar as they are objects of *my* experience. However, I do experience some purely temporal contents, such as moods and feelings, as states of myself that fill my consciousness without having any spatial structure of their own.

Kant was still operating within the dualistic framework of Descartes, according to which the world was divided between minds and material things, selves and external objects. If the flow of time could not be located "out there," in space or in bodies, then the only other possibility was to locate it in the mind as a universal feature of human consciousness. By contrast, I have been arguing that what we experience as the flow of time in ourselves is also present in all living systems insofar as we share with them the property of being *subjects* engaged in self-instantiation.

REFLECTIONS

What do you think of these objections to the arguments above?

Objection 1. Whatever disrupts the unity of a body is *bad* for that body. The blow of a sledgehammer is just as disruptive to the unity of a stone, and therefore just as *bad* for it, as the crushing pressure of a boot is for a bug. There were plenty of rocks on earth before the first cells appeared. So it's not the case that "the origin of life billions of years ago was the origin of value on this planet."

Objection 2. You say that the linear representation of time leaves out the successiveness of time because all the points (representing moments) on a line *coexist*, whereas each moment of time as we experience it immediately becomes part of the past and thus ceases to exist. If you are right, then how do we hear a *melody* or experience the *curvature* of the edge of something we are running a hand over?

AN ENCHANTED SPACE

> Swiftly the brain becomes an enchanted loom, where millions of flashing shuttles weave a dissolving pattern—always a meaningful pattern—though never an abiding one.
>
> —Sir Charles Sherrington

Another problem with the linear image of time is that it suggests that each moment, including the present (the Now), is like a point on a line. This implies that a moment has no magnitude. But that is not how we experience the present moment. The conscious present includes some of the immediate past—how else could we hear a melody *as* a melody or sense the *curvature* of an object as our hand moves along it? Just as there is a flow-through of matter and energy as a cell instantiates itself in each successive interval by incorporating new materials from its environment while discarding spent ones, so there is a flow of sensory input into and out of our consciousness as we go about the business of living from moment to moment and perception to perception. Self-instantiating activity gives an organism intrinsic unity in space and time (1) by operating over the various *coexisting* parts of its body and thereby uniting parts that are otherwise outside each other and (2) by doing the same thing with each successive part of the organism's duration, spanning the temporal interval represented by the linear distance from one point to another. It does this by bringing about at each point an *instance* of itself in the three-dimensional space or body represented by that point. The "streaming" of consciousness in the human brain is this spanning function become present to itself.

Critic: Stop right there! Before you spiral out of sight on the wings of your analogy, please notice the huge difference between cellular self-instantiation and consciousness. Mental life is about such things as perceptions and desires, whereas the a cell's adaptive behavior is about molecules and chemical reactions.

Author: Yes, there is a big difference. Let's talk about that. The adaptive control system of a cell interacts with the environment it regulates *at the same level* of magnitude and energy as events in that environment. It is nanomachinery dealing with nanoscale events, molecule to molecule. As I pointed out earlier, this would be impossible for organisms at the macrolevel.[10] If sensory and motor signals had the magnitude of environmental events, they would disrupt or destroy an animal's body. Instead, when stimulus events affect sensory receptors, they induce signals that are scaled down to microdimensions, as well as transduced into the standard signal unit of a neuron impulse. In the reverse direction, motor signals are amplified when they reach muscle tissue and trigger contractions that have sufficient force to affect the environment. Intervening between sensory and motor signals is, in humans at least, what you called "mental life." It is embodied in about 100 billion neurons, each of which has, on average, about one thousand connections with other neurons. Each neuron is like a little computer operating in parallel with all the others. It is constantly barraged with signals from other neurons, signals that have the effect of making the neuron more or less likely to initiate along its axon an impulse that will shower signals on a huge array of downstream neurons. Figure 3.1A shows what a few of the neurons in a slice of brain tissue look like *from the outside* (as external *objects* from a third-person point of view), and figure 3.1B shows what the entire array of neural activity constituting a perception would be like *from the inside* (from a first-person point of view, for the human *subject* whose brain it is) for someone looking at Old Centre. Of course, for the point I'm trying to make, you can substitute the experience you're having now for figure 3.1B.

Critic: Poof! Just like that, huh? Having those two photos side by side like that only brings out more clearly the immense problem you're skipping over with your analogy between unicellular and mental life. In the case of cells, you're talking about a sequence of *molecular* events all the way from input

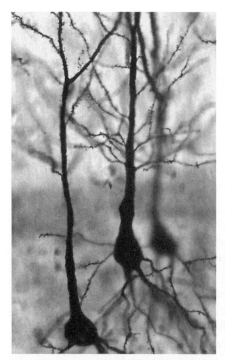

Figure 3.1A: Photomicrograph of three cortical cells isolated from the mass of neighboring neurons by a staining technique. Courtesy of Miles Herkenham, Section on Functional Neuroanatomy, National Institute of Mental Health, Bethesda, Maryland.

Figure 3.1B: Photograph of Old Centre.

to output. The content of the cell is molecular, and its processes are chemical, such as DNA getting involved in protein synthesis. With mental events, you also have molecular interactions among neurons like those on the left, but they give rise to *perceptions* such as that on the right, perceptions that are *contents* of the mind/brain in some totally different sense of "content" than we use when we speak of molecules inside a cell or neurons inside brain tissue. With a microscope, I can look inside a cell and find DNA and the other molecules, and I can find in the brain the cells depicted in figure 3.1A. But no microscope will let me observe a building inside the brain. You're being equivocal in your use of "inside" and "content."

Author: Of course, the building isn't inside the brain in the sense that neurons are inside it! I admit that I'm using "content" in two very different senses when I apply it to molecules and to perceptions, but the difference between these two senses of "content" is clear in this context—it is like the difference between the spatial notion of an *inside* and what I call the *inner* aspect of a self-instantiating system. What is spatially inside is the content of an external *object*, whereas the building is the content of a *subject*. One and the same body can have both kinds of content simultaneously, as in figure 3.1.

Critic: I think I'm beginning to understand where you're going.

Author: Insofar as molecules are inside the cell as a *subject*, insofar as they are part of its inner reality, they are as different from how they appear to us as the building is from the neurons in figure 3.1. The human brain and an individual cell are both *subjects*. The *objective*, scientific description of what is happening in the brain is imaged in figure 3.1A, whereas the same set of brain events is something quite different (like a building) insofar as it is content for the brain as *subject*. Similarly, the scientific description of a cell's content (molecular processes) is quite different from what these processes are as content for the cell as *subject*.

Critic: I suspected that was where you were going. I've heard of philosophers asking us to contemplate what it is like to be a bat.[11] But you're saying that there is something that it is like to be a bacterium. That's a bit weird. Or just flaky, like the short-lived fad in pet rocks.

Author: I'm just heeding the command of Parmenides' goddess to follow the argument wherever it goes. Of course, all arguments are reversible. If you reject the conclusion, and yet the conclusion follows from the premises I've been elaborating, go ahead and challenge one of them. But don't reject the conclusion just because it's "weird." What sounds weird is often a function of what you're accustomed to hearing and of the company you keep. People in the philosophical community haven't found it weird to hear from famous philosophers that "we're all zombies" or that "we can give a complete account of man in purely physico-chemical terms."[12] Moreover, the mind–brain relation has been one of the most intractable problems in philosophy. Any progress in solving it will inevitably stretch the conventional meanings of many of the terms used in the discussion. And your reference to pet rocks is totally beside the point, since what I've been talking about is the *ontological divide* between nonliving systems such as rocks and living, self-instantiating systems. Only the latter are subjects.

Critic: Fair enough. A brain[13] and a cell are both subjects, as you've defined that term. Something like figure 3.1B can be the content or perception of a brain *as a subject* and also be the sort of thing that is partially imaged in the three neurons of figure 3.1A when the same brain is given a third-person, *scientific* description. According to the parallel you suggest, what is described as a set of molecular processes in a cell can also be for that same cell *as subject* a . . . perception? Is that what you'd call it? I can't get my mind around that!

Author: I understand. Using "perception" in that context is like calling an acorn an oak. The acorn will *become* an oak under the right conditions, but it stretches the usual meaning of "oak" too far to apply it to an acorn. I'm not urging a radical revision in our use of "perception." However, we need to recognize that the kind of subjective state that occurs in a unicellular system *is* the evolutionary ancestor of what we call perception in a brain, and there is something very important in common between them, just as an acorn really is an early stage of an oak. As Thomas Nagel has pointed out, although we are increasingly able to understand the neural mechanisms of perception in other animal species, it is impossible to know *what it is like to be them.*[14] For instance, because a bat is the *subject* of sonar perceptions, we can't know what it's like to be a bat. We just have to admit the existence of something that our understanding can never penetrate. If that is true for fellow mammals such as bats, it is even more so for nonmammalian vertebrates, to say nothing of organisms without nervous systems.

Critic: It seems to me that your theory is a kind of dualism, with many of the same problems as GOFD. Instead of mind and body, you give us a duality of inner and outer in the makeup of every living system. As figure 3.1 makes clear, subjective and objective content have as little intelligible connection with each other as mind and body in Descartes. There is nothing about the content of figure 3.1A that would let you guess that it is the objective or outer aspect of what's in figure 3.1B, and vice versa. And you've compounded the unintelligibility of dualism by extending it to countless hosts of life-forms, all the way down to single cells.[15] Your dualism involves not just humans, but the entire biomass of the planet.

Author: Be careful about how you use the term "unintelligible." If you're saying that there is no *scientific* intelligibility about the relation between inner and outer in living systems, I agree. Science deals with the outer aspect exclusively, with what is observable and measurable. I don't agree that *only* science can make things intelligible—that's the dogma of scientism. I have argued that what we have learned from biological science about adaptive control systems in every organism from single cells to humans suggests a fundamental ontological difference between living and nonliving bodies. Ontology is not a scientific enterprise; it's part of philosophy. But the philosophical argument here continues where the science leaves off. As a philosopher, I see no reason why I should accept that there is nothing more to understand about organisms than what is yielded by the methodology of science. The inner and outer aspects of living bodies are *not* unconnected, as you suggest. Far from it. The notion of self-instantiation incorporates the general scientific facts about adaptive control systems into the vocabulary of philosophy, so that we can relate these facts to traditional philosophical questions about what kind of unity a body has in space and time. Biological science tells us *how* a body can be a subject. The notion of a self-instantiating system provides one answer to the longstanding philosophical puzzle about how a body that is changing can have temporal identity. Only by being a subject and having an inner aspect can a body have *intrinsic* spatiotemporal unity.

Critic: The notion of a self-instantiating system is purely functional—it doesn't specify which kinds of components will embody it. These systems function by responding to events in an environment in such a way as to retain the capacity to respond in the same ways to the same sorts of events. This suggests that there could be living, and even conscious, systems in a *virtual* environment. You have referred to genetic information as a self-instantiating *program*.[16] Do you really think that *programs* running in a computer could be alive? That the image on the screen could be a living body?

Author: Yes. And thanks for steering the conversation in that direction. With critics like you, who needs coauthors?

Critic: I'm still your critic, and I'm very skeptical of this implication of your argument. *The Matrix* did a lot of fantasizing about virtual reality. But even in that film the rebels navigating the virtual environment of the matrix could not stay alive without their real bodies, which were strapped into chairs underground. As Cypher demonstrated, kill the flesh and you kill the cyberbody also.[17] If a body is virtual, then it's not real.

Author: Pixels on a display screen, computer microcircuitry and the flows of electricity through it, all these are just as real and physical as the neurons and electrochemical events that are the physical ingredients of your mental life. As Descartes realized in the middle of the seventeenth century, as long as the relevant parts of your brain are stimulated in the right way, you would be having the very same experience that you're having now by interacting with an external, physical world that, you believe, is like what you're experiencing.[18] This is true not only of your perception of the external world, but also of your experience of your own body. As *experience*, it is physically constituted by neural events, specifically, by patterns of electrochemical currents that neurons induce in each other. And these are sealed off from the rest of the intracellular details in neurons. Artificial elements and circuitry with the same input/output relations to other elements would presumably sustain the same mental life and experiences you're now having, as long as *they* were interacting in the same ways as your neurons, whether or not they had input/output relations with an external world resembling the contents of those experiences.

The environment in which your mind functions as a self-instantiating system is rather similar to the kind of environment in which a computer program would operate: both consist of a flux of very low-voltage electrical events to which a program responds. If those responses are adaptive, then the system is alive. A life-form is always relative to an environment; it is an embodied repertoire of responses to a specific sort of environment.

Critic: It seems that *any* program would be alive, by your account. Programs respond to a specific input the same way each time, and they retain their capacity for such a response to such an input. Once loaded, a program is, to use your phrase, an embodied repertoire of responses.

Author: You left out something crucial. The phrase I used was "embodied repertoire of *adaptive* responses." An adaptive or self-instantiating program has certain requirements: (1) a boundary that sets its body or embodiment apart from the environment, giving it a spatiotemporal inside; (2) an environment in which *all* events, inside and outside the body, obey laws (even if those laws are different from the laws of nature that scientists constantly try to discover and accurately formulate); (3) a body that is engaged in constant interaction with its environment but is subject to harm or disruption from adverse environmental events; and (4) the ability to respond to environmental events in such a way as to secure the continuing existence of the body and environment that the program needs in order to run. Please indulge me here while I go to the board and diagram how these requirements are met by the internal domain of neural events that is the immediate environment of the life of a human mind (see fig. 3.2). From there, we can look at how a self-instantiating program would function within a computer.

Critic: OK. Let me check if I'm reading your diagram correctly. What you seem to have done is to simplify the lower box in your previous diagram (see figure 2.4) by leaving out the differences in sensory modalities, while you have expanded the brain icon on top of figure 2.4 into a box in which you nest a modulator and what you call the "model." What does that word mean here?

Author: It signifies the environment on which the brain's adaptive control system *directly* operates, an environment constituted by neural circuitry and electrochemical currents. Much of our sensory input, once it reaches the brain, is projected onto various "maps" of the inside, surface, and external environment of our bodies. For instance, sensory input from muscles or from

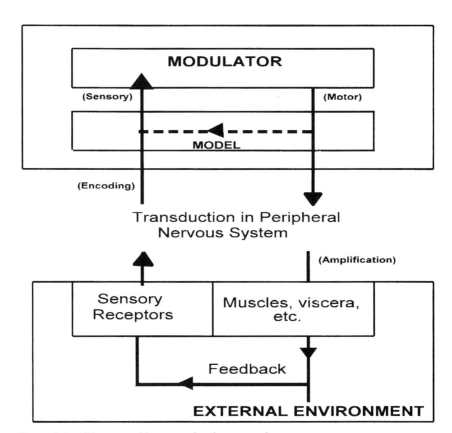

Figure 3.2.   Diagram of human adaptive control system.

pressure on the surface of the skin affects corresponding points on the brain's somatosensory maps of the body, and a spot of light on the wall activates a specific site on the retina of the eye, and that site, in turn, connects with a specific site in the brain's visual cortex that is stimulated by input from the part of one's visual field occupied by the spot of light (see figs. 1.1A and 1.1B). At every moment, alterations in the electrochemical signals among billions of brain neurons are being induced by input from sensory receptors all over our bodies. A wide variety of the energies at work in the world within reach of our senses gets transduced and scaled down to the medium of neural impulses, and these energies are thereby represented in the constantly shifting patterns of neural activity in the brain's model of its external environment. Adaptive responses to events represented in the brain's model come in the form of patterns of neural activity that do not register directly as contents of perception. Instead, they are transduced and amplified into muscle activity that affects sensory receptors in muscles and joints and that alters the environment in ways that in turn affect sensory receptors. In other words, the patterns of motor impulses in the brain normally give rise to sensation only by way of *feedback,* indirectly affecting the content of the brain's model. For instance, when I voluntarily wave my hand, I don't experience the outgoing pattern of signals to the relevant muscles; I merely sense the downstream *effects* of those signals—such as the tensing of muscles in my arm, the rotation of my elbow and shoulder joints, and the sight of my arm moving. This feature contributes to the *passivity* of human experience that I spoke of early in chapter 1.[19] We experience a desire to do something (e.g., we see a friend across the street and want to wave), and then we experience it getting done by our body, but we don't seem to be in on what intervenes between desire and execution.

Critic: Why the broken line creating a loop *within* the brain's model?

Author: In a word, imagination. I put the broken line there not so much to explain as to *acknowledge* a very important function I won't be able to discuss at length here. It's a capacity or set of capacities that we humans obviously have and other species seem to possess to some degree or other. Suppose I'm standing in the doorway to a room where a reception is taking place, and I'm surveying the people chatting and sipping in various groups. I can imagine going up to different people whom I recognize and I can anticipate what I might say to them, how they might react, how that would serve my agenda, and so on. In such a case, the motor impulses associated with my imagined movement don't get amplified into muscle contractions. Instead, they generate from my memory input to my brain's model of the room. This input serves as a pale but very useful proxy for the sensory input I would get from actually using my muscles to behave the way I'm imagining. I don't confuse this imagined behavior with the real thing, but I can learn from it all the same, assessing the consequences of alternatives without actually experiencing them from sensory input. It's the sort of thing involved in thinking over what we're about to say, and it is a pervasive feature of our mental life that incorporates past learning and memory to generate feedback within the brain in the absence of actual behavior.

Critic: OK. It seems pretty obvious that we and many other mammals have that capacity, though neuroscience still has a lot to learn about how the brain carries it out. You told me that your diagram would help you explain how a self-instantiating program would operate within the virtual environment of a computer. Let's go on to that topic now.

Author: Sure. By the way, what we're discussing now is another reason for accepting Descartes' claim that what we experience and call reality is the same stuff that dreams are made of.[20] What our minds (our self-instantiating programs) *directly* respond to when we're awake *and* when we're dreaming is content embodied in neural events. The difference is that when we're awake, the flux of neural events is, to a crucial degree, determined by sensory input from the external environment modeled by our brains. When this input is lacking or ignored, we are in the domain of dreams, daydreams, and fantasy. When the sensory input is from a computer, we are in a *virtual* environment; and when this input comes from the usual external events, we are experiencing reality in the real life (RL) sense.

If a mind were to be embodied in a computer, there are similar possibilities. If this mind were inside a robot and got sensory input through receptors that interfaced with the environment outside the computer, and if its effector mechanisms interfaced with the external environment, it would be instantiating itself in the external environment just as we do. Or its situation could be quite the opposite. All its input and output relations may be limited to a virtual environment inside a computer or network (perhaps as wide as the Internet). Or perhaps it would occasionally interface with RL just as we do with virtual reality (VR). It might be a superintelligent agent[21] with a very rich virtual life that is symbiotic with external users who maintain the computer system it inhabits in exchange for the useful data it regularly supplies to them.

Critic: According to your account, for something to be a mind, it must be alive. And life, you say, involves "constant interaction" with an environment. When I'm asleep at night, there are all kinds of physiological activities that still go on in my body, and the neurons in my brain and nervous system are in a standby mode, ready to cause me to respond to sensory stimuli by changing my position or even waking me up. However, once a computer that embodies a mind is disconnected from its power source, *nothing* is going on inside it—it's incapable of input or output. If I (or any other animal) were in that condition, we'd be *dead,* with no possibility of revival. Yet, if you reconnect the computer, it carries on as before. The word "alive" applied to the computer mind seems more like a metaphor than like the real thing—a bit like the way we use the word when we say that a car engine comes "alive" after ignition. I remember a cartoon that made fun of the idea that a computer could house a mind. The first frame showed a computer with a speech bubble around Descartes' dictum "I think, therefore I am." The second frame showed the computer with its plug lying outside the socket and with no speech bubble.

Author: Humans and other animals are just as dependent on physical inputs from their environments as the computer is on its electrical power source. The computer in the cartoon looks especially vulnerable because it depends on an easily interrupted electrical connection, rather like a patient in an intensive care unit. Let's make the computer more robust by giving it a long-lasting battery and the capacity to connect itself to securely stored chargers. And let's suppose that this computer has a standby mode in which it uses little power but is ready to activate whenever it detects anything relevant in its environment, just as we are when asleep.

The physiological processes and intracellular metabolism that continue even when we're asleep are manifestations of life *at a lower level* than the one we function at when awake. Because our sensory, motor, and cognitive functions are embodied in a multicellular body, a major part of our self-nstantiating activity is directed toward maintaining an internal environment in which our cells and tissues can live. We must do such things as eat, drink, sleep, and stay within a certain temperature range in order to preserve the high-maintenance body that evolution has saddled us with. But there is a seal between our mental functions and the lower-level physiology of our bodies. Our minds are only weakly coupled[22] with the seething multicellular community that embodies them. If they were housed in low-maintenance bionic brains and bodies, most of their self-instantiating activity would be devoted to maintaining the external environment in which their bodies operate—the workplaces and other physical and social spaces that enable them to do what they do. That's what being alive would mean not only for bionic humans, but also for any artificial system with a mind.

Critic: To the extent that these future mind scenarios you describe are credible, I find them rather disturbing in many ways. If we were able to populate physical space with robot persons and cyberspace with virtual persons, it would seem that we ought to regard them as having the intrinsic worth and dignity we attach to human persons. Yet these persons would, at least in the beginning, be products of human will and contrivance. Would we exercise property rights over them or feel free to destroy them when they outlasted their usefulness (like the replicants in *Blade Runner* or the mechas in *AI*)? To the extent that they become easy and inexpensive to produce, will the lives of persons lose their value because robot and virtual persons are in such plentiful supply? Persons are supposed to be autonomous—that's why we prefer democracy to dictatorship and abhor slavery. Yet would we risk giving autonomy to artificial persons? What might they ultimately do to *us*?

Author: I certainly don't claim to have a master plan for all these contingencies. We, all of us, need to do a great deal more thinking about the effects of future technology on our society and species. Here is one contingency I've thought about a great deal lately. At the present time, the supply of healthy human infants tends to fall a bit short of demand, at least within affluent societies in which birth control is widely practiced. Humans often experience difficulty becoming pregnant at a time of their choosing, and pregnancy requires a significant investment of time, energy, and money, especially on the part of a woman. How much of the value we place on the life of a child is a function of its relative scarcity and the opportunity cost that pregnancy imposes on a woman? The conventional philosophical explanation for that value is that the child is a (potential) *person.* However, perhaps we aren't being entirely honest by putting it that way. In her famous paper "A Defense of Abortion," Judith Thomson uses a striking image that poses this question almost in passing:

> Suppose it were like this: people seeds drift about in the air like pollen, and if you open your windows, one may drift in and take root in your carpets or upholstery. You don't want children, so you fix up your windows with fine mesh screens, the very best you can buy. As can happen . . . one of the screens is defective; and a seed drifts in and takes root. Does the person–plant who now develops have a right to the use of your house? Surely not.[23]

Although Thomson does not intend this point, her image suggests a world in which the equivalent of abortion would be routine and unavoidable, instead of being an agonizing personal and social issue. Her scenario, of course, bears no resemblance to any foreseeable world, and so it's hard to take it seriously. But imagine a future in which technology has rendered pregnancy obsolete—in which gestation in an artificial environment is inexpensive, much safer for the fetus, and much less demanding of a woman. Or one in which nanotechnology can quickly produce bionic humans (or superhumans) whose artificial components don't need to be grown from cells and tissues. The process is not expensive, and it also allows for replication of individuals. When persons are in such abundant supply, will they be the bearers of the kind of dignity and intrinsic worth we now ascribe to human persons? Would it be psychologically or politically possible to continue to recognize such a value?

If we are to have a future in which persons *can* be treated with dignity, we will have to be deliberate about creating conditions that allow for such treatment. We will have to restrict the supply of persons, keeping it well below our production capacity. People today are very resistant to this idea. Most Americans, for instance, believe it is their sovereign right to bring as many children into the world as they choose, even though each addition to our population further taxes increasingly scarce community resources such as water, clean air, green space, and agricultural land. We know better, but wisdom is a late and uncertain product of knowledge. Since the late 1960s, we have had photographs of our planet from orbiting satellites and ships returning from the Moon. They show us a very finite and fragile sphere with a thin surround of blue-green water and sky against the dark emptiness of outer space. This is the image of spaceship Earth, a vessel carrying us through a hostile environment with limited supplies on board. No rational person could insist that there be no limit *enforced* on the number of passengers aboard such a vessel.

We are going to have to accept a role something like that of God if we are to secure a future that is compatible with our most basic current principles and values. We can achieve the necessary viewpoint only from an elevation where the moral air is thin and the lack of landmarks may disorient us. Our task will be like that of Hobbes's sovereign or Machiavelli's prince, only more radical. In *Leviathan,* Hobbes writes of what the human condition would be in a "state of nature," in a place without a government empowered to use lethal force to command lawful and civilized behavior. Although his best-known phrase about the state of nature is that human life would be "solitary, poor, nasty, brutish, and short," what I find most striking is his remark that,

> The notions of right and wrong, justice and injustice, have there no place. Where there is no common power, there is no law; where no law, no injustice.

Force and fraud are in war the two cardinal virtues. Justice and injustice are none of the faculties neither of the body nor mind. If they were, they might be in a man that were alone in the world, as well as his senses and passions. They are qualities that relate to men in society, not in solitude.[24]

As with right and wrong, so with the dignity of persons: These values are not innate to persons; they can be realized only in a certain kind of society. The social requirements for morality and dignity to flourish include not only effective political institutions (which were the concern of Hobbes and Machiavelli), but also political control of technology so that its products will not overwhelm or debase us.

REFLECTIONS

Here are two more objections the critic might have posed. See if you can take the author's part.

1. You speak of a living subject, by its self-instantiating activity, "operating over" the coexisting spatial parts of its body and "spanning" the time between one point and another in its duration. That sounds like GOFD all over again. What you call a "subject" behaves like a non-physical thing distinct from the physical thing we call its body. That's dualism—the horse that won't die.
2. You say that the dignity of persons "can be realized only in a certain kind of society." Doesn't that imply that persons have *no intrinsic dignity*, no value that is specific to persons? If the dignity of persons is an artifact of certain kinds of societies, then is it simply a matter of personal or collective preference that we treat persons better than we treat mere animals and plants?

DESCARTES' SAILOR

We've been looking at technological developments that could drastically affect the way we value and treat persons. The word "person" is ambiguous in this context, because it has both a descriptive and a prescriptive meaning. In its *descriptive* sense, it picks out beings that are alive, conscious, and have certain cognitive or behavioral traits such as speech and tool use that let us infer that they are rational subjects. In its *prescriptive* sense, "person" signifies a being that is to be treated as a member of the moral community, with rights and obligations. We have seen that there are certain important but *contingent* features of the human condition (such as the cost and relative scarcity of children) that make it easier for us to accord great value or dignity to human persons as members of our moral community. But the prescriptive and descriptive senses of "person" could become dissociated if we acquire the capacity to produce or replicate persons. (We are already on the verge of cloning humans.) If persons fall under the category of products or commodities, we could become less inclined to accept all persons into our moral community. This dissociation would seriously erode our basic concepts of morality.

I now want to examine other *contingent* features of human personhood, this time from a first-person perspective. I will try to show that if the evolutionary history of the human brain had been somewhat different, the experience of being a self would be different. This suggests that as we acquire the capacity to alter and enhance our bodies and brains, the effect on our experience of *self* and embodiment may be more radical than we suspect. I know of no better place to begin discussing our experience of self and embodiment than Descartes' analysis, in meditation 6, of the experience of "pain, hunger, and thirst": "There is nothing which . . . nature teaches me more vividly than that I have a body which is ill affected when I feel pain, and stands in need of food and drink when I experience the sensations of hunger and thirst, etc. And therefore I ought not to doubt but that there is some truth in this."[25]

Sensations such as pain, hunger, and thirst presented a serious problem for Descartes' dualism. Earlier in his *Meditations*, Descartes had argued for the existence of an all-powerful and truthful God.[26] Now confident that it was God rather than a deceitful Demon who was causing him to have the sensations he passively experienced, he was readier to trust what his senses told him. However, he had also claimed to understand with maximum clarity and distinctness that *mind and body were completely different in nature,* as different as what is spatial and measurable from what is nonspatial and unmeasurable. Since God created him and God is not a deceiver, Descartes could not doubt what he clearly and distinctly understood. Yet, with a sensation like pain, he seemed to be getting from a truthful God a message that *contradicted* his mind–body dualism: for instance, I can verbalize the experience of cutting my finger both as "It hurts" and "I hurt (where my finger is cut)." In other words, I experience the cut finger not just as an *object* in space, but also as (part of) my*self*. It's an experience of *being* my body; and God, as the author of nature, has willed that I have this experience. "And therefore," says Descartes in the passage above, "I ought not to doubt but that there is some truth in this."

Nature likewise teaches me by these sensations of pain, hunger, thirst, etc., that I am not only lodged in my body as a pilot in a vessel, but that I am besides so intimately conjoined, and as it were intermixed with it, that my mind and body compose a certain unity. For if this were not the case, I should not feel pain when my body is hurt, seeing I am merely a thinking thing, but should perceive the wound by the understanding alone, just as a pilot perceives by sight when any part of his vessel is damaged; and when my body has need of food or drink, I should have a clear knowledge of this, and not be made aware of it by the confused sensations of hunger and thirst: for, in truth, all these sensations of hunger, thirst, pain, etc., are nothing more than certain confused modes of thinking, arising from the union and apparent fusion of mind and body.[27]

Descartes criticizes the traditional dualistic analogy according to which the mind is in its body like a pilot is in his vessel. He says this image fails to do justice to the way we experience our bodies. When my finger is cut, I *see* it as a thing with a cylindrical shape and a red mark where it is cut. My *visual* experience is of an object in space, like the side of the ship where the pilot can *see* damage from an impact with a rock. I and the pilot would both feel some concern and want to take care of our respective problems. But there is also a localized sensation of *pain* in my cut finger, one that causes me to experience the finger as part of *me*—as *being* me—and that's the difference between the way a human mind is present in its body and a pilot in his vessel. Of course, Descartes can't admit that this experience is true in the sense that his dualism is true. He clearly and distinctly understands that mind and body *cannot* be one thing. So he concludes that, although there is "some truth" to my experience of being one with my body, this truth is only of a *practical* sort: God wants me to take care of my body as if it were myself, and so I am given sensations like pain, hunger, and thirst to motivate me to do what is required. God is not deceiving me in this regard, because (for instance) my body really does need food when I'm hungry. But such sensations are "confused." They have little cognitive value. After all, what does hunger tell me about what's actually going on when my body needs food? And what does my toothache tell me about what's happening in my tooth? When it comes to understanding what tooth decay is, or how the mind and body are really related, I must use clear and distinct ideas, ideas that allow for mathematical analysis of a body.

As he hurries to save his dualism from an apparent contradiction, Descartes pays too little attention to a very important difference between two kinds of *sensory* modalities, one exemplified by vision and the other by pain. Notice that he does *not* say that if I were in my body the way a pilot is in his ship, then *all* my perception of damage to my body would be like the pilot's *visual* perception of a damaged hull. Instead, he says that I would "perceive the wound by the understanding alone." He compares *sight* in the sailor to *understanding* in the mind. There is a long tradition of using visual language to signify understanding or intellectual comprehension. For instance, we say "I see what you mean" and "I see your point." It would be useful to look closely at what it is about visual sensation that leads us to speak this way, and why pain and other sensory modalities do not serve as proxies for understanding.

When I look at my hand in front of me, what do I *see* in it that makes me experience it as *mine*? The complete perception of my hand contains tactile, muscular, and other kinds of sensation, but I'm concentrating on the *visual* awareness. I see that my hand is physically continuous with the rest of what I call my body. But the same question arises about my whole body: what do I *see* that makes it *mine* rather than just *a* body? Is it that I seem to be looking out from inside it, through eye sockets in the head? After all, no one else has *that* perspective! But this experience of looking out from within my head could be compared to gazing out from a close-fitting body suit with openings for my eyes. Having that visual experience doesn't lead me to regard the suit as part of me, as my body, even though I experience being inside it. What I don't experience through vision alone is *being* my body. Seeing my body is perceiving it as an *object,* as one of many things out there in space. How do I experience my body as a *subject,* as *me*?

In pain, hunger, and thirst, of course, just as Descartes told us in the paragraph quoted above. But what exactly is it about them that is so different from sight? Descartes calls these sensations "confused," which implies that vision is clearer. But he doesn't help us any further, since he contrasts these "confused sensations" with "understanding alone" rather than with vision. Descartes' use of the word "confused" is an unintentional pun, and is also question begging. The Latin term he uses is *confusi,* which derives from a Latin verb *(confundo)* whose first meaning is "to pour together," with secondary meanings such as "to obscure" and "to throw into disorder." In pain sensation, we seem to experience the mixing together of body and mind or self, an "apparent fusion" that Descartes cannot accept as true because he *knows* that his self is *not* his body. Since the self cannot be extended in space, it cannot literally be mixed with or poured into the body. So he labels the experience as "confused" in the intellectual sense, because it obscures the difference between mind and body. He ends the paragraph with a circular explanation of how such sensory confusion originates: it arises "from the union and apparent fusion of mind and body." Since there really is no such union, since the fusion is only apparent, it can't be a source of anything, not even of confusion. Descartes admitted to Princess Elizabeth of Hungary, one of his favorite correspondents, that the experience of mind–body union was a stumbling block for his dualism: "It does not seem to me that the human mind is capable of conceiving at the same time the distinction and the union between body and soul, because for this it is necessary to conceive them as a single thing and at the same time to conceive them as two things; and this is absurd."[28]

Back to the question: What constitutes my experience of my body as myself? Let's look again at the difference between pain and vision, without the dualistic preconceptions of Descartes. We call pain a *feeling*, but we would not (usually) use this word to describe seeing something. We can distinguish two kinds of feelings. The first includes pain, hunger, thirst, temperature, taste, and other modalities I will discuss later. The second includes feelings such as sadness, cheerfulness, or guilt. What these two kinds of feeling have in common is that they are states of one*self*, states one mentions in response to a question such as "How are you?" or "How do you feel?" The two kinds differ insofar as the first is more or less localized, whereas the second is not—it qualifies and permeates our consciousness without drawing our attention to a specific part of the body. Because all feelings are forms of *self*-awareness, whereas vision is a form of *object* awareness, I will call vision *perception*. Sensations such as pain or cold often seem like perceptions rather than mere feelings. For instance, I notice a pain in my ankle, or that a bottle is cold to the touch, just as I notice the shape of a box. However, I would argue that this similarity is due to our referring pain or cold to the *perceived* images of our bodies (especially the visual image, at least in those who have sight). In other words, pain and cold are like perceptions only because they are associated with, or referred to, *objects*. They are *localized feelings*. The scheme is in table 3.1.

Table 3.1. Sensory Modalities

(1) PERCEPTION: awareness of something as an object "out there" or *other* than self	(2) FEELING: awareness of something as a state of one*self* (a) Localized: the state is experienced as having a location or area in the body (b) Nonlocalized: the state is experienced as filling the present time, but with little or no location

I don't mean to imply that all sensory modalities sort themselves out cleanly into one or another of these categories. In fact, as we shall see, there are good neurophysiological reasons why they don't. The distinction between localized and nonlocalized feeling is more of a spectrum than a dichotomy. Toothaches are more localized than hunger, and hunger is more localized than fear. What we call moods are least localized, but they could be interpreted as involving a more or less vague awareness of some general condition of one's body, as in heightened alertness.[29] The somatic or somatosensory modalities of touch, pressure, muscle, and joint sensation belong to *both* the categories of perception (1) *and* localized feeling (2a), as shown in table 3.1. These kinds of sensation give us experience of our bodies as both subjects and objects.

Bodily contact (touch, pressure) induces a *sense of self* with noticeable affect. That is part of the reason why there is such a different social significance between looking at someone and touching them. The widespread awareness today of the beneficial psychological effects of muscle relaxation testifies to the affective quality of muscle sensation. Chronic muscle tension is an unpleasant, fatiguing state in itself, and it can precipitate depression or anxiety. The sense of self in bodily contact is probably the experiential basis for our use of the word "touching" to describe what arouses benign emotions in us. There is a similar metaphor derived from our sense of self in muscle and joint sensation (which together form a large part of *kinesthesia*—our awareness of motion in our bodies). Something is "moving" in much the same sense as it is "touching."

Yet, we can also use somatic sensation to identify *publicly observable objects,* especially by handling them (what neurologists call *stereognosis*). Blindfolded, I can perceive by handling alone that something is a pen, a cup, or a hand that happens to be my own. This identification is a perception rather than a feeling. It picks out an item as part of the public world. The observation that what I hold is a pen or a cup or a hand can be made by anyone else, since the features by which I distinguish these objects are the same for everyone. But, in my own case, the experience of these features is accompanied by a sense of self. And when I touch one of my hands with the other, there is a sense of self in both. Thus somatic sensation comes as both perception and feeling, often in the same experience (e.g., handling something).

Hearing belongs with sight and somatic sensation in the category of perception. Normally, we don't speak of a sound, or the hearing of a sound, as a feeling. We experience music and the sounds of birds or traffic as part of the public world that includes what we perceive visually and by handling.

We need to look at some further important features of these objective modalities to appreciate the role they play in the human experience of being a self and having a body.

Vision, hearing, and somatic sensation are strikingly *intermodal*. Our experience is saturated with isomorphism (identical relations or structures) across these modalities. For instance, when I notice the shape of my pen as I look at it, and then I handle the pen, I experience the visible and the tangible cylindrical shape as one and the same, not as distinct items between which I perceive a resemblance. This isomorphism is more than just the conjunction of two modalities of sensation in one experience, such as feeling weary *and* thirsty or feeling a toothache *and* hearing a voice at the same time. The toothache is not an awareness of anything about the voice. But the shape I see *is* the shape I feel.

The intermodal aspect of the perceptual modalities enables them to serve as channels for language and for mimetic or expressive behavior (nonlinguistic behavior that embodies thoughts or perceptions, such as dance, mime, or the simple drawing of a shape in the air with a finger). I will use the term *communication* for all these forms of behavior. Communication clearly involves a great deal of intermodal isomorphism. For instance, we perceive the same linguistic structures (sentences, etc.) embodied in speech sounds or handwritten characters. The complex sequences of muscular contractions involved in the production of oral or written speech must encode the sequences of sounds or characters to be produced. When we draw a shape that we see, the elements of the visible shape must be translated into elements of arm and hand motion that also register as elements of kinesthetic feedback as we execute the drawing. When we dance, we render the temporal structures of musical rhythm into spatiotemporal patterns of bodily movements. In general, our intermodal perception seems to be mediated by sensorimotor isomorphism—our brains map elements of visual, auditory, and somatosensory content onto sequences of motor impulses. Aristotle used the term "common sensibles" for properties perceived intermodally rather than by one or other "special sense." And he seems to have concluded that the common sensibles were perceived by sensorimotor analysis: "There cannot be a special sense-organ for the common sensibles, . . . i.e. the objects we perceive incidentally through this or that special sense, e.g. movement, rest, figure, magnitude, number, unity; for all these we perceive by movement."[30] For these reasons, the *perceptual* modalities can also be called *communicable*. *Feelings*, by contrast, are *incommunicable*.

Critic: Are you sure about that? Can't I communicate my mood with a facial expression or tone of voice? Or the pain of a cramp with a grunt and a gesture or two?

Author: Yes, but not in the sense that we communicate intermodal sensory content. Grunts and facial expressions are typical *effects* of certain inner states, and this enables us to use them as symbols of those states. But grunts and grimaces don't embody a structure or pattern that is part of a pain, not the way my pen's motion renders a shape I'm looking at.

Critic: Maybe. But can't I make a jabbing or pulsing motion to convey a similar feature in a headache?

Author: True enough. You're able to do that for the same reason that experiences of pain are sometimes called perceptions: just as I refer a toothache to my visual and somatic image of my tooth and its surround, so I sometimes experience a recurring sequence of pain sensations as a periodic motion through the visuosomatic space of a part of my body.

Critic: Your use of the word "refer" bothers me a bit. It sounds like you're saying that, when I have a toothache, I consciously "place" the ache on my visual or somatic image of my mouth and gums. Why not say instead that there are body maps or images for each of the localized feelings, such as pain and warmth?

Author: First of all, referring is not a conscious act. It's a perceptual mechanism that organizes the pain experience preconsciously. I can't choose not to experience a pain as referred in that way. Furthermore, we just don't experience localized feelings as having their own body images the way you suggest. There is even good experimental data demonstrating the dominance (in people with sight) of the visual over the somatic body image when someone is given conflicting sensory input. In an experiment performed by J. Victor and I. Rock, subjects looked at the upper surface of a cube through a reducing lens that made the square appear only half as large as it really was (see fig. 3.3). There were no other objects in the field of vision. When using touch alone, the subjects judged the size of the square surface to be twice the size of one they had seen through the lens.

> But when looking and grasping *simultaneously,* subjects experienced the square to be half its size, corresponding more or less exactly to how they perceived it by vision alone. Moreover, the square *felt* to them as if it were half-size. We did a similar experiment on *shape.* The cylindrical lens we used altered size along one axis, so that a square looked like a rectangle. The result was the same. The shape percept was dominated by vision and visual capture of touch occurred.[31]

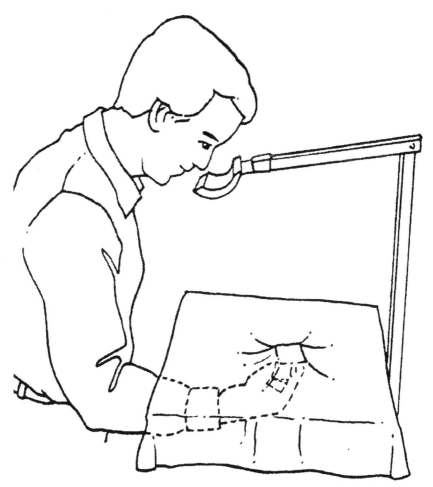

Figure 3.3. Subject views through a reducing lens the impression in cloth of the up-per surface of a cube while holding the cube in his hand beneath the cloth. When vi-sual and stereognostic input clash, vision dominates. [After I. Rock, *Perception* (1984).]

In localizing *sound* sources, there is also evidence that vision dominates hearing as it does somatosensory perception when someone is presented with conflicting sensory input:

> Whereas auditory localization is strongly influenced by visual displacement of a stimulus (for instance, as produced by a prism), visual localization is hardly influenced by auditory displacement. . . . Put simply, people try to make sense out of what they sense, and make simple sense at that. When making simple sense requires the resolution of a conflict, something has to

give. What gives, though, is typically not vision. Apparently, seeing is believing.[32]

Sight, then, is the most cognitive of the perceptual modalities, the custodian
of a master grid onto which input from other modalities (perceptions and
localized feelings) are referred and integrated. That is why "I see" so often
serves as a proxy for phrases such as "I understand."

There are questions that Descartes ignores in his discussion of the
pilot/vessel analogy: What if that analogy were correct and our experience
of our own bodies were like the pilot's visual awareness of his vessel?
What if our experience of a cut finger were purely perceptual, and our response were based merely on the belief that we needed to promptly repair the damage to that part of our "vessel"? Or if we had only perception
and nonlocalized feelings? What would happen to our sense of *self*? Because of his commitment to dualism, Descartes was convinced that ("seeing I am merely a thinking thing") he would be the very self he refers to
with the pronoun "I" absent a body and all sensation. However, as I argued earlier, the notion of disembodied life is unintelligible; only an embodied, self-instantiating system can be a *subject* with an inner aspect;
and the stream of consciousness is the presence of self-instantiating activity to itself.[33] Contrary to Descartes, there can be no "I" without a body.
I want now to argue that the particular kind of consciousness and sense of
self that we humans share could have been very different if mammalian
evolution had gone in a different direction, and that our sense of self
could be radically altered in various ways as we increase our ability to
modify our brains and bodies.

There is a certain ambivalence in what I experience as *my body*—it is both
public and private. When I've been doing a lot of heavy lifting, my arm (and
the rest of my body) can be suffused with more or less unpleasant feelings that
no one else can share. I'm all too aware of this arm and body as *me*. By contrast, the arm and hand I *see* before me resting on the surface of my desk are,
in fact, mine, and I expect that they will directly respond to my willing them
to move. Yet the *sight* of them is on a par with the sight of other *objects* on the
desk—they are among the things out there, and I am not them (especially
when the tactile sensation of my arm's contact with the desk has subsided, just
as the feeling of the clothing I'm wearing normally fades very soon after I put
it on). Anyone else can see my arm. I'm like a Cartesian pilot gazing at the
deck from a window in his ship's cabin. But then I decide to move my arm,
and two things happen: (1) it moves, which makes my arm different from the
book or the clock that are also on my desk but aren't part of my body, and (2)

the *combination* of visual perception and somatic feelings presents *it*, the arm, as *me*. I am out there, localized, part of the public world: "Here I am, as you can see." My body becomes the basis for my community with other bodies and selves. Both this community *and* the radical solitude of gazing on an external world are part of the reality to which the pronoun "I" refers. What we call a self is something, not nothing, and the only *thing* a self can be is a body. But it can't be a body the way a rock or a chair is a body. As strange as it may sound, a self must both be and not be the same body. These two essential aspects of human self-consciousness depend on having immediate voluntary control over one's body and on the joint occurrence of perception of that body and localized feelings.

We have come full circle. This book began with a discussion of the family of words surrounding the notion of *appearing*.[34] The words I used back then in discussing the contrast of reality and appearance belong here, too:

> *Appearing* means becoming present, manifest, or visible ("She appeared in the doorway"). However, it can also mean having an outer aspect that may be inconsistent with an inner aspect, as when things or persons seem to be what they are not ("He always appears to be happy"). How can something *not be* what it presents itself as? How can it be *hidden* by, or in the very process of, becoming *manifest*? This (apparent?) contradiction is a big part of what we understand about a *self*. As I use the pronoun "I", I'm aware of being other than what others can observe of me—I could pretend to feel what I don't, and anyway only I can know what it is like for me to be me right now. No matter how open and honest I am, the inner and outer me can always go their separate ways. Because of this gulf between observable and unobservable aspects, I am in a sense alone, even when I am with others.

The experience of having a body is the appearance of a self to itself and to others; it is the externalizing and objectifying of a human subject, a subject that nevertheless remains a subject while perceiving itself as object and so is not what it appears to be—it is not its body. The conjunction of feeling (localized or nonlocalized) and perception is essential to being a self. If the pilot/vessel analogy for the human mind/body relation were accurate—if I had perceptions and direct voluntary control of a body, but only *non*localized feelings—then I would still be a self, but not a human self. Direct voluntary control over a body would be enough to distinguish that body as *mine* and give me a presence in the public world. A human self has a further aspect, one that is contingent to the notion of a self in general, but is essential to *human* selfhood: I have pain, hunger, thirst, and other *localized* feelings in my body. It is these feelings, according to Descartes, that "confuse" my self-awareness by immersing it in my body.

Critic: You seem to be presenting a contradiction as if it were an improvement on Descartes' dualism. You're saying that it is an essential feature of a self that it both is and is not the same body. To quote Descartes: "for this it is necessary to conceive them as a single thing and at the same time to conceive them as two things; and this is absurd."

Author: Not really. Of course, it's impossible to conceive of one thing as two things. But I'm not saying that the self and its body are two *things*. A self is not a thing apart from its body. It's the inner aspect of a living body, with the added attribute of self-presence. The inner aspect is not the outer aspect—a body as object is really different from that same body as subject.

Critic: You're still saying that a self both is and is not one and the same thing—its body. Why isn't that a contradiction?

Author: Because I have argued that there is a duality in a living body, a duality of inner and outer. A self *is* the inner aspect of a living body, and therefore it *is not* that same body considered in its outer aspect. I sense that you're still bothered. Look, consciousness *is* a different kind of reality. That's what makes it so hard to understand. Or am I talking to a zombie?[35]

Critic: I won't dignify that with a response.

Author: I was going to say that even someone like Dennett would admit that funny things happen to the word "is" in the context of people's consciousness or awareness of something. Consciousness generates what is known as an "opaque" context. Suppose that the old house on the corner *is* the birthplace of Herbert Hoover. "Is" in the preceding sentence signifies identity. The referents of the subject and predicate phrases in that sentence are the same. Put abstractly, it's like saying "$a = b$." It follows that whatever is true of a is true of b and vice versa. So if I am standing in front of that old house on the corner, then I am standing in front of the birthplace of Herbert Hoover. However, from the fact that I notice there's an old house on the corner, it does *not* follow that I notice that Hoover's birthplace is on the corner (I might have no idea who has lived there). The "is" of identity doesn't behave normally in the opaque contexts of our awareness. All philosophers acknowledge that this is a fundamental fact about consciousness (or at least about sentences expressing certain states of consciousness). So the *peculiarity* of a self being and not being its body is not unprecedented.

Critic: Fair enough. I happen to agree with John Haugeland's paraphrase of Ockham's razor: *Don't get weird beyond necessity.*[36] You claim to have shown the necessity in this case, and I will think about it some more. A little while ago, you were talking about the peculiarity of the way the human sense of self is constituted and how it could have been different, or could be made so as we begin to acquire the capacity to fundamentally alter our bodies and minds. Please go on with that. I'm curious.

REFLECTIONS

1. What if we had only perceptions and *non*localized feelings? Can we imagine ourselves into that condition? What are some of the ways in which our ordinary, day-to-day experience would be different? How would that affect our sense of self?

2. Can feeling and perception be so neatly separated as awareness of a state of oneself and awareness of an object (nonself)? What about aesthetic pleasure—the kind you get from hearing music or from the sight of a painting by some great master? In these experiences, we seem to take pleasure in the object, in *its* attributes or structure, rather than in a state of ourselves. The pleasure seems, in other words, to be an integral part of the perception. Thomas Aquinas put it this way:

   > The beautiful is the same as the good, and they differ in aspect only. For since good is what all seek, the notion of good is that which calms the desire; while the notion of the beautiful is that which calms the desire, by being seen or known. Consequently those senses chiefly regard the beautiful, which are the most cognitive, viz. sight and hearing, as ministering to reason; for we speak of beautiful sights and beautiful sounds. But in reference to the other objects of the other senses, we do not use the expression "beautiful," for we do not speak of beautiful tastes, and beautiful odors. Thus it is evident that beauty adds to goodness a relation to the cognitive faculty: so that "good" means that which simply pleases the appetite; while the "beautiful" is something pleasant to apprehend.[37]

OUR MAMMALIAN BRAIN

Descartes was so right when he said, at the beginning of the sailor passage quoted previously,[38] that "there is nothing which . . . nature teaches me more vividly than that I have a body." The experience of having a body is the fulcrum on which the human mind raises an entire world. That world consists of *my* body, on which is projected a spectrum of localized feelings (most importantly, somatic sensations that cover the area of my visual body image and coincide with its visible boundary), and the great surround of *other* bodies and places—those that I perceive but in which I don't have those localized feelings.

The Holy Grail for philosophers and philosophically inclined scientists in fields such as psychology, neurobiology, and cognitive science is to understand how our brains carry out this world-making function. I don't pretend to have found the grail yet, but I believe that the way to it goes through intermodal perception and sensorimotor isomorphism.[39] They make *communication*[40] possible, and thereby the domain of communicable, public objects that we call the world. The same sensorimotor isomorphism that lets us draw a shape we see also made possible the earliest manifestations of technology, such as the shaping of a hand ax and its use in shaping materials such as wood.

In his provocative 1968 film *2001: A Space Odyssey*, Stanley Kubrick uses brief, wordless sequences of striking visual and auditory images to advance the story and its themes. In the "Dawn of Man" sequence, a group of ape-men wake up to the presence of a large monolith partly immersed in the ground by their den. It is a dark, perfectly regular and smooth, door-shaped object. They circle excitedly around the object until curiosity overcomes their fear and they begin touching it and running their hands over it. Then the scene ends. We next see a single ape-man glancing up occasionally at the monolith while handling the bones of a mostly intact tapir skeleton lying in the sand where the creature died. The hominid runs his hands over a leg bone and begins using it to move and hit the other bones. His excitement increases as he imagines a tapir falling to the ground under his blows. At the same time, we hear the slowly growing crescendo of *Also Sprach Zarathustra*, Richard Strauss's symphonic poem about the Superman that Nietzsche imagined as the culmination of human evolution. In the next scene, the ape-men are shown using their bone weapons to attack another group. They prevail and their leader triumphantly throws his bone into the air. As it drifts upward against the sky, in one of the most striking flash-forwards I have ever seen, it dissolves into the image of a spaceship drifting toward a slowly spinning, wheel-shaped space station in orbit above Earth. Now the background music is "Tales from the Vienna Woods" (by a very different and unrelated Strauss).

The film gives us no narration to explain the interaction of the hominids with the monolith. Many viewers interpreted the mysterious object as very much a deus ex machina that upgraded the hominids' central nervous system to the level of tool use. I prefer to think of the monolith as providing a special stimulus for a hominid brain that had already evolved into a state of readiness for the next great step in terrestrial life. My interpretation is something like Roger Ebert's in his 1997 retrospective on the film: "I have always felt that the smooth artificial surfaces and right angles of the monolith, which was obviously made by intelligent beings, triggered the realization in an ape brain that intelligence could be used to shape the objects of the world."[41] We don't need to suppose that the hominid was capable of thinking about intelligence as such. But it had a rich intermodal perception of its hand moving over the smooth surface and lines of the monolith, a dynamic image constituted by visual, tactile, and kinesthetic sensations (from all those joints in its fingers, wrist, elbow, and shoulder). What it got from its experience of handling the monolith was a visuosomatic perception of a physical object that, in its geometrical perfection, was so strikingly abstract that it thrust the common sensibles[42] of line, shape, magnitude, and motion into the foreground. The visible regularity of the edges mapped onto the smooth succession of uniform tactile and kinesthetic sensations generated in the hominid an image of *making* that shape, and something similar happened as it hammered the leg-bone of the tapir against the rest of the skeleton. It could use its hand to embody a shape into something it could use to . . . build a rocket.

We humans belong to the primate order that arose from the mammalian class more than sixty million years ago. The traits that distinguish primates from other mammals include well-developed binocular vision (reflected in the face by large eyes and reduced snout area, and in the brain by a larger cortical area dedicated to vision),[43] excellent manual dexterity, good hand-eye coordination, prehensile hands with opposable thumbs, an expanding neocortex that enables a complex and wide range of learned behavior, long infant dependency periods, and complex social organization. Nearly thirty million years ago, the hominoid superfamily branched off from other primates to evolve into hominids and apes. The hominid family originated about seven million years ago, and humans are its last surviving species. Hominids developed even larger brains than other primates, especially in the frontal lobes dedicated to motor abilities; greater prehensile capacity, aided by a lengthening of the thumb; and true bipedalism, which freed hands and arms for the kind of sensorimotor isomorphism discussed above. There is evidence that they used tools. However, the first hominids had brains that were only one-third the size of the average human's today, even though their bodies were approximately the same size as ours. Only in the past 500,000 years did the human brain reach its current size.

So far, we've been focusing on a dramatic increase in brain size resulting from expansion of the neocortex—that part of the brain that is the major player in the distinctively human functions of language and technology.[44] But something else was going on (or, perhaps more accurately, *not* going on) during this same evolutionary progression. As the human brain was being readied for novel and unprecedented perceptual and motor functions, the human *animal* continued to have the needs of an animal—food, drink, protection from predators, and sexual reproduction. Successful strategies for these had already evolved and been genetically programmed into the primate brain. There was no need for reinvention here. It was possible for the hominid brain to hang on to these proven mammalian functions while it explored the new possibilities opened up by its expanding neocortex. As Joseph LeDoux tells us in *The Emotional Brain:*

> The brain systems that generate emotional behaviors are highly conserved through many levels of evolutionary history. . . . Within the animal groups that have a backbone and a brain (fish, amphibians, reptiles, birds, and mammals, including humans), it seems that the neural organization of particular emotional behavioral systems—like the systems underlying fearful, sexual, or feeding behaviors—is pretty similar across species. This does not imply that all brains are the same. It instead means that our understanding of what it means to be human involves an appreciation of the ways in which we are like other animals as well as the ways in which we are different.[45]

Copulation, eating and drinking, urinating and defecating, what to do when in contact with a body that threatens us or when a sudden noise signals a possible danger—we and other mammals have similar body parts with which to deal with similar situations relevant to our well-being. There are large differences, of course, in how humans and nonhuman animals go about doing these things. There are tools and culturally variable rituals that surround *our* biological functions and *our* fighting. But the anatomical, emotional, and behavioral legacy of our mammalian ancestors is pretty obvious. Examples abound.

Our emotions are often like buttons people and other animals can press. A certain facial expression or gesture elicits feelings of anger or fear in us before we can even think through what's happening. To have these feelings is to find oneself, independently of any reasoning process and without a conscious interval, predisposed to behave in a certain way toward their object. Certain kinds of perceptual stimuli seem hardwired in our brains to specific responses.[46] For instance, mammalian babies have distinctive features—unlike baby reptiles, they're not just scale models of adults. Their young bodies and faces help elicit in their parents and other adults of their species nurturing responses and a tolerance for behavior that would not be permitted in adults. Humans typically feel this way not only toward babies and infants of their own species but also toward kittens, puppies, lambs, and fawns. As humans long ago began adopting wolves into their circles, they favored those that were more submissive and less aggressive; conversely, wolves with these traits were more likely to remain in the company of humans. Wolves became domesticated dogs by a process of *neoteny*—retention in adults of juvenile characteristics. Wolves with puppy-like temperaments tended to make better helpers and pets than wolves whose ferocity and fighting ability made them candidates for dominance in their packs. That is how we find ourselves at home with dogs that elicit in us nurturing feelings and behaviors and often excessive tolerance for misbehavior. A dog's pleading gaze fixed on us presses our buttons as effectively as would a wolf's snarl. (I say all this with full knowledge that there are some humans in whom animals, and even human infants, don't arouse tender feelings. Most of these people seem healthy in other respects. The philosopher in me is frequently fascinated by primates and other nonhuman mammals because they are *partly* alien subjects. While I can guess but never understand *what it is like* to be them, I sense that we have much in common. It seems to me that, because we are mammals, our human *self-respect* commits us to a degree of respect and empathy for *them*.)

The drawings in figures 3.4 and 3.5 are graphic testimony to what evolution has wrought in our psyche. The phrase "limbic system" needs some explanation. Like many other neuroanatomical terms, it is somewhat imprecise and laden with theories that are not universally accepted among neuroscientists. The limbic system is often referred to as the "emotional brain." This language can suggest too great a degree of functional independence from the rest of the brain. Like other areas demarcated on functional maps of the brain, this "system" can do what it does only through complex interactions with other parts of the brain.

The originator of the term "limbic system" was Paul MacLean, one of the most prominent neuroscientists of the twentieth century. He produced an elegant synthesis of decades of research, by him and others,

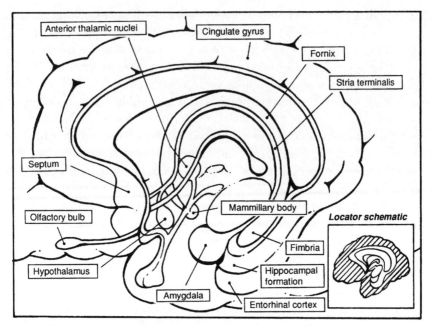

Figure 3.4.   Schematic drawing of limbic system.

into the brain structures and processes involved in emotional behavior and experience.[47] We can get a useful but very simplified notion of MacLean's theory from the diagram in figure 3.5. According to this "triune brain" model, when mammals evolved from reptiles, their brains conserved many reptilian structures and functions that were useful to the self-preservation of both reptiles and mammals. MacLean calls the most ancient area of the brain the R(eptilian)-Complex. It includes the brain stem (an expansion at the top or forward end of the spinal cord) and the cerebellum. As figure 3.5 indicates, the cerebellum (which rises from the brain stem at the base of the cerebral hemisphere) has its own triune structure and has greatly evolved from its reptilian origins. The traditional view was that the cerebellum functioned as a timer and coordinator of complex movements. However, recent research suggests that it may have a role in sensory processes as well.[48] The brain stem is strongly connected to the autonomic nervous system and thereby influences such functions as respiration, swallowing, sleep, and heartbeat. It affects the brain's level of alertness and can trigger behaviors such as the startle reflex, aggression, and territoriality, all of which occur in reptiles as well as in mammals.

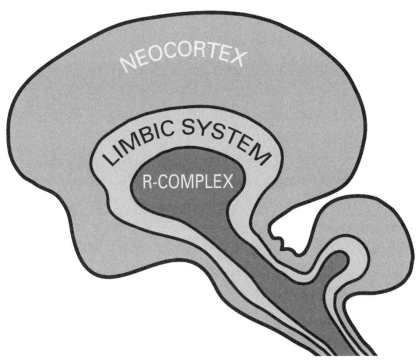

Figure 3.5. Paul D. MacLean's "triune brain" model. It depicts three levels of structure and function in the human brain that recapitulate the evolution of the brain from reptile to mammal to primates (incl. *Homo sapiens*).

Epilepsy is a brain disorder that causes abnormal discharges of electrical activity in the brain. The part of the brain from which this activity originates is called the *epileptogenic focus*. The brain areas to which the discharge spreads are rendered dysfunctional until shortly after the seizure has run its course. Epileptics frequently experience *auras*—abnormal sensations and affects immediately preceding their seizures. These auras strongly correlate with the location of the epileptogenic focus. For instance, a somatosensory aura may indicate a focus in the parietal lobe of the neocortex. In complex partial seizures (what is often called psychomotor epilepsy) the focus is on the inner (mesial) side of the anterior temporal lobe, and the discharge spreads into the limbic system. The auras include "feelings of hunger, thirst, nausea, suffocation, choking, retching, cold, warmth, and need to defecate or urinate. Foremost among the secondary affects are feelings of terror, fear, sadness, foreboding, familiarity, strangeness, unreality, wanting to be alone, and persecution."[49] Psychomotor seizures often include *automatism*—a kind of behavior that is accompanied by diminished consciousness. Most of this behavior is primitive and purposeless, such as lip-smacking, chewing, or manipulating a shirt button. These persons typically don't remember what they do in their automatic states. However, because psychomotor seizures often don't spread to the sensorimotor neocortex, there are occasional instances of intellectually demanding automatic behavior, including speech. Here is Wilder Penfield's description of one patient, P. Ge:

> [P. Ge's] wife had become a domestic servant. She sent her husband to get her belongings from the house where she had just given up employment. When he arrived there, no one was at home and the house [was] locked. He broke in a window and entered to carry out his mission. Then he went to hospital to have his hands dressed because of cuts from the glass. He said he had no recollection of receiving the cuts or having them dressed. Presumably this was erased by the amnesia of automatism.[50]

When P. Ge bloodied his hands while smashing the window, his response seems to have been like that of a Cartesian pilot who "perceives by sight when any part of his vessel is damaged."[51] Apparently, he either did not at first notice the lacerations or else merely took note of them and sought "repair" once his mission was accomplished.

This case also suggests how important a role the limbic system plays in *motivating* our behavior. P. Ge formed a particular intention—to retrieve his wife's belongings—just prior to his seizure. During the seizure, the intention became an *unconditional* imperative to be carried out in spite of any standing prohibitions, legalities, proprieties, discomforts, or other unfavorable circumstances. It was as if the goal intended before the onset of the seizure became the only possible goal for the psychomotor automaton. He was unable to reevaluate his original intention in the light of changing circumstances. Intellectual functions are normally exercised in conjunction with affects that determine such things as the object, importance, and urgency of a particular intellectual task. In P. Ge's case, there is no reason to think that his specifically cognitive functions were deficient—he showed a tactical flexibility in his choice of means toward his goal when he broke into the house, and he remembered what he came for. What he could not do was divert his intact neocortical functions from the task undertaken when his limbic system was last functional.

We need not conclude from these clinical examples that the human mind is an intelligence in the service of brute feelings inherited intact from our mammalian ancestors. The relationship between emotions and cognition is reciprocal, as we can see from another clinical example. The prefrontal cortex is a phylogenetically recent area strongly interconnected with the limbic system. When a patient suffered from intractable and intense pain, neurosurgeons in the middle of the twentieth century often either excised the prefrontal lobe (lobotomy) or else severed its connections with the limbic system (leucotomy). Although these procedures actually lowered their pain thresholds, the patients reported that they no longer *suffered* from their pain.[52] It would seem that the integral experience of pain and suffering is profoundly influenced by the neocortex. Until the advent of psychoactive drugs, these surgeries were often performed to relieve a variety of extreme and uncontrollable emotional and psychotic disturbances.[53] They are seldom if ever performed any more, because of advances in antipsychotic and antidepressive medication and because of their drastically negative effects on the patient. These include flattened affect, inability to plan ahead, and disregard of the consequences of behavior. These cases tell us not only that the quality of our affects is greatly influenced by cognition and reason, but also that our reasoning works in tandem with our emotions. This is a major theme of Antonio Damasio's 1994 book *Descartes' Error: Emotion, Reason, and the Human Brain.* It is true that emotions often interfere with reason, as conventional wisdom tells us. Nevertheless, "the *absence* of emotion and feeling is no less damaging, no less capable of compromising the rationality that makes us distinctively human and allows us to decide in consonance with a sense of personal future, social convention, and moral principle."[54]

Needless to say, the major role played by the limbic system in emotional behavior and experience requires a great degree of connectivity with the brain stem and thereby with the autonomic nervous system. Let's take a look at two important limbic components, the *hypothalamus* and the *amygdala*. The hypothalamus (see fig. 3.4) provides much of the limbic system's interface with the brain stem. For example, experiments by Cannon and Bard in the late 1920s showed that cats in which cortex, thalamus, and all of the limbic system except the hypothalamus had been excised would engage in displays of rage (including bared teeth, hissing, and clawing) accompanied by associated internal adjustments such as increased blood pressure and heart rate. The cats responded even to inappropriate stimuli and became immediately placid once the stimulus was removed. For this reason, Cannon and Bard called the behavior "sham rage."

The amygdala (or amygdalae—there is one in each hemisphere), like other components of the limbic system, is a higher-level modulator of behaviors and internal adjustments such as those generated by the hypothalamus in Cannon and Bard's cats. The effects of bilateral destruction of the amygdala in monkeys and in humans demonstrate the complex linkages among the three parts of the triune brain. In the late 1930s, Klüver and Bucy reported that monkeys with this condition seemed incapable of anger or fear, became hypersexual, and were unable to recognize food by sight, although they had no visual impairment.[55] When hungry, they would put almost any object in their mouths and discard it if inedible. Their inability to recognize the significance of objects for their welfare had a drastic impact on their social relations with other monkeys. The first report of a human version of the Klüver–Bucy syndrome came in 1955, when a patient underwent a bilateral temporal lobectomy (including the amygdala and hippocampus), as treatment for uncontrollable psychomotor epileptic seizures.[56]

When bilateral amygdalar damage occurs in a human's early years, the symptoms are not as extensive as in the Klüver–Bucy syndrome, probably because other parts of the brain compensate. In *The Feeling of What Happens*, Antonio Damasio describes the case of S, a young woman with calcified amygdalae. Although mentally and physically healthy in other respects, S exhibited far less fear or anger than the average person. She was often unable to recognize the facial expression of fear or anger, nor could she imitate it herself or draw it (even though she had excellent drawing skills). This impairment in reading facial expressions made it difficult for her to analyze and learn from social interactions: "Immersed in a secure Pollyanna world, these individuals cannot protect themselves against simple and not-so-simple social risks and are thus more vulnerable and less independent than we are."[57]

Cases such as these tell us something profound and important about the human mind. Consider the difference between two sorts of judgments. The first sort is a largely cognitive appraisal such as "There's a squirrel on the lawn" or "This table has an oval shape." The relevant sensory input registers in our highly evolved neocortex and activates our store of related memories and facts. But that's not enough for judgments based on facial expression, such as "He is offended" or "I don't trust this person." These appraisals aren't merely cognitive; their cognitive content incorporates the speaker's *emotional* response. As the case of S suggests, they require that visual input to the neocortex also engage the amygdala. It's possible that in some situations we may calmly note a negative facial expression and act accordingly with minimal emotion (e.g., "Something I said alarmed her"). Yet even these situations have their meaning for us only because we, unlike S, have been able to emotionally experience negative facial expressions in other cases. S was not deficient in her ability to reason or to recognize patterns in space. She recognized faces and could recognize other emotions in faces. But she often *could not see* the particular configuration of facial features that we easily categorize as fearful, angry, or hostile, and she was thereby deprived of a great deal of important social knowledge.

Joseph LeDoux argues very persuasively that our *experience* of fear in response to what we perceive depends on two things. The first is that the amygdala activates the nearby nucleus basalis as well as other arousal systems in the brain stem that raise the level of sensitivity of neurons in the neocortex. Although the increased sensitivity is widespread over the neocortex, it has the effect of highlighting the sensory stimuli that are currently engaging a specific part of the brain. However, many different kinds of emotionally relevant stimuli, as well as novel stimuli in general, are attention getting. Something else is necessary to distinguish *fear*. That further specification comes in the form of *feedback* from amygdalar activation of various responses in the autonomic nervous system and associated endocrine processes. When we are afraid, we experience such things as muscle tension, elevated heart rate, sinking or tightening feelings in the stomach, perspiration, and rapid, shallow breathing. The neural and biochemical mechanisms involved in these responses are ancient and common among mammals.[58] They prepare our bodies to fight or flee.

In summary, *we can't evaluate and respond appropriately to what goes on around or within us without being able to respond physically and physiologically like the mammals we are.* This fundamental fact about humans makes me wonder what a techno-optimist like Ray Kurzweil has in mind when he predicts that, by the end of the twenty-first century, it will be common to "scan someone's brain to map the locations, interconnections, and contents of the somas, axons, dendrites, presynaptic vesicles, and other neural components. Its entire organization could then be re-created on a neural computer of sufficient capacity, including the contents of its memory."[59] As we have seen, the emotional systems of the human brain are to a significant extent devoted to the maintenance of a suitable internal environment for the *metabolic* processes of our multicellular body. These parts of the brain even interface with the endocrine system, causing hormonally induced body states that feed back to the brain in the form of neural impulses. Would we want to create the functional equivalents of all these processes in the neural net computers that would house our downloaded minds? Feelings such as hunger, thirst, warmth, and cold would not have much relevance to a mind embodied in synthetic materials. Would we still want to have these experiences for sentimental reasons? Would we want to continue having experiences such as Cypher has in *The Matrix*—savoring the delicious flavor of a steak that we no longer eat for nourishment, or of a VR steak? Without our various flesh-related feelings, human consciousness would be unimaginably different from what it is now. The final chapters of Kurzweil's book *(The Age of Spiritual Machines)* are filled with imaginary conversations between him and late twenty-first century fictional personae with various kinds of artificial embodiments. They sound very much like us, but I wonder why.

REFLECTIONS

Try to imagine how different the content of our everyday experience would be without the activities, feelings, and sensations associated with our needs as animals—the care and nurture required by a body made up of trillions of living organisms. If we humans were to acquire increasingly bionic bodies, would it be worth preserving some or all of these animal experiences, even though they would no longer have any relationship to what we were?

FEAR AND LOATHING

> Human infirmity in moderating and checking the emotions I name bondage: for, when a man is a prey to his emotions, he is not his own master, but lies at the mercy of fortune: so much so, that he is often compelled, while seeing that which is better for him, to follow that which is worse.
>
> —Baruch Spinoza

The human condition is to have a brain that is the interface between (1) a rapidly expanding cognitive and technological capacity and (2) motivational systems that evolved for behaviors such as fighting, fleeing, eating, drinking, establishing social status, and mating. In this regard, nonhuman mammals have it much easier. The structure of their bodies and the capacities of their sensorimotor systems have evolved to enable what they are genetically determined and motivated to do in order to survive and reproduce. Their behaviors and goals are set in DNA—they do "what comes natural," even if the detail of their goals and behaviors is further specified by learning (e.g., when an animal learns where there is water to drink or learns the social status of specific individuals in its group). In a very important sense, humans have no nature; there is no genetically determined self-instantiating program for us to act out consciously or not. Instead, our "nature" is to create a variety of *cultures*—sets of beliefs, customs, stories, technologies, and institutions that constitute the framework for a human life and mark the pathway from birth to death. There is an increasingly loose connection between the primary drives affecting us as mammals and any culture's ways of satisfying them. In a technologically advanced society, people divide their time between tending to biological needs, indefinitely many specialized occupations, and whatever leisure they can salvage. In these societies, the distance between basic mammalian drives and human culture becomes an abyss out of which come questions such as the ones that Paul Gauguin used as the title for his 1897 masterpiece *Where Do We Come From? What Are We? Where Are We Going?* (see fig. 3.6).

Gauguin had gone to Tahiti believing that it was an earthly paradise in which the native islanders lived a life close to nature and unspoiled by European civilization. The scenes depicted in his paintings from this period seem to confirm that he found what he believed was there. But, in fact, Tahiti was heavily colonialized, and French religion, clothing, customs, and architecture were taking over the native culture. Gauguin simply concentrated on what remained of traditional culture and left out the European influence. His knowledge of religious practices and idols such as the one

Figure 3.6.   Paul Gauguin, French, 1848–1903. *Where Do We Come From? What Are We? Where Are We Going?* 1897–1898. Oil on canvas. 54 3/4 x 147 1/2 in. Museum of Fine Arts, Boston. Tomkins Collection: 36.270. Photograph © 2003 Museum of Fine Arts, Boston. According to Gauguin, the three groupings in the picture should be viewed from right to left. The first represents birth, the second adulthood, and the third old age and death.

depicted in figure 3.6 came from books. To a large degree, he created an imaginary world animated as much by his distinctive use of color, scale, and thick, flat, simply drawn human figures as it was by the actual locale. He was alienated from his own culture by the poor reception his work received in France, and he was alienated from his wife and family, whom he had left behind when he went to Tahiti. During the time he painted *Where Do We Come From?* he wore native clothing when at home and European clothing when he went to town in nearby Papeete. Shortly after he completed the painting, Gauguin attempted suicide.

Gauguin's masterpiece invokes, in a most profound way, what I described at the beginning of this book as the *pathos of the senses*.[60] I said then that the passivity in our sense perception extends to our awareness of our existence, our having come into this world at a certain point in space and time. Our existence is a happenstance that imposes itself on our senses as we get old enough to think at this level. As a *conscious* being, I was less present in my coming into being than I am in the fashioning of my sentences or the recovering of my memories. Much less so, since I couldn't even have chosen to exist; I just found myself here, much as I see willy-nilly what's there to be seen when I open my eyes. We find ourselves with hands that can do anything and a mind to match. We also find ourselves more or less urgently needing to satisfy various animal needs. Under the right circumstances, most of us can simply accept what a particular culture directs us to do with our hands and minds and be content that our efforts are rewarded with satisfaction for our animal needs. But we don't have to be geniuses like Gauguin to be alienated by our culture and wonder about the meaning of life. Many different kinds of experience, such as injustice, illness, or the prospect of death, can cause anyone to ask Gauguin's questions.

There is a very loose fit between human emotions and the perceptual content that arouses them. To have an emotion is to feel an urge to respond in some way. Suppose I see anger or aggression in the face and body language of someone coming up to me. I feel a tinge of fear. What to do? Fight or flee? That's ridiculous—I'm at a reception! But my body feels like it's getting ready to avoid or resist something. I don't know this person. What's his problem? Even if I were about to literally fight, what would I do? Thanks to our advanced neocortex, there are numerous tactics and weapons, even for physically weak humans. Our flexibility in combat led Thomas Hobbes, with his typical cold-blooded realism, to attribute a "natural" equality to all human beings because even the weakest could kill the strongest "by secret machination or by confederacy with others."[61] If my fear is too strong, my judgment about what to do will be clouded, and I will become a victim of what Spinoza, in the passage quoted on p. 129, called my "human infirmity."

Aristotle was deeply aware of the delicate relationship between reason and emotion in deciding how to respond to a situation. He argued that a large part of human happiness and fulfillment consisted in (moral) virtue, which he described as a harmonious relationship between feeling and reason. A virtuous person is one who responds in the right way to a situation out of a desire to act in the right way. Aristotle recognized that we can't act at all without the appropriate emotion. Too much or too little feeling will result in misconduct. So the virtuous person will experience just the right degree of feeling—one that generates just the right behavior for those circumstances. For instance, in a dangerous situation, someone who is *fearless* will be unresponsive to the objective hazard facing her. She exhibits a vice called recklessness. But *too much* fear gives rises to cowardly behavior. The *rational* response is what Aristotle called the "mean" between these two extremes: having enough fear to do justice to the danger, but not so much that I can't do what's needed. Courage is rational fear, the *harmony* of fear and reason.

Aristotle was one of the few great philosophers to make peace with the human *mammal*, with its flesh and reservoir of raw feeling. He seemed to believe that a proper upbringing in a good political community could instill moral virtue in just about anyone (or at least any adult male citizen of a Greek polis—children, women, and barbarians could not be expected to be *fully* human). He was willing to call someone with moral virtue and superior talent happy and blessed, living a life that was beautiful and good. Yet even he thought there was something much better, something we could experience only in limited intervals before the demands of human life recaptured us. This was the life of contemplation, which should not be confused with the laborious activity of acquiring knowledge. It is always better to *have* what we are striving for than to be still striving. Contemplation is the exercise of knowledge possessed, the ongoing experience of understanding. It is an activity for its own sake, like an accomplished dancer going through her steps for the sheer enjoyment of it. Moral virtue makes us good citizens, friends, spouses, or parents; but practicing virtue entangles us in a net of dependencies on other people and external resources. Contemplation is different:

> Firstly, this activity is the best (since not only is reason the best thing in us, but the objects of reason are the best of knowable objects); and secondly, it

is the most continuous, since we can contemplate truth more continuously than we can do anything. And we think happiness has pleasure mingled with it, but the activity of philosophic wisdom is admittedly the pleasantest of virtuous activities; at all events the pursuit of it is thought to offer pleasures marvellous for their purity and their enduringness, and it is to be expected that those who know will pass their time more pleasantly than those who inquire. And the self-sufficiency that is spoken of must belong most to the contemplative activity. For while a philosopher, as well as a just man or one possessing any other virtue, needs the necessaries of life, when they are sufficiently equipped with things of that sort the just man needs people towards whom and with whom he shall act justly, and the temperate man, the brave man, and each of the others is in the same case, but the philosopher, even when by himself, can contemplate truth, and the better the wiser he is; he can perhaps do so better if he has fellow-workers, but still he is the most self-sufficient.[62]

There is a tension within Aristotle's ethical system, and it shows in this passage. To the extent that we accept what he says about contemplation, how do we balance this good against our roles and responsibilities in the community? Should a good person perform *less* well his roles as a citizen, friend, and family member in order to create more leisure for contemplation? Aristotle recognized that the contemplative life is more proper to gods than to humans: "But such a life would be too high for man; for it is not in so far as he is man that he will live so, but in so far as something divine is present in him; and by so much as this is superior to our composite nature is its activity superior to that which is the exercise of the other kind of virtue." As Aristotle saw it, we have no choice but to accept our human nature and make the best of it by cultivating a harmonious relationship between emotions and reason and developing our talents as best we can. What would he have thought if he were alive today, at the beginning of an era in which we will be able to enhance our minds and bodies and ultimately shed our mammalian legacy altogether by transforming ourselves into bionic bodies and brains? His rhetoric suggests that he would recommend maximizing what is "divine" in us, rather than conserving our "composite" nature as *thinking animals*.

Aristotle understood the soul to be the "form," or organization, of the human body. Had he been familiar with today's neuroscience, he would have regarded the very complex connections among neurons as a prominent feature of the human soul, since these connections are a kind of organization of bodily parts that enables us to function mentally. He did not have our concept of neural organization as *information* that could be "scanned" and "re-created" or downloaded into a different physical substrate (as in the predictions of Moravec and Kurzweil).[63] He did not see how the "form," or organization, in our bodies could exist except as embodied in our kind of flesh. So when humans die, there is no soul that can survive the death of the body. While they are alive, some of them have the leisure and ability to ignore practicalities for a time and be contemplative. But no one can really escape his animal nature, so humans must make the best they can of it through moral virtue.

By contrast, Aristotle's predecessor, Plato, was a dualist. He held not only that the soul *could* exist apart from the body, but also that it is hindered in its search for truth by having to perceive through the body's senses instead of beholding the forms directly.[64] He regarded death as liberating the human soul from imprisonment in the body:

> While we are in the body, and while the soul is mingled with this mass of evil, our desire will not be satisfied, and our desire is of the truth. For the body is a source of endless trouble to us by reason of the mere requirement of food; and also is liable to diseases which overtake and impede us in the search after truth: and by filling us so full of loves, and lusts, and fears, and fancies, and idols, and every sort of folly, prevents our ever having, as people say, so much as a thought.[65]

It is a commonplace that discomfort with, and even loathing for, the human body and its animality is one of the central themes of the Christian tradition. This theme comes in many variations, and I cannot hope to portray it adequately here. The mainstream of Christian thought rejected as heretical the Platonic doctrine that human misconduct and vice are due entirely to the soul's falling under the dominance of the body's emotions and appetites, and that the conflict of good and bad in us is reducible to the contrary tendencies of soul and body. As St. Augustine (354–430) explains it, the original sin of our first parents, Adam and Eve, was one of *pride* and *disobedience*—a disorder of the mind rather than the body. One of the consequences of their sin and expulsion from the Garden of Eden was that their bodies were "corrupted": their emotions became unruly, and they were subject to disease and death. All of humankind have inherited this corruption and need redemption. Augustine doesn't share Aristotle's optimism that the right sort of upbringing in a good community can instill a virtuous harmony between reason and feeling. Only with God's help and our constant struggle can we manage to curb our appetites and live virtuously. God created humans as embodied spirits. So there is nothing intrinsically bad about humans having bodies.

But humans lost the pristine goodness of their bodies when Adam and Eve sinned. The gap between our limbic emotional systems and the cognitive/sensorimotor functions of the neocortex that I have described as a natural outcome of primate evolution is interpreted by Augustine as a *corruption* of nature. For him, embodiment is good in principle because God willed it, but our animality is a sin-induced degradation. For instance, he explains that there would have been sexual intercourse in paradise, because God wanted the human race to multiply. And it would have been a joyful and loving interaction, but it would *not* have been what he calls *lust*:

> So possessing indeed is this pleasure, that at the moment of time in which it is consummated, all mental activity is suspended. What friend of wisdom and holy joys, who, being married, but knowing, as the apostle says, "how to possess his vessel in sanctification and honor, not in the disease of desire, as the Gentiles who know not God," would not prefer, if this were possible, to beget children without this lust?[66]

Augustine complains that lust is so out of harmony with reason that we often can't get aroused when, in the context of love sanctified by marriage, it would be good to have intercourse. Sometimes, we are psychologically aroused, but our lust (as he delicately puts it) "leaves the body unmoved." He could have added that we often can't like people who deserve our affection for their objective merits and are attracted to people we should avoid. We can't summon feelings at will; instead, we *undergo* them. (The word "passion" comes from the Latin verb for "suffer.")

At the end of created time, the souls of the just will be reunited with bodies that are spiritual rather than animal, bodies that will express and manifest the spirit rather than constrain and resist it. The glorified body will respond

> in all things to the will that has entered on immortality—all reluctance, all corruption, and all slowness being removed. For the body will not only be better than it was here in its best estate of health, but it will surpass the bodies of our first parents ere they sinned. For, though they were not to die unless they should sin, yet they used food as men do now, *their bodies not being as yet spiritual, but animal only.*[67]

In effect, Augustine is saying that only in heaven can humans possess the kind of harmony between feeling and reason that is Aristotelian moral virtue. Aristotle set a very high standard for calling someone virtuous. In the case of courage, for instance, someone who manages to conquer a strong urge to flee when she should stand and fight does the right thing, but is not yet courageous. A person doesn't have the virtue of courage until she habitually and *spontaneously* feels the right degree of fear to motivate her to do what is called for in a dangerous situation. In such a person, mind, feeling, and body respond in unison. For Augustine, the legacy of original sin makes this chronically virtuous condition unattainable in this world. Only when we exchange our animal bodies for "spiritual" ones will we automatically feel like doing what it is good to do.

Discomfort with, or blindness to, human animality is common in the Western philosophical tradition. Since Descartes, this theme is complicated and masked by the reduction of the categories of life and sentience to that of (inanimate) body.[68] But it emerges with striking clarity in the very influential ethical theory of Immanuel Kant. His theory divided the world into two kinds of beings: (1) *persons,* who have intrinsic or unconditional value, and (2) *things,* which have only an extrinsic or conditional value. *Animals* fall under the category of *things.* Persons are rational beings—they have reason and will, which enable them to act according to the *consciousness* of law. All things act according to law in the sense that they behave according to the laws of nature, but only rational beings are *motivated by the conception of law.* For example, a book drops when I release my grip on it (behaving according to the law of gravity), plants grow toward the light, and animals eat when hungry. They do what they do necessarily, and we can express the regularity and predictability of their conduct in the form of laws that they *un*consciously follow. An animal may experience something like what I call hunger in myself, but it isn't motivated to eat by *awareness* of a *law* governing the circumstances. It just does what it can't help but want to do. We are different.

We regularly choose to do or refrain from doing something because we *ought* or *ought not* to do it, even when we have desires to the contrary. What motivates us in such cases is some law-like statement of how to behave under certain circumstances. However, in some cases, we do what we ought rather than what we desire only because an even stronger desire prevails. For instance, I may have such a strong aversion to being overweight that I consciously obey the principle that I ought not to eat a second dessert. In that case, it could be said that I'm not essentially different from a nonhuman animal that can't help but yield to the stronger of two conflicting desires. However, according to Kant, there is a *moral* sense of the word *ought* that sets us far apart and above mere animals.

Kant would have liked the 1999 film *The Insider.*[69] It presents the true story of Jeffrey Wigand, a senior researcher at Brown and Williamson Tobacco who

decided that he had to speak out about what he regarded as the company's falsified reports of what they knew about the harmful effects of smoking. In doing so, he broke a confidentiality agreement and lost his highly paid job, his
wife, and his social status. The company threatened legal action against him
and, he claims, threatened to harm him. Nevertheless, he went public in an interview on *60 Minutes* with information that helped launch a multibillion dol-
lar lawsuit against Big Tobacco. Here is how Kant would analyze this story:
Wigand acted on the belief that he ought not to certify statements that smoking was not harmful or addictive when he knew otherwise. The "ought" in this
belief was an *unconditional* imperative. Under no circumstances should he or
anyone engage in such a falsehood, no matter how much it would harm their
interests to speak the truth. The "ought" in this case expresses a law binding on
all persons. As a *moral* man, Wigand would not make an exception of himself.
If an act is morally wrong for me, then it is wrong for all persons, and if an act
is wrong for others, it is wrong for me—so speaks the voice of reason in me, re-
quiring that I act only according to an intention that I could will anyone and
everyone to act on in the same circumstances. This is the fundamental moral
principle in Kant's theory, and it is often referred to as the Categorical Imperative or universalization test. A moral or good-willed person is someone who is
always ready to subject her intentions to this test. In Wigand's case, if everyone
felt free to lie about the results of health-related research, such reports would
be automatically ignored. So if Wigand were to universalize the intention to
come out with a false report, he would be choosing to publish a report in a
world in which such reports would not be believed. In effect, he would be
choosing for and against the same action. His will would be in conflict with itself, and therefore, as a rational being, he *ought not* to falsify the report.

Kant doesn't present an argument for his basic moral principle. He assumes
that all human beings, insofar as they are rational, experience a sense of obligation to behave according to the principle. Since being able to act according
to the consciousness of law is a defining characteristic of a rational being, the
Categorical Imperative says, in effect, BE RATIONAL! Fulfill your rational
nature by always acting lawfully! The word *ought* suggests not only the necessity of doing something, but also that it is good to do it. In other words, *ought*
implies *value*. When it is used unconditionally, it implies unconditional value.
Since the Categorical Imperative commands us unconditionally to be rational,
it places unconditional value on our rational nature. This brings us to Kant's
second formula for the basic moral law: Always treat rational nature, whether
in yourself or others, as an end and never as a means only. In other words, always treat rational nature as having intrinsic value—don't treat persons like
things, don't exploit them. It's alright to be useful to one another—this is the

cement that bonds a community. But this mutual usefulness has to be based on *voluntary* transactions, not force or deception. For instance, I can agree to work for someone for a specified compensation. If my employer later chooses not to pay me, he has *used* me, gotten me to do something that I, as a rational being, would not have done without compensation. His behavior violates my *dignity* as a person. If Jeffrey Wigand had cooperated in the falsification of reports on the health effects of smoking, he would have been willing to exploit people by misleading them into paying for cigarettes that harm them.

Kant's concept of a person is one of the great achievements of the Enlightenment and a milestone in the history of Western culture. It articulates and refines an idea that was implicit in the 1688 Glorious Revolution in England and in the American and French Revolutions. There is a grandeur and sublimity to the notion of individual human beings as autonomous agents obligated, and therefore entitled, to act only according to laws they can legislate for themselves. This notion has major implications not only for how we treat one another, but also for how governments treat their citizens. It provides a support for the declarations of human rights adopted by the United Nations and numerous governments. But it has a dark side also, one that takes us back to the topic of human animality.

Let's look again at Wigand as he is depicted in *The Insider.* Our hero isn't very virtuous in the Aristotelian sense. He feels afraid and alone; he is extremely reluctant to do what he perceives as his duty and is inclined to look for an excuse to back off. Aristotle would say that he didn't yet have the *virtue* of courage, even though he finally did the right thing. Kant, however, would take the internal conflict Wigand felt as a good sign that he was doing the right thing for the right reason: he did what he did because he *ought* (unconditionally) to blow the whistle on his company, no matter how much he shrank from the consequences. Strange as it may seem, if Wigand had possessed Aristotelian courage so that his feelings had harmonized with his decision to speak out, Kant would have doubted the moral worth of his decision. Why so? Because *feeling like* doing something, *desiring* or *fearing* to act a certain way, all these are mental states that are not directly under the control of a person's will. Of course, I can attempt to manipulate myself into having a certain feeling by putting myself in a state or situation that usually generates it. I might, for example, concentrate on a recent success in order to feel more energetic or hopeful. But I can't simply decide to feel a certain way. Kant's general term for feelings and affects is *inclination*. Inclinations *happen* to us—we *find* ourselves with desires or feelings about particular objects or even the world in general. In a passage discussing the Christian injunction to love one's neighbor, Kant calls inclinations "pathological," not in the medical sense, but in the etymological sense that we *undergo* them rather than will them:

> It is in this manner, undoubtedly, that we are to understand those passages of Scripture also in which we are commanded to love our neighbour, even our enemy. For love, as an affection, cannot be commanded, but beneficence for duty's sake may; even though we are not impelled to it by any inclination—nay, are even repelled by a natural and unconquerable aversion. This is practical love and not pathological—a love which is seated in the will, and not in the propensions of sense—in principles of action and not of tender sympathy; and it is this love alone which can be commanded.[70]

The will is *practical reason*—a capacity to act according to the consciousness of law. Since the will cannot command inclinations, and yet they influence our wills, inclinations belong to us not insofar as we are rational beings but because we are *animals*. They are inherently irrational. We would be better off without them: "The inclinations, themselves being sources of want, are so far from having an absolute worth for which they should be desired that on the contrary it must be the universal wish of every rational being to be wholly free from them."[71] Even Kant had to admit that human animals could not act morally without the concurrence of some feeling. In his theory, there is only one feeling that does not compromise the moral worth of an action: *respect*. In relation to reason, it alone is *not pathological:*

> Although respect is a feeling, it is not a feeling received through influence, but is self-wrought by a rational concept, and, therefore, is specifically distinct from all feelings of the former kind, which may be referred either to inclination or fear. What I recognise immediately as a law for me, I recognise with respect. This merely signifies the consciousness that my will is subordinate to a law, without the intervention of other influences on my sense. The immediate determination of the will by the law, and the consciousness of this, is called respect, so that this is regarded as an effect of the law on the subject, and not as the cause of it. Respect is properly the conception of a worth which thwarts my self-love.[72]

According to Kant, the will directly commands respect for itself as the source of its own law (the Categorical Imperative). This respect is felt by us as *sentient* beings—it is the animal in us submitting to reason in us. Submission is far from guaranteed, of course. Animal inclinations always threaten to overcome respect. That is the human condition, and Kant is alienated by it. Finally, his ethical theory, for all its brilliance, is *inhuman*. It implies that being naturally empathetic and amiable, for instance, is an ethical *peril* because such qualities *incline* us to treat others well, thus compromising the moral worth of our beneficence. Worst of all, it could inspire a chronic anxiety in a conscientious person who regularly does what is right. Such a person acquires *habits* of good behavior, and humans always like to do what is habitual rather than its opposite. Thus the strength of a habit of good conduct subtracts from the moral worth of that conduct. What Aristotle would regard as the achievement of genuine virtue becomes morally worthless in Kant's theory.

Without animal inclinations, the Kantian feeling of respect would be irrelevant. There would be no "self-love" to "thwart." But then, what would be left? Can there be any sense of self or awareness of value, indeed anything like *consciousness* without feeling? Even Augustine, despite the distaste he shares with Kant for the human condition, looked forward to a "spiritual" embodiment in which feelings would be spontaneously aligned with reason, "all reluctance, all corruption, and all slowness being removed." According to Kant, a purely rational being, a person that is not an animal, would have no experience of moral *obligation,* because such a being would have no possibility of internal conflict with irrational inclinations. In fact, this "holy will" would have no inclinations at all. It would be "of itself necessarily in unison with the law."[73] Is this a person or merely a machine with practical judgments as output?

Whether we talk about the human condition in terms of corruption from original sin, about the opposition of rationality and feeling, or the conservation of mammalian emotional systems as the primate neocortex evolved into an organ of language and thought, it is hard to deny that *something is very wrong with us.* Mammalian emotional systems may have been very effective at keeping *Homo sapiens* alive while it learned how to use its new brain, but those same systems now make us liable to overpopulation, famine, and global war. Our moral evolution lags woefully behind our scientific and technological progress. As a result, our laziness, greed, fear, and aggressiveness often lead us to think illogically, ignore or misinterpret our collective knowledge, and use our technology to degrade our environment and destroy each other (often in the name of what is "holy" or "just"). More than 800 million persons are malnourished today, and millions of these are starving to death on a planet that still can grow more than enough food for its surging population. "Inequalities in consumption are stark. Globally, the 20 percent of the world's people in the highest-income countries account for 86 percent of total private consumption expenditures, while the poorest 20 percent account for a minuscule 1.3 percent."[74] The same Western culture that spawned the notion of an intrinsic and unconditional worth of persons coexists with and, at least in part, contributes to the misery and premature death of hundreds of millions of persons.

In affluent and technologically advanced societies, our bodies seem less and less relevant to the typical work and lifestyle of the new millennium. It isn't just the old drawbacks of having to spend so much time asleep or tending to biological needs. As Linda Hasselstrom remarks:

> We take a body with a hunter/fighter history, prop it upright for eight hours while the fingers lightly punch buttons, then seat it in a car where moderate foot pressure and a few arm movements take it home. Once it's home it slumps down on a cushiony surface and aims its eyes at a lighted screen for two to six hours, then lies down on another soft surface until it's time to get up and do it all again. No wonder we're sick.[75]

Get some exercise! Of course, anyone living this way needs exercise to restore a healthy balance between mental and physical effort. Yet, isn't the exercise a diversion, hopefully enjoyable, but finally irrelevant to what we *really* do? Arguably, our bodies, like our emotional systems, are obsolete. Are *we* then obsolete? Massive change is upon us. With only *some* tweaking— a few bionic supplements or replacements—the future could still be a mostly human one, *our* future. Of course, we're in a race with our increasingly intelligent machines, so the respite would be temporary. The hard fact is that any consciousness substantially like ours must be the subject of bodies like ours. Then should we accept the inevitable and try to secure for *Homo sapiens* the kind of future Richard Brautigan longs for in his poem quoted at the beginning of chapter 4, one in which we will be looked after "by machines of loving grace"? Humans would be like great-grandparents in a superbly equipped retirement community, maintained out of respect and gratitude for having made a new world possible.

In *Escape Velocity: Cyberculture at the End of the Century* (1996), Mark Dery provides an excellent panorama of the subculture that has grown around the increasing influence of electronic technology in daily life, and he offers extensive commentary on this subculture's visions of the future. One of the most striking characters in Dery's book is the Australian performance and body artist Stelarc (born Stelios Arcadiou), who has lectured, taught, and performed in a long list of venues around the globe over the past thirty years. Stelarc is clear and articulate about the message he intends to convey with his performances: in language heavy with Augustinian and Cartesian overtones, he is proclaiming that the human brain and body are obsolete because they drastically limit the mind and are ill suited to make efficient use of future technology. His performances explore what it would be like to have different sensory organs or limbs, a virtual body, or a weightless body suspended in the air. His premise is that, with a different body and different sensory organs, our minds would have fundamentally different thoughts. So the rather startling things he does to and with his body are his way of exploring new realms of consciousness. Here is Dery's description of one of Stelarc's events:

> A welter of *thrrrups,* squeals, creaks, and *cricks,* most of them originating in Stelarc's body, whooshes around the performance space. The artist's heartbeat, amplified by means of an ECG (electrocardiograph) monitor, marks time muffled with a metronomic thump. The opening and closing of heart valves, the slap and slosh of blood are captured by Doppler ultrasonic sound transducers, enabling Stelarc to "play" his body. . . . A kinetic-angle transducer converts the bending of his right knee into avalanches of sound; a microphone, placed over the larynx, picks up swallowing and other throat noises; and a plethysmogram amplifies finger pulse.[76]

He has converted his body (heart, arteries, joints, throat, and skin surface) into a complex musical instrument. This sort of performance does funny things to the notion of an instrument or prosthesis. Both of these terms suggest something that is coupled to what is not itself an instrument or extension of the body, namely the natural body itself. Yet the monitors, transducers, and amplifiers he is connected to break down the distinction between the instrument being used and the user's body. The performance as a whole conveys the idea of a conscious will treating its entire embodiment as an instrument. He is playing his body as a pilot navigates his vessel. To break down the distinction between space inside and outside the body, Stelarc twice (in 1992 and 1993) had a "sculpture" with a flashing light and beeping noise inserted into his stomach. On his web page, Stelarc titles this performance *Hollow Body/Hollow Space.* His statement on the meaning of this event is worth quoting:

> The intention has been to design a sculpture for a distended stomach. The idea was to insert an art work into the body—to situate the sculpture in an internal space. The body becomes hollow, with no meaningful distinctions between public, private and physiological spaces. The technology invades and functions within the body not as a prosthetic replacement, but as an aesthetic adornment. One no longer looks at art, nor performs as art, but contains art. The hollow body becomes a host, not for a self or a soul, but simply for a sculpture.[77]

His most famous or notorious performances came during the 1970s and 1980s, when he staged several variations of the Native American sun dance. These performances involved hoisting the naked artist by cables attached to hooks embedded in his flesh. Needless to say, these experiences were quite painful for him, perhaps none more so than the suspension depicted in figure 3.7. In this case, Stelarc used only horizontal cables. In his comment on this event and similar ones, Stelarc uses deliberately impersonal, objective

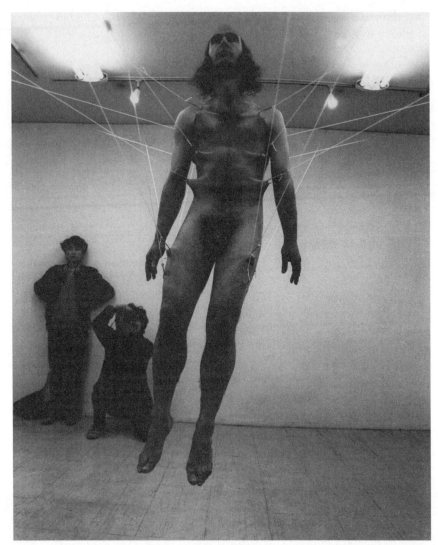

Figure 3.7. Stelarc. Event for Lateral Suspension. Tamura Gallery, Tokyo. 12 March, 1978. Photo: Tony Figallo. © STELARC.

language to emphasize his alienation from the body as subject: "The body was on the verge of passing out when it was lowered down after only 60 seconds of suspension."[78] The artist explained in a 1995 interview with the online magazine *CTHEORY* that it is incidental to his purpose that the suspended body is his own: "I've never felt that I am the artwork. In fact the reason why my performances are focused on this particular body is that it is difficult for me to convince other bodies to undergo rather awkward, difficult and sometimes painful experiences."[79]

REFLECTIONS

While the traditional concept of original sin and the notion of a loose fit between neocortical and limbic functions in the human brain both address the same phenomenon of humans behaving irrationally and making selfish choices, they present what seem to be very different analyses of it. The former asserts that human reason is itself corrupt and dysfunctional (as a result of the first sin of Adam and Eve), so that our wills tend toward evil choices independently of the influence of animal desires and appetites. The latter claims that our selfishness and misbehavior are due to an evolutionary lag between the brain mechanisms of emotion and of thought (neither of which is inherently evil). Are these alternative analyses really different (apart from the reference to Adam and Eve)? If so, which do you think is more plausible?

THE ENDGAME OF MULTICELLULARITY

> Constancy of the internal environment is the condition for free life.
>
> —Claude Bernard

Multicellularity is the attribute shared by organisms that are composed not only of many cells, but also of different cell types with different functions. Every cell in a multicellular organism has the same DNA—the same set of genes—but the cells are differentiated into types according to which subset of those genes is active in them. Cells of the same type form tissue, tissues combine to form organs, and organs work together in organ systems, such as the stomach and intestines in the digestive system. The first living systems, 3.5 billion years ago, were *unicellular* organisms much like today's bacteria. Unlike the DNA in the cells of our bodies, bacterial DNA isn't contained in a nucleus. Cells *with* nuclei *(eukaryotes)* did not appear until 1.9 billion years later. Although some kinds of bacteria managed to develop a primitive multicellularity, eukaryotes were better equipped to exploit it. That is why today's animals and plants are descended from unicellular eukaryotes.

Each of *us* is a multicellular community of about 50 trillion eukaryotic cells differentiated into more than two hundred kinds, including several varieties of neurons. Cells of this kind specialize in stimulating each other, and other kinds of cells, with electrochemical signals. About 100 billion neurons form the brain tissues that enable us to consciously perceive, think, and move. With this recent evolutionary product, multicellularity may have run its course. The mind that it made possible is on the threshold of creating for itself an *artificial, noncellular* embodiment, one that will both enhance its power and free it from the limitations and distractions of a multicellular body. The human species may be an *endgame* of multicellularity and the *beginning* of a new kind of evolution. Before we look ahead in chapter 4 to what might happen next, let's take a last look backward at how we got to where we are.

To help us look backward, we can focus on a fascinating organism that is found on the normally cool and moist floors of a forest or in piles of bark mulch. It's a rounded, gooey blob that looks like dog barf. Its official name is *Dictyostelium discoideum*, but it is more familiarly known as slime mold. According to the Douai–Rheims version of Genesis 2:7: "The Lord God formed man of the *slime* of the earth: and breathed into his face the breath of life, and man became a living soul." "Slime" is probably not an accurate translation, but it suits my purpose here because the life cycle of the unlovely *slime* mold encapsulates much of what happened over the billions of years it took unicellular organisms to become *us*.

This slime comes into being when unicellular amoebae that normally feed as individuals on bacteria in the soil begin to starve from a depleted food supply. The starving amoebae secrete cyclic adenosine monophosphate (cAMP), which acts as a pheromone, drawing as many as a hundred thousand cells to the area of highest cAMP concentration. There they aggregate and form a slimy sheath around themselves, constituting a single organism that is capable of slowly moving. The cells then *differentiate* into stalk and spore cells, thus exhibiting true *multicellularity*. The stalk cells eventually die off, but first they segregate themselves to form the stalk of a fruiting body that raises the spores into the air for wind dispersal. If a spore lands in the right conditions, it begins a unicellular amoeboid existence, starting the cycle again.

This very complex behavior, including movement of the slime mold across ground, internal shifting of tens of thousands of cells into different configurations, and coordinated differentiation of stalk and spore cells, requires an elaborate adaptive control system. The slime mold must be able to *detect* changes in its internal and external environments, *select* and *execute* adaptive responses to these changes, and detect and respond to the *results* of its responses *(feedback)*. A response is adaptive to the extent that it promotes the structural and functional continuity of the individual organism or of a population of such organisms. The adaptive responses of the slime mold typically consist of genes being turned on and off in individual cells by changes in their environment, including chemicals secreted by neighboring cells. This is essentially the same kind of *hormonal* control system that is found in plants and still operates at some levels in humans and other animals. But *animals* needed faster and more flexible control systems in order to move around instead of clinging to one place as plants do. So they evolved increasingly sophisticated nervous systems, including a brain and spine, consisting of billions of neuron cells suited by their structure and behavior for the function of adaptive control. That function has reached a level of power and refinement in *us* that we call *thought* and *consciousness.*

In these pages, I have argued that

- The function of adaptive control or self-instantiation is the defining criterion of a *living* system.
- What we call the human *mind* is a highly evolved version of the self-instantiating function that defines a system as alive, a function that was present even in the very first unicellular organisms.
- Therefore, just as there is a strong *evolutionary* connection, so there should be a strong *conceptual* relation, between having a mind and being alive.

As the mental function in humans is on the verge of creating artificial embodiments for itself, it is in a sense going back to its origins in bacterial life: once again, self-instantiation will take place in a body that is not composed of living systems. However, the orientation of this new form of life will be completely different from that of bacterial or multicellular systems. From the perspective of biological science, the bottom line for the adaptive control function, in us and in all other animals, is *the preservation of the multicellular community within.* Our vertebrate nervous system has had such a long evolutionary run because it is good at keeping this cellular community alive long enough to reproduce. We breathe, drink, eat, sleep, excrete, seek shelter, and clothe ourselves, all to keep the extracellular fluids in our bodies within the narrow parameters required for intracellular metabolism. Much of how we feel and what we sense from moment to moment has to do with these needs. As the great nineteenth-century French physiologist Claude Bernard (1818–78) famously said, "La fixité du milieu intérieur est la condition de la vie libre" [The constancy of the internal environment is a necessity for independent life]. And our brains evolved as the guardians of this internal domain.

The concept of life has strong connections with the metabolic processes that go on ceaselessly in unicellular and multicellular organisms. It is somewhat jarring to attribute *life* to a humanoid robot—a *Robo sapiens* whose low-maintenance body is made of lifeless internal parts.[80] The *functional* concept of life as self-instantiation detaches it from the historical link with metabolic processes in cells, while retaining what I believe are its essential features. Functional concepts characterize a system entirely in terms of its interactions or input/output relations with its environment. It is important that such concepts do not specify what kinds of physical or chemical components a living system must have. We do not want to be terrestrial or even carbon chauvinists who limit life and personhood to beings with our kind of metabolism, or to bodies with organic, carbon-based parts.

Such phenomena as beaver dams, bird nests, and bee hives foreshadow a turn that life takes with *finality* in human beings: a turn away from the cells and tissues of Bernard's *milieu intérieur* toward the external environment as an embodiment of the living system's repertoire. Self-maintenance comes to include maintenance of a dwelling, workplace, tools, social and political relationships, and other external essentials of self-instantiation. As the ecologist G. L. Clarke said in 1966, "The exchanges that the organism has with its external environment may be thought of as an 'external physiology,' and they are just as essential as its internal physiological adjustments."[81] The substitution of a low-maintenance synthetic body for the old multicellular body will mark a permanent reorientation of life from an *inner* physiology based on metabolism to an *external* physiology based on technology. If the endgame of multicellularity plays out as I am now projecting, the crowded 3.5 billion years it took life to get where it now is on earth will pale in comparison to what comes next.

The increasing orientation of vital processes toward the *external* environment gave rise to a new kind of *milieu intérieur* as animal brains developed ever more complex representations of the external environment to enable animals to move about safely and anticipate events relevant to their survival. This new internal milieu is a model of the external environment; it consists of rapidly changing patterns of neural impulses reflecting stimulation of sensory receptors adapted to different forms of energy impinging on the boundary of the animal.[82] Adaptive responses to external events are, in the first instance, responses to representations in the brain's model of the environment. With the development of imagination, animals could rehearse behavior within the brain without externalizing the behavior.[83] At what point in brain evolution we should call the internal milieu a *mind* is a matter of convention. Certainly the development of intermodal perception[84] in primates brings us very close to what we call mind in humans.

So there are two paths that the endgame of multicellularity opens up for the future orientation of life toward an external environment, paths that may converge or diverge in unpredictable ways. The *first* path is toward increasingly powerful minds with various embodiments and technologies that will interact with the environments of Earth and outer space in ways that are beyond what *Homo sapiens* could hope to do. Call this the way of *Robo sapiens.*

The *second* path is indefinite enhancement of experience—living in an increasingly virtual environment richer and more diverse than anything we can now imagine. Minds will have virtual bodies navigating virtual external environments. The RL environment will still be out there, of course. Virtual communities will need to secure and stabilize their physical embodiments and must therefore interface with the RL external environment and respond adaptively to it. But these interactions will be means toward the end of cultivating experience of a virtual universe. The enormous impact of the film and television industries and (more recently) computer messaging, MUDs, and online gaming demonstrate how much time and energy people are willing to devote to interacting with virtual worlds, especially when the interaction is communal. South Korea, the most wired nation in the world, is currently leading our way on this second path. About 70 percent of South Korean households have broadband Internet connections, compared with about 15 percent in the United States and 30 percent in Canada. In this small nation of forty-eight million, there are twenty-five thousand cyber cafes open around the clock. *Lineage,* the leading online game, has 2.2 million subscribers in South Korea. Many players show signs of addiction, as the Toronto *Globe and Mail* reports:

> Kim Soo-hwan, a 28-year-old man who plays seven to eight hours of Lineage each day, sometimes finds the on-line world more rewarding than the real one. "Once you are into it, you just can't be bothered to show up for appointments," he said.
>
> In an extreme example, a 24-year-old South Korean man died in October after playing the on-line game *Mu* virtually nonstop for 86 hours—three and a half days. Police said he died from a blood clot triggered by lack of physical activity.[85]

REFLECTIONS

How much of your daily experience is constituted by artifacts (including interior spaces of buildings and vehicles, and audio or visual images generated by electronic systems such as televisions, sound systems, and VR technology)? Is there something inherently bad or deficient about the progressive substitution of artificial for natural environments? If so much of RL is artificial, isn't the second path opened up by the endgame of multicellularity already well traveled enough that we can get an inkling of what it would be like?

NOTES

1. See "Can Machines Think? A Nanoresponse," chapter 2.
2. See "*E.T.* and *Alien*," chapter 2.
3. See "Liberation from the Cave," chapter 1.
4. Daniel E. Koshland Jr. of the University of California at Berkeley's Department of Molecular and Cell Biology uses the word "program" in a similar sense in a recent essay in which he attempts to define the category of *life* from a biologist's standpoint. He describes what he calls the "pillars," or essential principles, of life. "The first pillar of life is a Program. By program I mean an organized plan that describes both the ingredients themselves and the kinetics of the interactions among ingredients as the living system persists through time. For the living systems we observe on Earth, this program is implemented by the DNA that encodes the genes of Earth's organisms." D. E. Koshland Jr., "The Seven Pillars of Life," *Science* 295 (22 March 2002): 2215.
5. See p. 88.
6. As I said in chapter 1 (see "Levels of Reality"), a living system can be both one *and* many organisms *at different levels*, which is always the case with multicellular organisms. A higher-level subject can be composed of many lower-level subjects.
7. Antonio Damasio makes a similar point: "Sensing environmental conditions, holding know-how in dispositions, and acting on the basis of those dispositions were already present in single-cell creatures before they were part of any multicellular organisms, let alone multicellular organisms *with* brains.

Life and the life urge inside the boundary that circumscribes an organism precede the appearance of nervous systems, of brains. But when brains appear on the scene, they are still about life, and they do preserve and expand the ability to respond to changes in the environment that surrounds brains. Brains permit the life urge to be regulated ever so effectively and, at some point, knowingly." A. Damasio, *The Feeling of What Happens* (New York: Harcourt, 1999), 139.
8. Isaac Newton, *The Mathematical Principles of Natural Philosophy*, trans. Andrew Motte (London, 1729), Scholium to Definitions, 1, emphasis added.
9. Immanuel Kant, *Critique of Pure Reason*, trans. Norman Kemp Smith (New York: St. Martin's, 1990), B49.
10. See "*E.T.* and *Alien*," chapter 2.
11. See Thomas Nagel, "What Is It Like to Be a Bat?" *Philosophical Review* 83 (1974): 435–50.
12. Daniel Dennett (see "Scientism," chapter 2); David M. Armstrong, "The Nature of Mind," in *The Nature of Mind and Other Essays* (Ithaca, N.Y.: Cornell University Press, 1981), 1.

13. Or brain-endowed human being. Some metonymy is inescapable on this topic.

14. See Nagel, "What Is It Like to Be a Bat?"

15. In 1987, Edward O. Wilson estimated that in addition to the million inverte-brate species already described, there may be thirty million yet to be classified. E. O. Wilson, "The Little Things That Run the World," *Conservation Biology* 1, no. 4 (December 1987): 344–46.

16. See "E.T. and Alien," chapter 2.

17. As part of his betrayal, he kills two of his fellow rebels by shooting their phys-ical bodies while their avatars are in cyberspace.

18. See "The Demon as Evil Scientist," chapter 1.

19. See "The Pathos of the Senses," chapter 1.

20. See "Descartes' Meditation," chapter 1.

21. See the discussion of agent programs in "The Imitation Game," chapter 2.

22. The notions of a seal and weak coupling are discussed "Levels of Reality," chapter 1.

23. Judith Jarvis Thomson, "A Defense of Abortion," *Philosophy and Public Affairs* 1 (1971): 47–66.

24. Thomas Hobbes, *Leviathan* (London, 1651), chapter 13.

25. Descartes, *Meditations on the First Philosophy* (Paris, 1642), trans. J. Veitch (with small modifications), med. 6, at www.class.uidaho.edu/mickelsen/texts/Descartes/Descartes%20-%20Dedication.txt (accessed 18 September 2003).

26. See "Descartes' Meditation," chapter 1.

27. Descartes, *Meditations,* med. 6.

28. Descartes to Princess Elizabeth, 28 June 1643, in *Descartes: Philosophical Letters,* trans. and ed. Anthony Kenny (Oxford: Clarendon, 1970), 142.

29. The autonomic nervous system can bring about such general effects as constricting or dilating blood vessels and channeling more blood to either the muscular or digestive systems, depending on the kind of situation and adaptive response called for by that situation. Joseph LeDoux, *The Emotional Brain* (New York: Simon & Schuster, 1996), presents a very clear and accessible survey of dif-ferent theories about the role of autonomic responses in the experience of emo-tion.

30. Aristotle, *The Basic Works of Aristotle,* ed. Richard McKeon (New York: Random House, 1941), 425a.

31. Irvin Rock, *Perception* (New York: Scientific American Library, 1984), 137.

32. Lawrence E. Marks, *The Unity of the Senses* (New York: Academic, 1978), 32.

33. See "The Flow of Time," this chapter.

34. See "The Pathos of the Senses," chapter 1.

35. See "Scientism," chapter 2.

36. John Haugeland, "Ontological Supervenience," *Southern Journal of Philosophy* 22, supplement (1983): 1–2. The original principle, attributed to William of Ockham (1285–1349), is known as Ockham's razor: Don't multiply entities beyond necessity.

37. Thomas Aquinas, *Summa Theologica* I of II, 27, 1, ad 3, at www.ccel.org/a/aquinas/summa/FS/FS027.html#FSQ27A1THEP1 (accessed 14 September 2003).

38. "Descartes' Sailor," this chapter.

39. See "Descartes' Sailor," this chapter.

40. Earlier (see "Descartes' Sailor," this chapter) I defined communication as including language and mimetic or expressive behavior (nonlinguistic behavior that embodies thoughts or perceptions, such as dance, mime, or the simple drawing of a shape in the air with a finger).

41. Roger Ebert, "2001: A Space Odyssey," *Chicago Sun–Times* (1997), at www.suntimes.com/ebert/greatmovies/space_odyssey.html (accessed 14 September 2003).

42. This is an Aristotelian phrase for those aspects of bodies that are perceived in more than one sensory modality. They are closely related to Locke's notion of primary qualities. See "Descartes' Meditation," chapter 1.

43. The early primates' "large eyes faced forward, and their visual resolving power was greatly improved by an increased density of photoreceptors in the center of their retinas. Emerging from this dense array of photoreceptors was a strong set of connections from the central retina via the optic nerve to the brain. . . . Another innovation in the early primates was a specialized cortical area devoted to the visual guidance of muscle movement." John Morgan Allman, *Evolving Brains* (New York: Scientific American Library, 1999), 122–23.

44. See fig. 1.1.

45. LeDoux, *Emotional Brain*, 17.

46. As LeDoux puts it, "The hallmark of cognitive processing is flexibility of responses on the basis of processing. Cognition gives us choices. In contrast, activation of [emotional] appraisal mechanisms narrows the response options available to a few choices that evolution has had the wisdom to connect up with the particular appraisal mechanism." LeDoux, *Emotional Brain*, 69.

47. MacLean's most comprehensive account is found in his *The Triune Brain in Evolution: Role in Paleocerebral Functions* (New York: Kluwer Academic, 1991).

48. See Henrietta C. Leiner and Alan L. Leiner, "The Treasure at the Bottom of the Brain," at www.newhorizons.org/blab_leiner.html (accessed August 2002).

49. Paul D. MacLean, "Man and His Animal Brains," *Review of Modern Medicine* 32 (1964): 116. "In everyday life the affective feelings that guide our behavior have relevance to something in particular, but under ictal conditions [i.e., as auras] the affects are usually free-floating feelings unattached to specific individuals, situations or things. Hence the phenomenology of psychomotor epilepsy provides a strong argument against . . . those who would claim that it is inadmissible to make a sharp distinction between 'emotion' and 'reason.'" MacLean, *Triune Brain*, 452–53.

50. Wilder Penfield and Herbert Jasper, *Epilepsy and the Functional Anatomy of the Human Brain* (Boston: Little, Brown, 1954), 449.

51. See "Descartes' Sailor," this chapter.

52. According to MacLean, "the relief of emotional symptoms following frontal lobotomy is primarily attributable to the relief of anxiety. . . . It might be inferred

that . . . intractable pain, although still experienced, is alleviated because there is no longer the anxiety associated with the anticipation of continued suffering." Paul MacLean, "Contrasting Functions of Limbic and Neocortical Systems of the Brain and Their Relevance to Psychophysiological Aspects of Modern Medicine," *American Journal of Medicine* 25 (1958): 613.

53. They may also have been used to control rebellious temperaments. Ken Kesey vividly presents this scenario in his 1962 novel, *One Flew Over the Cuckoo's Nest.* A much altered version of the novel appeared in a film in 1975.

54. Antonio Damasio, *Descartes' Error: Emotion, Reason, and the Human Brain* (New York: Putnam's Sons, 1994), xii.

55. See H. Klüver and P. C. Bucy, "'Psychic Blindness' and Other Symptoms Following Bilateral Temporal Lobectomy in Rhesus Monkeys," *American Journal of Physiology* 119 (1937): 352–53, and "Preliminary Analysis of Functions of the Temporal Lobes in Monkeys," *Archives of Neurology and Psychiatry* 42 (1939): 979–1000.

56. H. H. Terzian and G. D. Ore, "Syndrome of Kluver and Bucy Reproduced in Man by Bilateral Removal of the Temporal Lobes," *Neurology* 5 (1955): 373–80.

57. Antonio Damasio, *The Feeling of What Happens: Body and Emotion in the Making of Consciousness* (New York: Harcourt, 1999), 67.

58. LeDoux, *Emotional Brain,* 132.

59. Ray Kurzweil, *The Age of Spiritual Machines* (New York: Viking, 1999), 124.

60. See "Pathos of the Senses," chapter 1.

61. Hobbes, *Leviathan,* chapter 13.

62. Aristotle, *Nicomachean Ethics,* trans. W. D. Ross, X, 7, at classics.mit.edu /Aristotle/nicomachean.10.x.html (accessed 14 September 2003).

63. See note 59 and "Posthumanity" in the introduction.

64. See "Liberation from the Cave," chapter 1.

65. Plato, *Phaedo,* trans. B. Jowett (1871), at classics.mit.edu/Plato/phaedo.html (accessed 14 September 2003).

66. Augustine, *City of God,* New Advent Translation, XIV, 16, at www.newadvent .org/fathers/1201.htm (accessed 14 September 2003).

67. Augustine, *City of God,* XII, 20, emphasis added.

68. See "*E.T.* and *Alien,*" chapter 2.

69. *The Insider* (1999), dir. Michael Mann, Touchstone Pictures.

70. Immanuel Kant, *Fundamental Principles of the Metaphysic of Morals,* trans. T. K. Abbott, sec. 1, 1934, www.class.uidaho.edu/mickelsen/texts/Kant%20-%20 Fundamentals%20.%20.%20.txt (accessed 14 September 2003).

71. Kant, *Fundamental Principles,* sec. 2.

72. Kant, *Fundamental Principles,* sec. 1.

73. Kant, *Fundamental Principles,* sec. 2.

74. United Nations Development Programme, *Human Development Report 1998,* at www.undp.org/hdro/hdrs/1998/english/e98over.htm (14 September 2003).

75. Quoted in Mark Dery, *Escape Velocity: Cyberculture at the End of the Century* (New York: Grove, 1996), 234.

76. Dery, *Escape*, 155.

77. "Stomach Sculpture," Stelarc, at www.stelarc.va.com.au/stomach/stomach .html (accessed 14 September 2003).

78. Stelarc, "Stelarc," at www.bmeworld.com/flesh/suspensions/public/stelarc/ Stelarc.html (accessed 14 September 2003).

79. Paolo Atzori and Kirk Woolford, "Extended-Body: Interview with Stelarc," *CTHEORY* (6 September 1995), at www.ctheory.net/text_file.asp?pick=71 (accessed 14 September 2003).

80. The phrase *"Robo sapiens"* is part of the title of a fascinating book by P. Menzel and F. D'Aluisio: *Robo Sapiens: Evolution of a New Species* (Cambridge, Mass.: MIT Press, 2000).

81. George Leonard Clarke, *Elements of Ecology* (New York: Wiley and Sons, 1966), 1.

82. See *"E.T.* and *Alien,"* chapter 2.

83. See "An Enchanted Space," this chapter.

84. See "Our Mammalian Brain," this chapter.

85. *Globe and Mail* (Toronto), 12 May 2003, at www.globetechnology.com/ servlet/story/RTGAM.20030512.gtogmay12/BNStory/Technology (accessed 14 September 2003).

4

POSTHUMANITY

I like to think (It has to be!) of a cybernetic ecology where we are free of our labors and joined back to nature, returned to our mammal brothers and sisters, and all watched over by machines of loving grace.

—Richard Brautigan

Technical civilization, and the human minds that support it, are the first feeble stirrings of a radically new form of existence, one as different from life as life is from simple chemistry. Call the new arrangement Mind. Unlike Life alone, which learns from its past, but is blind to its future, Mind can choose among alternatives to imperfectly choose its own destiny—even to amplify that very ability.

—Hans Moravec, *Robot: Mere Machines to Transcendent Mind*

[A] dream of robotics is that we will gradually replace ourselves with our robotic technology, achieving near immortality by downloading our consciousness. . . . But . . . what are the chances that we will thereafter be ourselves or be human? It seems to me far more likely that a robotic existence would not be like a human one in any sense that we understand, that the robots would in no sense be our children, that on this path our humanity may well be lost.

—Bill Joy, *Wired Magazine*

PLANET AI: THE SECOND DAY

The visitor told his hostess yesterday that he would call her Persona, because this Latin word's two meanings—*person* and *mask*—seemed to suit
her well. After all, he had no idea what kind of reality to attribute to her
other than her role as a manifestation of the kind of mind controlling this
mysterious planet. She smiled at the name and explained that she would call
him Human, because what was most important about their encounter was
the interaction between such different life-forms. As he wakes up this
morning, he hears her speak to him in that soothing and encouraging voice
he remembers from yesterday.

P.: I hope that food and sleep have restored your cells so that you can understand and enjoy all that I have to tell you. Having accessed our database
on your planet and civilization, I think I can now communicate with you
more effectively.

H.: I've never felt better! I feel energetic yet relaxed, and passionately curious about all that I'm experiencing here. Did you put something into my
food or drink? I'm not complaining, but I somehow don't feel like myself.

P.: Through a noninvasive procedure, we were able to make minor adjustments to your nervous system so that your feelings harmonize better with
your cognitive and rational processes. We've given you Aristotelian moral
virtue[1] as an immediate gratification! You're a more rational animal than
you used to be. You'll notice that you won't get tense for no reason or feel
restless when you need to be still. But you remain capable of a full range of
emotions, even intense ones, when appropriate. You can even remember
with amazement what it was like on occasions when you lost your temper or
were otherwise in the grip of some unhealthy feeling.

H.: Yesterday, I would have said that I was unwilling to undergo such tam-
pering. I would have seen it as a violation of my dignity as a person. Yet now
I feel liberated.

P.: Many humans had similar concerns about the early psychoactive drugs,
even relatively benign and effective ones such as Prozac. They worried that
whatever positive changes such drugs brought about in them were coming
not from themselves but from some alien source. If a pill made them feel
more optimistic or energetic, they regarded such feelings as inauthentic because they did not come from facing up to and resolving their problems. It
wasn't enough for these people that the pill often enabled them to actually
deal with their problems.

H.: They had a point. It's still a controversial issue among us. Just as I would not want to drink so much alcohol that it disinhibits me from doing what I believe is wrong or foolish, so I don't want the action of some medication to substitute itself for my rational choices. I want to be, as far as possible, the sole author of my actions. I want it to be me, and not alcohol or drugs, that originates my choices. Otherwise, what gets done by this human is not *my* doing; I just get to experience it from the inside, as it were. A person is not just a stream of consciousness registering the behaviors of its body. No agency, no self.

P.: Then what do you think of your current situation? Would you like me to reset your psyche to yesterday's condition?

H.: Perhaps later. The rational tranquility you've induced in me makes me want to talk this matter over and do what seems best.

P.: You sound like Socrates examining whether he should escape from prison!

H.: Perhaps, but you are no Crito.[2] I know that my intellectual powers are no match for yours, even though you may be a downsized version of the mind that animates this planet. I appreciate your indulgence as I try to grasp what's happening in my own terms.

P.: You're doing fine. Let's get back to our topic. You said that needing repeated doses of a pill or therapy suggests that the beneficial effect isn't part of the "real" you. This attitude reminds me of Bill McKibben's recent book *Enough.* McKibben argues that humans should be willing to accept the mix of attributes they receive from their genetic lottery and should *not* develop the power to genetically or otherwise implant superior attributes. He claims that if humans bestow on themselves enhanced abilities, they will become "engineered automatons" and "consciousness as we know it—including the ability to make our own decisions, to say no—will eventually disappear."[3] But what if an enhancement is permanent—a *transformation*—instead of being a transitory state that will lapse unless you keep medicating yourself? In that case, wouldn't *you* be the author of the actions and achievements made possible by your transformation?

H.: Let's maximize that scenario. What if I could have *any* ability for the asking? Or I could just wish for something to get done and it would happen? In such a case, *I* wouldn't be *doing* anything. It would be a kind of wish fulfillment in which I call on some power outside me that would not only do what I wanted but also give me a first-person experience of doing it. As I said before: no agency, no self.

P.: Every human is involuntarily born with certain traits and abilities and undergoes training and education by a family and a society, thereby being made into a certain kind of person. Each human then gets the first-person experience of making the choices that kind of person would make. Does that mean that no one is a self or agent? At least in the case of what I have called "transformations" you could get to *choose* what kind of person to be. Of course, you would not want to have a rapid succession of unrelated wish fulfillments. That would be meaningless. The experience of deciding on a project and seeing it through is essential for a healthy mind. Whether it's solving a complex theoretical problem, going on a journey, or building a house, a mind is a *living* system. It must have *continuity* through diversity and constant interaction with an environment.

H.: I remember that Aristotle said "the actuality of thought is life."[4] And I realize that the ultimate evolutionary ancestor of human brain function is the adaptive control function of DNA in unicellular organisms.[5] But I don't really understand how there is anything more than a weak analogy between life in the biological sense and what is sometimes called the "life" of the mind.

P.: As you know, the adaptive control function enables a living system to unify itself in space and time by responding to events in its environment in such a way as to retain the capacity to respond in the same ways to the same sorts of events. As the system progresses from one point in its duration to the next, it repeatedly embodies the same repertoire of responses, so that each point is an instance of the same kind of system. That is why it is called a *self-instantiating* system. It exists in and through constant interaction with its environment.

As terrestrial animals evolved in the direction of your species, their brains developed an increasingly powerful model of their external environment. From the very beginning, there was an enormous degree of *abstraction* in this model, insofar as it reduced all the original physical detail of events in sensory receptors to patterns of a single unit—the nerve impulse. Animals instantiated themselves *by* instantiating successive representations of themselves within their model of the environment. The self-instantiating program in an animal's brain works like a concept of what it is to be that animal, a concept that causes each stage of an animal's life to be an instance of itself.

In the course of primate evolution, a sequence of species emerged that became increasingly capable of walking upright. This growing bipedalism freed arms and hands from their roles as supports for the torso, allowing a more sophisticated prehensile capacity and progressively finer innervation of the joints of fingers and wrist and of the skin surface of the hand. This, in turn, provided feedback for greater neuromotor control of the hand. With increasing flexibility of wrist and fingers came a vast increase in the variety of possible orientations of the hand and fingers to objects in the environment. This increased variety was due to the combined movement of the wrist and multiple finger joints in tandem with the movements of elbow and shoulder joints now free of the burden of holding up and moving the front portion of the torso in harness with legs. This world of possible movements generated a vast array of configurations of kinesthetic and tactile stimuli from handling an object. Without even looking at what was in their hands, these hominids could detect such features as line, shape, and size with an acuity approaching that of vision.[6] And this, in turn, made possible a new kind of perception, one that incorporated both motor and sensory neocortex.

Have you ever wondered about the *insensibility* of the *motor* areas of the human neocortex?

H.: I don't understand.

P.: Although the neural architecture of motor areas appears quite similar to that of sensory areas, patterns of neural events in motor cortices don't give rise directly to sensations the way they would if they occurred in sensory cortex. For instance, an electrode inserted into the visual cortex will give rise to the sensation of a flash of color in a part of the visual field corresponding to the point of insertion. While an electrode inserted into a specific part of the motor cortex may give rise to a motion of a corresponding body part, the insertion doesn't directly generate a sensation. The only sensation you will get is by way of feedback from the bodily motion caused by the electrode insertion. Yet the frontal (motor) cortex is just as busy as the sensory areas while you're awake and about, even when you're just thinking or looking at something. But all those patterns of neural events in the frontal cortex run silently in the dark—they don't register as sensation.

H.: OK, that's one of the major differences between the two kinds of cortex. But I don't see the relevance of all this to our topic, especially to the relationship between biological and mental life.

P.: Let me put in the form of a thesis what I want to explain next: Among the patterns of neural events in the more recently evolved portions of the human neocortex are the nonsensory or conceptual ingredients of your perceptions of objects.

H.: What do you mean by the "conceptual ingredients" of perceptions?

P.: The easiest way to explain it is with the examples of a couple of perceptual ambiguities. Figure 4.1 alternates between a pair of faces looking at each other and a black goblet, depending on which shape is foregrounded. The staircase in figure 4.2 seems to go in alternating directions. These alternations occur in spite of constancy in the visual stimuli. The oscillating interpretations relate to how you would *handle* or otherwise *interact* with what is seen. In general, all perception of visible objects incorporates motor representations of the interactive relationships between the human body and its surround. As far as we can tell from our study of your central nervous system while you slept, it appears that there is automatic, subconscious activity in the motor cortex whenever there is sensory perception.[7] This activity is similar to what goes on in the conscious rehearsals humans engage in when they deliberately imagine doing something without actually

Figure 4.1.   Goblet/faces perceptual ambiguity.

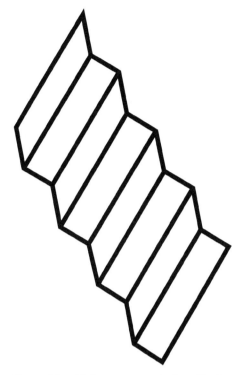

Figure 4.2. Staircase perceptual ambiguity.

engaging in the behavior. The activation of motor representations by sensory input (e.g., viewing the staircase above) seems to have the further effect of generating a weaker form of the sensory feedback that would occur from muscle contractions in actual behavior or interactions with objects. That feedback amounts to a concomitant kinesthetic and tactile content in addition to the visual. It is weaker than actual sensation, of course, just as visual content is much less vivid when it is imagined rather than actually seen. The motor representation of an object is the nonsensory ingredient of perception; it is a *concept* of that object. Notice that a common English word for knowing or understanding is "grasp(ing)" something.[8] The French *comprendre* and Latin *comprehendo* have a similar association with perception by handling. Human vision is prehensile.

The mediating role that the concept or motor representation plays between visual and (weak) tactile/kinesthetic content in visual perception also explains how humans perceive a shape that is seen to be the *same* as one that is perceived by handling. As the hand moves over a visible object, units of motion and its feedback are mapped onto segments of visible shapes, so that what is seen is felt and vice versa. This capacity for concept formation might have developed slowly among the ancestral hominid species. One early manifestation might have been movements of arms and hands in imitation of visible shapes or motions. Finely innervated, flexible hands and fingers would have enabled hominids to exercise detailed control over an object in their grasp. They could maintain a constant pressure on, and orientation of, an object they were moving in various directions. Suppose that the object was a stick being held above a surface of sand and that the stick had a shape and size that allowed it to function as a stylus. Such a situation would invite the transition from a mimetic motion expressing the shape of some other object to a *drawing* of that shape. Suppose instead that the object in hand was a rock with a shape that allowed it to function as a hand ax. Here the transition from a motion expressing the shape of another object could be to a *shaping,* carving motion directed at a malleable material. This transition would open the way to creating a variety of practical artifacts.

Sensorimotor representation is also prominent in auditory perception. The movements of a dancer or a conductor's baton are examples of the human capacity to render patterns of sound as movements of the body. Furthermore, dancing and the baton demonstrate how audiomotor representation can make what is heard visible. Properties such as shape, pattern, speed, and frequency are examples of what Aristotle called *common sensibles,* properties that are perceptible across modalities. He said, "There cannot be a special sense-organ for the common sensibles, . . . i.e. the objects we perceive incidentally through this or that special sense, e.g. movement, rest, figure, magnitude, number, unity; for *all these we perceive by movement,* e.g. magnitude by movement, and therefore also figure, . . . what is at rest by the absence of movement; number is perceived by the negation of continuity."[9]

H.: We got onto this topic of sensorimotor representations as part of your explanation of the strong evolutionary relationship between life as its is found in unicellular organisms and the activity of the mind. You seem to be saying that three levels of self-instantiation have occurred in the course of evolution on my planet. The first level was *genetic,* consisting in DNA's adaptive control over the metabolic processes in cells. Next came the *neural* level, in which a self-instantiating program was embodied in the brain, instantiating the animal's body by means of a representation of that body in a model of the environment. This model is constituted by shifting patterns of neural impulses, with input from sensory receptors and output to muscles. The third level is still neural, with the important difference that the main activity is at a *conceptual* level, involving motor representations that integrate the visual, auditory, and tactile/kinesthetic fields by means of various sorts of intermodal perceptions. The earliest manifestations of this sensorimotor capacity would have included hand movements imitating shapes and motions, drawing, dancing, and carving malleable materials. In more general terms, it was the origin of human communication, art, and technology. But I'm still unclear about how the third level is a distinct kind of *self-instantiation,* one that we could call *mental life.*

P.: [*She smiles as never before.*] Although we are so different, you and I, I felt so much in common with you as you spoke just now. I felt the *life* we have in common, the life you manifested in the way you gathered all the points we had covered and arranged them into a single journey from a question toward an answer. You presented each different point as a successive instance of the same process. What you did was, in its own brief way, an *odyssey.* You remember Homer's poem, don't you?

H.: Yes, it was part of a humanities course I was required to take as a college freshman.

P.: Then you remember how, through all the strange places and often frightening adventures depicted by Homer, there is always *one* thing going on in his book-length poem: the return of Odysseus. This return is on many levels, of course. He is returning to his home on Ithaka, to his wife and son, and thereby to himself, his very identity. His coming back is the completion of a journey he began twenty years earlier, when he set out to fight at Troy. People in the Dark Ages of ancient Greece loved to hear a bard sing such stories. Most of the audience was already familiar with the content and plot, just as later Greek audiences were who attended the performances of tragedies. Their primary interest was not in the novelty of the content, although they were always on the lookout for particular twists that a bard or playwright could bring to familiar material. What they wanted, what *all* minds want, is the heightened consciousness, the enhanced unity that a great narrative has in comparison to the clutter of ordinary experience. A real-life Odysseus would have experienced his odyssey as ten years of mostly uninteresting details such as sails flapping in the wind, overheard conversation of shipmates, the endless cycle of hunger and eating, thirst and drinking, other bodily functions, minor aches, chores, and countless other things, infrequently punctuated by special occasions of danger and triumph. Only the latter make it into *The Odyssey*—only the content that can be interwoven with the theme of return. Humans' personal memories of their pasts are much like this, narratives that seek meaning by leaving out the irrelevant and trivial, though seldom encompassing heroic deeds. In the world of Homer, heroes such as Achilles and Odysseus could look forward to a likely violent death in combat followed by an eternity of listless existence as shades in the underworld. What counted as *fulfillment* within this tragic vision was having the kind of life and death that could be transformed by memory and the narrative skill of a bard into a level of consciousness worthy of being shared by all who listened to the song.

Socrates, the patron saint of your philosophers, sought the same sort of fulfillment, even though he seemed not to share the dismal Homeric image of afterlife. At his trial, he identified the driving force behind his prosecution as anger over his persistent questioning of traditional values and beliefs, and over his inspiring others to do the same. He invoked the figure of Achilles to explain why he would not stop this behavior in exchange for his life being spared. In *The Iliad,* Achilles is warned by his goddess mother that if he rejoins the Greek army in front of Troy and kills the Trojan leader, Hector, it is fated that he, too, will be killed. Socrates reminded the jury that Achilles, despite this warning, resolved not to disgrace himself by shunning battle:

> Had Achilles any thought of death and danger? For wherever a man's place is, whether the place which he has chosen or that in which he has been placed by a commander, there he ought to remain in the hour of danger; he should not think of death or of anything, but of disgrace. And this, O men of Athens, is a true saying. Strange, indeed, would be my conduct, O men of Athens, if I who, when I was ordered by the generals whom you chose to command me at Potidaea and Amphipolis and Delium, remained where they placed me, like any other man, facing death; if, I say, now, when, as I conceive and imagine, God orders me to fulfil the philosopher's mission of searching into myself and other men, I were to desert my post through fear of death, or any other fear; that would indeed be strange.[10]

In *The Apology,* Socrates is casting his identity in terms of a search for truth to which he has sacrificed everything. The worst kind of death for him would be to stop living that story and no longer instantiate the concept of Socrates the philosopher. Socrates fought for his narrative in the public venue of a trial, and Plato preserved it in his dialogue. Humans should be grateful to Plato just as they should thank the unnamed scribes who committed to writing the great poems of Homer.

H.: We *are* grateful, especially because most of us don't get to be heroes. But you seem to imply that even ordinary, day-to-day consciousness is a form of life or self-instantiation. Even heroes have mostly ordinary experiences. The great narratives you've been talking about are, I presume, just special cases of what goes on all the time in the life of the mind.

P.: Yes. Let's look at the most ordinary sorts of experience such as seeing a *chair*. To recognize something as a chair involves a considerable unification and organization of what you perceive. In the here and now, your concept of a chair ties together the various parts of the chair as working together to support a human body in a sitting position. At the same time, it groups your present experience with a set of similar ones—other chairs you've encountered or will encounter. Suppose this chair is in the middle of what you recognize as a *classroom*. It stands in various spatial relations to tables and to other chairs, a blackboard, walls, floor, ceiling, and a lectern on a desk. All these different items belong both to the space and the function of the room. The concept of a classroom does, on a larger scale, what the concept of a chair does—it unifies and integrates. If you also see a doghouse in the classroom, there will be something that is out of place, not part of the unity of a classroom, and you won't (yet) understand. A really big concept such as the *world* will always extend to a great many objects and events that you can't yet fit into a greater context. But you have faith that they can in principle be assigned their place in the scheme of things. To think or understand or even perceive is to experience a unity in the multiplicity of what you perceive.

As Immanuel Kant repeatedly emphasized, every experience involves a *concept*, which he understood as the unity or *unification* of the content of a sense perception. To think is to conceptualize—a unifying *activity* he often referred to as "synthesis." This was Kant at his most revolutionary.[11] He did much to close the great gap between thought and action that I noticed in so many of your seventeenth- and eighteenth-century philosophers. For Kant, the object of perception is, to a great extent, the *product* of the mind's synthetic activity.

H.: Stop there, please. I can accept as obvious that thinking is *finding* or looking for the unity in experience. But your transition to the Kantian notion of synthesis is more controversial. It makes the unity a *product* of the thinking process. And, of course, that is an echo of what you were talking about earlier when you explained the origin of mental life on my planet in terms of the sensorimotor capacities of my hominid ancestors. And that, in turn, reminds me of our main topic: how genetic self-instantiation in simple organisms is the evolutionary ancestor of mental life.

P.: Considering everything you've been through in coming here, I'm amazed at the vitality of your mind, at how well you link earlier and later parts of our lengthy conversation. And these two words, "earlier" and "later," are crucial for our main topic—the relation between self-instantiation and thought. The genetic self-instantiating program in the genome of a unicellular organism secures the continuity of the organism by embodying itself in *successive* instances. In that way, the organism continues to be able to respond to the same sorts of events in the same ways, ways that are characteristic of that organism. A nonliving system such as a chair or a classroom also continues to exist only insofar as it continues to behave toward its environment in the ways that are characteristic of that sort of thing. As John Locke pointed out, the ideas of individual concrete things ("substances") are largely made up of what he called "powers"—the ways in which these things act on our senses and interact with other things.[12]

The self-instantiating program in a cell functions like a concept of what it is to be that sort of cell, a concept that brings about its own instances by continuously embodying a repertoire or set of "powers." There is no such thing in a nonliving system, whether artificial (like a chair) or natural (like a pebble). Whether we see such systems as collections of parts or as single things is a function of our interest in and interaction with them.[13] As long as a system continues to behave according to the specifications in *our* concept of such a system, we recognize successive instances of the same thing and attribute continuous existence to it. But these specifications are not imposed by the system on itself. Its continuity is *hetero*instantiation. It gets its unity from the mind of a perceiver. I'm not claiming that a thing is created ex nihilo by the perceiver. Just as self-instantiating programs in the first terrestrial organisms had to work with extant molecules and within the physical laws governing the behavior of these molecules, so our concepts (as heteroinstantiating programs) have to operate within a range of interpretations and expectations allowed by the laws of nature that govern the constituents of the physical environment. For example, the face/goblet and staircase ambiguities we talked about previously allow only two alternative conceptualizations at the lowest level. Above that level, of course, we could have many more competing interpretations of what is going on in such a case.

Since a nonliving system is *hetero*instantiated, its spatiotemporal unity is *extrinsic* and relative to a perceiver. Because a living system is *self*-unifying, we can say that it has an *intrinsic* unity in space (within its boundary, such as a cell membrane) and in time. The externality of part outside of part in space and time is cancelled[14] in the body and duration of a living system, insofar as these parts become the expression of a self-instantiating program.[15] Because of this inner aspect, a living body is a *subject,* whereas nonliving bodies are only *objects.*

H.: I don't understand what you mean by "inner." There's a perfectly clear sense in which one thing is inside or outside another, depending on where the relevant boundary is. A body doesn't need to be alive in order to have an inside.

P.: Quite right. But the notion of an inside as opposed to an outside is not the same as the inner aspect I spoke of. The former is a spatial relation between all or part of the space within a boundary and the space outside the boundary. That relation doesn't address the problem of intrinsic unity we were discussing. A part inside the boundary of a body is just as much outside or external to other parts as it is to what is outside the boundary. The boundary of a nonliving body is a function of how we classify and distinguish objects around us (such as regarding the same system as either one thing or a collection). It is not something established from within the body itself. By contrast, a living body is a subject that maintains its own boundary and thereby creates the distinction of inner and outer.

H.: OK, I'm beginning to understand some of the connections that were puzzling me about your account of visuomotor concepts. By handling and otherwise interacting with things I see around me, I distinguish them from each other, learn what to expect from them by way of responses to my interventions, and conceptualize in the form of motor programs such features as their shape, volume, relative location, velocity, and weight. The boundary between perceiving and doing is fluid. I wasn't paying enough attention to the essentially *temporal* nature of concepts. When I recognize something by its shape and location, for instance, I am doing more than just labeling a momentary spatial configuration. I am also expecting it to behave in certain ways, depending on future circumstances, such as its interaction with me, or changes in its appearance as I get closer to or farther from it. To use your term along with Locke's, I am *grasping* it as a locus of *powers*.

P.: That's right. Recognizing an object for what it is amounts to correctly instantiating it. It's a case of what I have called *heteroinstantiation*. By way of relating this term to our previous discussion of narrative unity in *The Odyssey* and in the life of Socrates as presented in *The Apology*, let's think of inanimate objects (heteroinstantiated systems) such as pebbles and chairs as *centers of narrative unity*.[16] When I label something as a chair or pebble, I expect that it will have one of a set of possible histories, depending on its next interactions with its environment. Each possible history unfolds, within the constraints of the laws of nature, according to the attributes that define the system (e.g., something with a certain weight, shape, and size will have different apparent shapes from different angles and will be displaced or not depending on the features of what collides with it). The continuing presence of these attributes does for a physical object what a theme does for a narrative poem. Insofar as the attributes are part of a *scientific* description of a system, they achieve a precision unavailable in other kinds of narrative. As consciousness streams from moment to moment, countless histories unfold as objects interact within a world organized around a perceiver's point of view. Nearly all go as expected, to the extent that perceivers correctly and completely conceptualize their environment.

H.: It sounds as though you're saying that the world is the embodiment of my mind.

P.: Yes. Just as the *repertoire* of a unicellular system consists of metabolic pathways being deployed and regulated by a genetic self-instantiating program, so the *repertoire* of a mind consists of concepts generated by a sensorimotor self-instantiating program. A *genetic* self-instantiating program interacts *directly* with, and at the same level as, the cellular body it instantiates. The *neural* self-instantiating program of a terrestrial animal with a brain has an *indirect* relation to the animal's body. It instantiates the animal *by* instantiating a model of its body and of the events affecting it. Bipedalism, and the corresponding evolution of the hand and sensorimotor capacities of hominid brains, gave rise to *mental* self-instantiation. Human minds instantiate their bodies within a model that includes an external environment—a world of other bodies that they also instantiate. A mind instantiates itself by instantiating a world in which its body can continue to respond in the same ways toward the same sorts of events. At each point in the duration of its world, a mind embodies its conceptual repertoire.

H.: Why, then, do I experience only one of those bodies as *mine,* if my mind instantiates all of them?

P.: For two reasons, one of which is peculiar to the human mind. The *first* reason is that the body that I call mine is the embodiment of my sensory and behavioral capacities. I act, I initiate behavior with that body alone, and it alone is the ultimate medium through which all my sensory input comes. This central position of my body is manifest in such things as the perspectival arrangement of the visible world and the chains of means and ends that link me to distant bodies and places with which I might interact.

The *second,* specifically human reason is one that Descartes happened on in his sixth meditation when he analyzed the experiences of pain, hunger, and thirst.[17] These belong to a set of localized feelings (including a level of tactile sensation) that humans inherit from their mammalian ancestors and that aid in maintaining the cellular community that makes up a human body. A human gets these feelings only about her own body. They map onto each human's visuomotor percept of her own body, and they vary with the well-being of that body. For instance, you would say "*I* hurt where *it* hurts," and are inclined to elevate the well-being of your cellular constituents to a central place in your world, even though these cells are so much lower forms of life than the mind that must constantly tend to them.

H.: As you describe it, the situation of a mind seems to be one of abject solitude—a subject alone with a world of *objects* it instantiates from moment to moment. And yet here I am having the experience of interacting with another *subject*—a mind very different from mine.

P.: Of course! And my human-like embodiment makes the interaction more comfortable and intelligible for you. My description of a person's world as the self-instantiation of her mind accommodates your everyday experience of other subjects, both human and nonhuman. As you try to *understand* and successfully interact with the things in your environment, you find that you can't conceptualize them in whatever way you wish. There are laws of nature and local conditions that determine the outcome of your interaction, and you ignore or are ignorant of them at your peril—if, for example, you try to walk on water. Even the *objects* we instantiate have a certain independence. However, a living body, the body of a subject, has even more independence. Call it autonomy. Its behavior can be interpreted only as *self*-instantiating, as bringing about the continuity of a body with a certain repertoire. A *hetero*instantiated body has no intrinsic value; it has value only as part of the self-instantiation of another body—the body of a subject. It is a mere object.

There is no other way in which a subject can be present in the world except as an object. The *inner* aspect of a living system cannot as such be part of the world—it can't appear in space. An alien subject is *present* to a mind only insofar as the behavior of its body calls for that mind to recognize that the body is *self*-instantiating and thereby has intrinsic value. You as subject would be alone in your world only if nothing in it called for such a recognition.

H.: Yesterday, you said that once the ancestral species on this planet had freed its mind from the confines of an animal body, it became a virtual community in the cyberspace of the planetary computational machinery that seems to be at work everywhere. You added that you ("we") could still create embodiments such as yourself when needed. I haven't noticed any other such beings. Is there no one else out here, unless more guests arrive? Forgive me for saying so, but such a world strikes me as desolate.

P.: Let's pick up on that tomorrow. We still have so much to talk about, but I can tell that you're feeling tired again. In the meantime, feel free to explore the home entertainment center we've set up for you. In addition to a vast library of digital books, music, and films, we've also set up an advanced version of the virtual reality (VR) body suit being developed on Earth. You can use it to get multisensory input from various robots we have sent into outer space to probe nearby planetary systems. Telepresence is experientially every bit as good as physical presence, but without the fuss of getting one's physical body out to distant and dangerous places. That's one of the many reasons why we've largely dispensed with RL physical embodiments for ourselves.

REFLECTIONS

1. P. sees no fundamental difference between a world in which persons strive to achieve goals by working within the limits of their genetically endowed talents and attributes and a world in which technological "transformations" could allow persons to accomplish much more. P. says that as long as a person is given a suitable amount of time to work within the limits of her enhanced capacity, that person can still have the experience of real accomplishment. After all, whether we have a certain ability due to the natural lottery of the human gene pool or to human technology, our achievements will be based on abilities that are given to us.

   Bill McKibben strongly disagrees. He argues that the kind of technology that would enable these "transformations" will be constantly improving, and these improvements will result in unacceptable situations such as this:

   > The first child who has been "enhanced" from what came before—that's the first child who will glance back over his shoulder and see a gap between himself and human history.
   >
   > But here's the really awful part: he won't be able to look forward, either. He won't be able to imagine himself connected with those who come after him. Because, of course, by then there will be better upgrades.[18]

   What do you think? If there is going to be such technology, is there any way our society can avoid what McKibben warns us of?

2. Is there a contradiction between P.'s claim that the world I experience is the embodiment of *my* mind and her claim that other living subjects, including minds, can be present in that world? If *their* embodiments are part of my world, then how can they be part of *my* embodiment?

PLANET AI: THE THIRD DAY

In the happiness of the sight of God there is perfect delight, all the more perfect than the pleasure of sense, which brute animals also can enjoy, as intellect is higher than sense; . . . all the more perfect again as the delight is more pure and free from all admixture of sadness or harassing solicitude; and of this it is said: *They shall be inebriated by the plenty of thy house, and thou wilt make them drink of the torrent of thy pleasure* (Ps. xxxv, 9). Nothing in this life is so like this final and perfect happiness as the life of them who contemplate truth so far as possible.

—Thomas Aquinas, *Of God and His Creatures*

P.: Did you sleep well?

H.: Yes. At first I felt hyperstimulated by the scenes transmitted from one of your outer-space probes. But once I became accustomed to the body suit, I was surprised at how relaxed I felt, even as I reveled in movements and vistas that my own body could never have given me. I could feel the pressure exerted by its arm and hand as it steadied itself against a rock on the icy surface of some planet I didn't recognize. I was even more enthralled by my experience with a robot on the surface of your own planet because it was responsive to my voluntary movements and gave me kinesthetic feedback. The robot really seemed to be my body, except that I knew I could separate from it. What would Descartes have thought of this body–body dualism? After a few hours of this body tripping, I was overtaken by a pleasant drowsiness. [pause]

Are you *in* your body or merely telepresent?

P.: The latter. Is your question prompted by your virtual voyage last night or by something about my appearance and behavior?

H.: It was the memory of last night's experience. Just as the robot felt like *my* own body, so you seem to be *in* your body. I'm having a hard time adjusting my concepts here.

P.: The body in which you see me, like the robot you entered last night, is only an instrument, a machine designed to transmit sensory input and be responsive to motor output from a remote mind. We didn't want to populate outer space or the surface of our planet with robots that were alive with minds of their own. We had to be sure that they would carry out *our* intentions rather than being able to form their own. Anything else would have been irresponsible and perhaps even dangerous for us. So these robots, like my humanoid body, don't have self-instantiating programs of their own. My self-instantiating repertoire is embodied in the hardware of our planet's computational system, just as yours is in your brain. You would have survived the destruction of your robot bodies last night, just as I would survive the destruction of the body you see before you.

H.: You seem to *be here*—or are we talking about bilocation?

P.: It depends on what you mean. Simultaneous instantiation in two places is just as impossible for me as for you. But the *presence* of a physically distant person is something that your technology has been making possible to an increasing degree ever since the invention of the telephone. The degree of presence is a function of how much it can provide of the kinds of interaction two people can have when sharing the same physical location. In principle, the first kind of presence can be as complete as the second. If someone had walked in on you while you were in the body suit last night, they would have found you physically present, but otherwise absent.

H.: You seem completely and really present here and now, I admit. I wouldn't have been able to conclude that your real body is elsewhere if you hadn't told me.

P.: It helps that input from the sensory receptors in this humanoid robot reaches me as quickly as your sensory input reaches your brain. Same with motor output. Our technology would allow for an even quicker transmission rate, but we slowed it down in this case to make our interaction more natural for you.

H.: I think I'm still having trouble thinking of a virtual body inside a computer as a *real* body.

P.: Keep in mind that the bodies and environment we experience in our virtual world are very close to what our ancestral species had. There is a large population of persons and a rich variety of plant and animal life. We eliminated some negative features and enhanced some positive features of the bodies of our ancestors and their natural environment. We don't have such things as food chains, infectious diseases, and scarcity of natural resources.

H.: You seem to have achieved the vision of Isaiah: "The wolf will live with the lamb, the leopard will lie down with the goat, the calf and the lion and the yearling together; and a little child will lead them."[19] But it's all just an image created by a computer.

P.: We need to clarify our terminology here. Let's say that VR is what someone experiences when their sensory input is generated entirely from within a computer, in such a way that they feel present in an environment other than the one they occupy physically.[20] The word "virtual" is strongly tied to the phrase "computer generated." And that, in turn, may be evoking in you the sense of a momentous difference between human perceiving and ours. Perhaps you think of the content of human perceptions as *resembling* the external domain that generates your sensory input, while ours does *not,* since we don't perceive ourselves as inhabiting a computational machine.

H.: Yes, I had in mind that contrast, though I realize that it's easy to overstate the degree of resemblance.

P.: Right. What you perceive, the world you instantiate from moment to moment using your conceptual repertoire, is in your brain, even though you don't perceive it that way. What could be more unlike the world you interact with on a daily basis than patterns of neural impulses? Furthermore, the way your physical science describes the world has little resemblance to the visible world of things you can touch, hear, taste, and smell. The physicist's world of mostly empty space with a thin scattering of imperceptibly small particles doesn't have much similarity to the solid objects and continuous surfaces that you see and handle. Of course, those scientific descriptions do enable you to predict and—to some degree—control what you experience. But so does our understanding of the programs that generate *our* experience. Those programs are rather like the laws of nature in their operation, except for alterations we have made to make the virtual environment friendlier to mental life. The programs impose the same constraints on all of us here. That constitutes a shared reality in which the bodies that we experience as *ours* are just as adequate a representation of our sensory and motor powers as are the ones that humans experience as theirs. As you know from your teleimmersions of last night, we haven't turned our backs to the outer world. We continue to explore it and increase our scientific understanding of it. We're also on guard against a particular kind of intelligent life-form from some other planet. Our concern is that there may be *aliens* in which intelligence and animal life have coevolved in a way that subordinates intelligence to the biological imperatives of an animal species. Such a species might not respect us as persons and might even want to harm us.

But we relate to the outer world from the interior of our well-protected computational system, a far more secure place than the inside of a human cranium exposed to the vicissitudes of raw nature. The principal difference between our situation and yours is that the physical systems embodying human minds are constantly interfacing with an outer environment operating according to laws beyond your control and heedless of your well-being. Your bodies are vast cellular communities that each of you must keep alive and well. Humans have evolved biologically and technologically in ways that enable most of them to survive such an environment. But I don't need to remind you of the toll in suffering and death by disease, starvation, and violence that blind nature continues to exact from your species.

H.: Our science and technology are making significant progress in reducing that suffering. What seems more intractable is the suffering created by *moral evil,* by the deliberate psychological and physical harm that humans inflict on each other. For that reason, I would be reluctant to replace natural laws over which none of us has any control with laws or programs devised by humans. Irrationality and ill will too easily infect our political and legal systems. I am glad to have laws of nature beyond our control.

P.: When we freed our minds from the animal legacy of our ancestral species, we eliminated the root cause of what you call moral evil. To show you what I mean, let's discuss the teleportation thought experiment Derek Parfit made famous in the late twentieth century.[21] Do you recall it?

H.: Vaguely. Perhaps you could summarize it for me.

P.: You're supposed to imagine a teleportation machine that is capable of scanning the complete molecular structure of your body. It then instantly and painlessly destroys it at the departure point and replicates it at the destination point. The body's molecular formula is transmitted at the speed of light to the arrival station, but there is an interval when the person exists only as a formula.

In what is called the "branch case," you imagine that the teleporter malfunctions in a very important way. It manages to replicate you at a station on Mars, but you find yourself still alive at the departure point on Earth. A technician explains to you what has happened and that the malfunction has damaged your body in a way that will cause you to lose consciousness and die in about an hour. He attempts to console you by dwelling on the fact that your replica is alive and well and will continue your life. He can even arrange for you to have an audiovisual conversation with your replica on Mars. The question posed by the branch case is what you are to think of your situation on Earth. You're about to die. Is this prospect just as bad in the branch case as it would be *without* a replica continuing your memories, goals, character, and personality?

H.: It's coming back to me now. I remember an intense discussion in which some of my classmates adamantly claimed that death on the branch line would be nearly as bad as normal death. Our instructor suggested we might think of the issue in light of another little story. Imagine that John and Mary have just come in from jogging a few miles in warm, sunny weather. Both are very thirsty. Mary goes to the cooler and picks up two cans of the very same kind of soda. She offers John the bottle in her left hand. To her surprise, John firmly asks for the one in her right hand instead. Mary draws back, slightly annoyed, yet also curious. "Why? What's the difference?" she asks. John can't articulate any difference, but insists on the bottle in Mary's right hand. She yields, but their relationship is never quite the same again.

The instructor's point seemed to be that to claim that death on the branch line is as bad (or nearly so) as normal death is (nearly?) as irrational as John's insistence on one can of soda over another. The two bottles were intrinsically the same. No difference due to being in one hand rather than the other could be relevant to making the choice. Similarly, for me to regard my death on the branch line as bad even though my replica lives on is irrational, since there is no relevant difference between me and my replica. No one I know would notice any difference, and presumably there would be no difference between what it would be like for me to continue alive and what it will be like for my replica. There are minor differences, of course, since my replica won't have the memory of being left behind on Earth, but such a difference is too inconsequential to matter, just as are the minuscule differences between two bottles of the same kind of soda coming off the same production line.

P.: Were you and the others convinced by this analogy?

H.: I was nearly convinced, at first. But the more I put myself in the position of the person left to die on Earth, the more I rebelled at the instructor's suggestion. I and the others argued that the analogy was simplistic. After all, the bottles are just *things,* whereas humans are conscious subjects—they're aware of them*selves* and want those selves to continue. In relation to my self-awareness, my replica would be *someone else* just as much as any other human being would be. *I* would die, not him.

P.: I don't understand. In neither case can you specify a relevant difference between the paired items. You admitted just now that there wouldn't be any difference between what it is like to be yourself continuing to live and what it would be like to be your replica.

H.: I see your point, but I'm still reluctant to agree. My mind keeps looking for some fault in your argument to justify my belief. It *matters* very much that I am not my replica. I find your analysis disturbing.

P.: Don't be offended by what I'm about to say. When you find yourself clinging anxiously and without reason to a belief, you may be helped more by a *diagnosis* than by further argument. The diagnosis I have in mind is of a universal human problem. Do you recall the distinction I made yesterday between two different ways in which humans experience their own bodies as unique?[22]

H.: Yes. The first way we experience our bodies is as originators of our behavior and receptors of sensory input. The second way involves a range of sensations inherited from our mammalian ancestors—such as the Cartesian trio of pain, hunger, and thirst. You included in that list a lower-level, affective aspect of tactile sensation. I thought about that last night. This tactile sensation maps onto the visible surface of my body, but not onto other visible bodies. Just as I don't feel thirst when another body is dehydrated, so I don't feel the pressure of a cup against the surface of the table, although I do feel it against my hand. Such experience presents me with a precise boundary between *my* body and other bodies, between self and other.

P.: Very good. Now think how it would be if, like us, you didn't have any of those lower-level body sensations. Just suppose that all the modalities in which you sense *your* body were the same ones that gave you perceptions of *other* bodies. You would experience *your* body purely as a thing, just as when you concentrate exclusively on what you *see* as your body. Of course, *it* would be a very special, perspectivally central thing; it is the only body that is directly responsive to your will, and its motions would be the beginnings of all you do. It would be your channel of communication with other minds and your most fundamental form of property and self-expression. Imagine that this body was designed specifically and entirely to facilitate the kinds of behavior that are distinctively human, such as speech, athletics, and dance. Perhaps you can begin to understand the kind of liberation our ancestral species bequeathed when it ceased to reproduce its animal body. We were freed from selfishness and irrationality.

H.: You're going a bit too fast for me. I understand how the human brain retained certain structures that served the needs of our mammalian ancestors for food, drink, mating, and safety from predators. The imperfect relationship between those brain structures and the neocortical functions that enable us to think often causes irrational behavior. It has always been a challenge for humans to harmonize such feelings as fear and anger with what we know we should do. Meeting this challenge is what Aristotle called moral virtue. But I'd like to hear more about the connection with selfishness.

P.: Let's go back to the branch-line case. When you imagined yourself as the one left behind and soon to die, you couldn't help judging that outcome to be nearly as bad as death, despite the ongoing existence of your physical and psychological replica. That was the desire of the *animal* in you—calling for self-preservation and unable to recognize that self in your thought of a replica. The brain mechanism for the desire to ward off harm evolved long before hominids developed conceptual awareness. This awareness enabled humans to be conscious of an instance *as* an instance. For example, each time your hominid ancestor saw a tree, it invoked the same anticipatory motor program in his brain, whether or not he actually carried it out. These activated programs gave rise to the same low-intensity tactile and kinesthetic images of feedback from executing the program. For that reason, each perception of the tree included an *abstract* image of the tree, one that applied just as well to an indefinite number of trees.

H.: I understand how a concept can be abstract. But I always thought an image was concrete and particular by its very nature. My image of a tree is always of this or that particular tree, not of a tree in general.

P.: Yes and no. Remember that your visual image or perception is undergoing motor analysis, generating a *way* of handling (literally or metaphorically) what you see. A *way* of handling is by its very nature abstract or universal—a way of handling *any such* object.[23] And the forebrain's rehearsal of that way of handling (i.e., that motor program) generates a correspondingly abstract feedback image of what's being handled. It's not only the tactile/kinesthetic feedback image that is abstract. The motor program also determines how and what you *see,* as we noticed in our discussion of perceptual ambiguities.

H.: And that is how we get the perception of what Aristotle called "common sensibles"—shape, size, motion, and so on.

P.: Yes, exactly.

H.: All kinds of animals respond in the same ways to similar items in their environments. Otherwise, they would not be self-instantiating systems. So they, too, have generally applicable motor programs that are activated by similar things. What's so different about *conceptual* awareness?

P.: In a word: *handling.* Remember our discussion about the revolutionary effect of true bipedalism.[24] It was through the wonderful flexibility and fine innervation of the hand that humans acquired intermodal perception of the common sensibles. It's true that a quadruped's perceptions of similar events would stimulate similar adaptive responses. However, those responses would generate feedback images not of the *object* of the response, but only of the sequence of movements anticipated or executed by the animal. *That* was the beginning of mental life on Earth—when behavior itself constituted perception. That was when consciousness began to instantiate objects.

H.: OK. Humans, and minds in general, have perceptions that are both particular and universal—they are conscious *of* instances *as* instances. You said that our minds were unlike yours in that *we* had feelings based on mammalian brain mechanisms not fully integrated with the mental functions of the neocortex. Are you saying that *all* our feelings are like that, or are there feelings that relate specifically to our mental life insofar as it is distinct from our animality?

P.: You, like us, do have specifically mental feelings, desires, and satisfactions. Many of your best philosophers have been eloquent on the subject. Plato thought that true philosophers were driven by a passion for the eternal forms their souls had contemplated prior to being immersed in bodies. When a philosopher catches sight of something beautiful in this life, he "is transported with the recollection of the true beauty; he would like to fly away, but he cannot; and he is like a bird fluttering and looking upward and careless of the world below; and he is therefore thought to be mad."[25] Aristotle wrote of "pleasures marvellous for their purity and their enduringness" that come to us when we can contemplate what we know without having to attend to practicalities.[26] Aquinas describes the vision of God that the blessed will enjoy in heaven as "inebriation" and a "torrent of pleasure."[27]

John Stuart Mill was very articulate about the qualitative superiority of mental over animal sensual pleasures: "it is an unquestionable fact that those who are equally acquainted with, and equally capable of appreciating and enjoying both, do give a most marked preference to the manner of existence which employs their higher faculties. Few human creatures would consent to be changed into any of the lower animals, for a promise of the fullest allowance of a beast's pleasures."[28] Like Aristotle, Mill recognized that our animal needs must be attended to. The best sort of life should contain moderate animal pleasures and a minimum of pain, with most of our happiness based on cultivation of our minds and of the ability to share in the happiness of others. That's why he saw ignorance and selfishness as the greatest obstacles to any individual's happiness.

Unlike Kant, Mill does recognize that moral decision making must consider the effect of one's conduct on the *happiness* of others.[29] But his moral principle demands as much unselfishness as Kant's: "The happiness which forms the utilitarian standard of what is right in conduct, is not the agent's own happiness, but that of all concerned. As between his own happiness and that of others, utilitarianism requires him to be as strictly impartial as a disinterested and benevolent spectator." He urges humans to strive through education and social propaganda "to establish in the mind of every individual an indissoluble association between his own happiness and the good of the whole." Of course, this association could never be indissoluble, because of the partial *dis*sociation of animal feelings and mental life in the human brain. By contrast, *we* on this planet have managed to maximize this association by shedding our animal past. Mill would regard our virtual world and its community life as a utilitarian paradise.

H.: Let's pause there. I remember that you were on the verge of saying something similar when you argued that my "irrational" reaction to being left to die on the branch line was due to animal feelings. And now you're again claiming that when your ancestral species shed its animal past, all minds became naturally unselfish. I still don't see the reasons for that claim. Many animals seem to behave quite unselfishly—for example, there are many animal species that exhibit cooperative breeding behavior, and an individual primate will endanger itself by crying out a warning to its group at the approach of a predator.

P.: Nonhuman animals are neither selfish nor unselfish as I am using those terms. They do as their genes and brain mechanisms dictate. There is obvious survival value for a breeding population when its members engage in certain kinds of altruistic behavior. It isn't difficult to understand how natural selection could favor the retention of such traits.

The selfishness I am talking about is defined quite well by Kant and Mill. In Kantian terms, a selfish person is one who wants to privilege himself by choosing to do what he could not be willing to have everyone else do under the same circumstances. Or, as Mill would put it, the selfish person has a greater regard for his own happiness than for that of anyone else. Selfishness in this sense requires conceptual awareness. Only a mind is capable of viewing its behavior as an instance of a kind of behavior and its well-being as the fulfillment of a kind of being. The belief that dying on the branch line is nearly as bad as death is an extreme case of selfishness—it prefers one's own happiness over that of another person who is one's physical and psychological replica. It is a preference without basis for the mind, one that is driven by animal feelings that cannot relate directly to conceptual content and so must cling to the dying original on the branch line with all *its* pains, hungers, and thirsts. That scenario brings out in a very pure way the irrationality of selfishness.

H.: I can appreciate the beneficial effects of the psychic tune-up you performed on me during my first night here. Normally, I would feel resentment when told that something I had said was selfish and irrational. But I can see your point, and the negative feelings just don't arise. I understand why you describe my belief about the branch-line case as irrational, since there is no intelligible difference between the original and the replica. But in the usual sort of situation in which I have to weigh my happiness against that of others, there are plenty of intelligible differences between them and me, and I often use those differences to justify preferring *my* happiness.

P.: And that preference may well be justifiable. Being unselfish does *not* require you to rank the happiness of another *above* your own. If you are dangerously dehydrated while another person is merely somewhat thirsty, and there's only one bottle of water available in the next several hours, it would create more unhappiness if you were to let the other person drink than if you drank it yourself. An unselfish person could decide that way—she would not be regarding her own happiness as more important than the other person's. She would merely be preferring the alternative that brings about the greater happiness, *regardless of whose happiness it is.*

Let's try to generalize from the kinds of cases we've been discussing. It doesn't matter which individual person has any particular attribute or experience, which individual person gets to do something, or even which one lives or continues to live. What matters is that all these things get distributed among persons in such a way as to maximize the happiness of the community. For instance, it is better for a person able to put an ability to its best use to have that ability than it is for someone not in a position to use the ability well to have it. But, other things being equal, it does *not* matter which person is in a position to use the ability.

The philosophers among our ancestral species added one important qualifier to the utilitarian principle: no person should ever be treated *merely* as a means toward the happiness of anyone else, not even for the greater happiness of the vast majority.

H.: I have a problem with your extrapolation from the relation between myself and my replica in the branch-line case to the relation between *any* two persons. You're claiming that my negative assessment about death on the branch line is the same kind of irrationality and selfishness as believing my own happiness to be more important than that of others. Aren't you just *assuming* there is the same degree of identity between me and everyone else as between me and my replica? That seems clearly false. In normal situations, people aren't dealing with their replicas.

P.: You're right to press me on that issue. Our entire civilization on this planet is built on our conviction about a fundamental identity of all minds. I think you fail to notice how many *human* institutions and practices imply the same belief. How do you explain what you're trying to achieve when you attempt to *communicate* what you're thinking to another person? Suppose you're trying to explain Newton's law of gravitation. Your criterion for success in communicating that idea may be that the other person now correctly paraphrases what you just said or successfully applies it to some problem. But such behavior is not the same as the *understanding* you were trying to communicate; instead, the behavior is an indication of something occurring *within the mind* of the other person, something that is the same as what goes on in you when you think of what you were trying to communicate.

H.: And yet I am sure that you could not communicate to me much of what you and others on this planet can understand. How, then, can you claim that *all* minds have a fundamental identity?

P.: I can tell that I'm succeeding in communicating my thoughts to you in this conversation, and I understand you in turn. To make that possible, I had to do something analogous to donning lenses that greatly reduced my visual acuity—I'm seeing through a glass murkily. At least, that's how it is for me, though it is your normal level of perception. Think of it this way. If you were a combat veteran trying to explain to someone with no such experience what war is really like, you would have to try to construct the experience out of elements of what is familiar to the nonveteran. You would encounter similar difficulties in communicating with a child or explaining a complex concept to a person with a low IQ. All these are nevertheless acts of communication, because each is an interaction between minds, between systems that instantiate themselves through sensorimotor representations of a world.

Because of our shared nature as minds, what it would be like for you to have my intellectual ability is the same as what it is like for me to have it—just as you can appreciate how a human with less ability than you could very well be you. Insofar as these abilities are *good* because they enhance the life of a mind, what *matters* is that minds have these abilities, not that you or I, rather than someone else, have them. This perspective is natural for us on this planet because we don't have animal feelings to contend with. Our ancestral species understood that releasing minds from animal brains would be a liberation of the self.

H.: That phrase reminds me of something Derek Parfit said about how liberated he felt once he understood that *his* continuing existence wasn't very important.

P.: Yes, and I agree with his conclusions about the unimportance of one's own death, but for different reasons. He analyzes the self reductively, as *nothing but* a set of relations among memories, beliefs, intentions, and other psychological states and attributes. For him, the continued existence of a self is no more than the continuity of a sufficient percentage of those psychological relationships. The self is not a substantial entity that is destroyed or falls into a void when I die. So death loses its sting. Contrary to Parfit, I have argued that there *is* a "deeper fact" behind my psychological continuity: a living, self-instantiating system bringing about the continuity. However, the conclusion I draw about death is similar to his because I argue that there is no more than a numerical difference between any one mind or self and another, and such a difference is not a rational basis for my preferring *my* continued existence over that of any other person. For my own reasons, I agree completely with Parfit's elegantly worded description of death as "merely the fact that, after a certain time, none of the experiences that will occur will be related, in certain ways, to my present experiences. Can this matter all that much?"[30]

H.: It's hard for me to imagine what it would be like to be unselfish in that way. I have a constant tendency to make my own happiness central—not that I would explicitly say or believe it's that important, but I have a strong inclination to feel and act that way. When I think of the billions of human persons alive today, and the billions that preceded them, and when I add in the vastness of the universe—all those galaxies blinking at me from billions of years ago—my sense of self-importance scurries away like a startled ant. But I usually have more pressing things to concentrate on. My bouts of unselfishness too often come as moral victories rather than spontaneous outpourings. This problem seems to be part of the human condition.

P.: The mirror image of selfishness is *alienation*. Selfishness is a false consciousness of one*self* that creates an equally false sense of *otherness* or estrangement toward nature, social reality, and other selves. Insofar as a mind is in the grip of animal feelings, it finds *itself* only in the particular body about which it has feelings such as hunger, thirst, and pain. And yet, insofar as it is a mind, it instantiates *itself* by instantiating a *world* of which its own body is only a minuscule part. The sense of otherness that animal feelings cause a mind to have toward its world is an alienation of the mind from *itself*. This alienation is made worse by the fact that the world that humans instantiate is governed by laws of nature over which humans have no ultimate control, so that nature itself can seem to be an oppressor. We have minimized that factor by living in a virtual world governed by laws of our own creation.

When one human experiences another human body behaving (or even seeming to behave) in ways that manifest a mind in the service of its animal feelings, the encounter is one of reciprocal alienation—a potentially adversarial relationship in which each may attempt to exploit or harm the other. Thomas Hobbes went so far as to call this sort of encounter the *natural* condition of humans when they are not coerced by the power and lethal force of a government. And yet humans commonly experience government as exercised by persons over whom they have little or no influence and who are using that power for selfish ends.

Nevertheless, humans do manage to have true friendships—two people really can have a passionate and abiding interest in each other's well-being, and there can even be small communities of such friends. Because selfish motives can arise in any human animal, establishing the trust that is essential to friendships takes skill and time. These relationships grow around shared activities and reciprocal contributions to shared goals. For that reason, they work best between equals. All of us on this planet are equal in status and have the same level of intelligence. Yet there is a rich diversity among us because we have different personalities and can participate in different communities and circles of friends united around specific activities and projects.

H.: I would guess that you are immortal.

P.: No, actually. Our ancestors realized that immortality would be a curse, and we have never been tempted to bestow it on ourselves. You look puzzled. Let me put it this way. We didn't want to be like Homer's gods and goddesses. The *Odyssey* is saturated with the contrast of mortal human life, the immortality of the gods, and the shadow life of the dead in Hades. Much of the poignancy in Odysseus's struggle to *return* to his life and identity in Ithaka comes from an awareness of the dreary fate that awaits even heroes such as Odysseus or Achilles once death drags them into the underworld. When Odysseus voyages to Hades to consult with the prophet Teiresias, he summons the spirits of the dead by pouring sheep blood into a pit. A crowd of spirits draws near, but each talks to Odysseus only after easing its thirst for life by drinking from this blood. When Achilles comes up,

Odysseus is filled with pity for this greatest of warriors and tries to console him by describing him as a "great prince among the dead." But Achilles will have none of this: "'Say not a word,' he answered, 'in death's favour. I would rather be a paid servant in a poor man's house and be above ground than king of kings among the dead.'"[31]

H.: Surely the immortal gods and goddesses have the happiest and most enviable existence in the world of Odysseus.

P.: Aren't you struck by the way these deities seem to have nothing better to do than be an active audience for the lives and deeds of humans? They take sides in human quarrels and often intervene on behalf of their favorites. And Greek mythology is full of stories about gods having affairs with humans.

H.: Perhaps that is due to the much greater number of partners available among humans. The number of gods and goddesses is small, and they have an eternity together.

P.: I suppose so. But that way of putting it masks a far deeper problem. The gods are going to live forever, and there is no scarcity of whatever resources they need for their divine way of life. So (to borrow a phrase from your economists) there is no opportunity cost to their choosing to do one thing rather than another or spend time with one person rather than another. They have endless time and resources to pursue other alternatives and relationships later. Consequently, they can't take anything or anyone very seriously. They can have pleasures and amusements, but nothing can have great value for them. Moreover, their lives lack meaning because they are condemned to living an *unending* story, one that can never have narrative unity. What Odysseus struggles so hard to achieve by getting back to Ithaka is simply unavailable to the gods. Their only recourse is to become involved in the lives of humans as spectators, lovers, friends, or enemies. It is vicarious experience, no closer to the real thing than what the spirits of Hades experience by drinking blood before conversing with Odysseus. That is the fate we avoid by fixing a standard limit to our lives. Immortals cannot have what Kierkegaard called "passion."

H.: I seem to remember that Homeric gods were quite anthropomorphic. Like humans, they, too, have their rages, lusts, and enthusiasms.

P.: Yes they do. But these feelings are not what Kierkegaard meant by "passion." States such as rage and enthusiasm are intense feelings that can help a person to accomplish good and even great deeds, but they can also overwhelm the mind and cause irrational and immoral behavior. We on this planet don't have such feelings, though our ancestral species did. What Kierkegaard was talking about was something good, and even necessary, for a mind. As he put it, "It is impossible to exist without passion, unless we understand the word 'exist' in the loose sense of a so-called existence."[32] A human can "exist" in the sense of being one of many occurrences of that *sort* of being, and the kind of self-instantiation going on in that human's mind will be specifically mental. But this person may be without passion and never really *exist* as an *individual* in Kierkegaard's sense. A mind is aware of limitless possibilities—it can think of itself as doing *anything* conceivable, and it can think of a limitless time in which to do it all. To *choose* a life—one that will progress like a story from its beginning to its end—is to give up the infinite for the finite. Such a choice leaves the eternal for the temporal; it focuses onto a finite existence a desire as boundless as the realm of possibility. That focusing is what Kierkegaard meant by "passion," and it could not happen without the prospect of death. That is why we have decided we wouldn't want to live without death.

Because we don't have animal feelings, this passion arises in us spontaneously and inevitably. We don't have desires to avoid the truth and we don't fear death. So we can look unblinkingly at it and choose a life. Humans are easily distracted, and their fear of death makes distraction welcome. That's why, in Kierkegaard's sense, it's rare to find a passionate, existing individual. It is all too easy for a human to happen into an unchosen life shaped by a combination of social expectations, peer pressure, consumer preferences, and personal whim.

H.: I think you're leaving out something important about humans—something that would make them even more interesting to the gods. Homer's epics are about *heroes,* and gods cannot be heroes. Part of the grandeur of heroes is that they *overcome* their fear of death and injury and their aversion to hard truths, and they are not deterred by the prospect of pain and suffering in pursuit of their goals. Heroism is measured not so much by the greatness of the deeds performed as by the obstacles overcome, especially those posed by animal feelings such as fear, pain, and fatigue. Neither the Olympian gods nor *you* can enter this inner battlefield. You can't be heroic. And, despite the mortality you've imposed on yourselves, I find it hard to equate *your* passion in choosing a finite existence with the passionate choice that a human makes. To make the choice that funnels infinite desire into a limited life, *we* must overcome irrational fears and other animal feelings. And this choice can always come undone. We have to renew our commitment in the face of future temptations. There is no such triumph in *your* affirmation of life, only effortless spontaneity. As I listened to you discussing Homeric deities, I wondered whether you had something in common with them in spite of your mortality: desire for the vicarious experience of a kind of passion unavailable to you. Perhaps that explains your abiding interest in *us* despite our selfish inclinations and intellectual inferiority. Your rationality and unselfishness are not achievements, they are only the preset modes of a highly advanced psychological machine. Perhaps you are drawn to the fact that *we can fail as persons* and must *choose not to*. This is a freedom you lack.

P.: I admire your spirited defense of human nature, but I can't view this freedom you speak of as a positive attribute. The possibility of failure, or of choosing failure, is a liability, not an asset. If this freedom is an attribute that is better to have than not to have, why does the religious tradition of your Western civilization deny it to God? Is God imperfect for being unable to do wrong? *Both* you and I are psychological machines. But there are parts of *your* machinery that don't work well together because they originated at different stages of evolution on your planet. We consider ourselves free because we were liberated from the possibility of irrationality and selfishness.

Relax now, and get some sleep. Tomorrow I'd like to get your final impressions of what you've experienced here and your opinion on how your species will react to your report of our encounter.

H.: I look forward to that.

REFLECTIONS

1. Do you think that H. is right about the lesser nature or intensity of passion in beings such as P., who live in a much more secure environment and don't have to cope with irrational feelings like those of humans? Is there a greater nobility and value in humans overcoming themselves than in the rational spontaneity of P.? After all, without our weaknesses and the hazards of our environment, we could not be *heroic*. Is P.'s response to this objection adequate? Is she more like Homer's gods than she is willing to admit?

2. P. claims that feelings, such as pain, hunger, and thirst, that are localized onto our bodies give us a false sense of *self* and a correspondingly false sense of the *otherness* of the rest of the world, including other humans. She calls this *alienation*, something that seems intrinsically false and bad. Yet, could there be such a thing as a self without a corresponding otherness of everything else? Has P. left room for *any* sense of self in her analysis of the mind's relation to its world?

PLANET AI: THE FOURTH DAY

P.: Good morning. Are you looking forward to being back on Earth?

H.: Yes, though I'm still trying to digest all that I've experienced here. I find it hard to anticipate what effect the report of this encounter will have on the human race. We're still far from having the scientific and technological capacity to bring about a transformation on Earth such as the one your ancestor species did, though I believe we will eventually acquire this knowledge and power. There are two reasons why I don't expect that a majority of humans in the foreseeable future would be willing to let human nature die off and be replaced by posthuman beings in a world like yours. *First,* there is a strong Christian tradition in many of our most advanced societies. The core doctrine of Christianity has God assuming human nature, and it makes the redemption of the human race the *central* event or process in all of creation. Those societies also have a strong humanistic culture inherited from Greco–Roman civilization. Their values and ideals are strongly rooted in human nature. *Second,* we are still very far from having the kind of global political community that could achieve consensus on such a monumental change.

P.: The first obstacle you mention doesn't strike me as insuperable. Humanistic ideals, whether based on Greco–Roman or Judeo–Christian texts and narratives, can be reinterpreted to apply to broader communities of persons, much as the phrase "all men" in the American Declaration of Independence came to be understood as applying to Africans, women, and all other persons on Earth.

The second problem is urgent and far more difficult. It is the reason we chose to bring you to our planet. We're concerned about the survival prospects of the human race—we're very afraid you may not make it to the point where a transformation such as ours would be possible. There have been countless planets on which rational life ended catastrophically after reaching your stage of evolution. As far as we can tell, failure is more common than success in making the difficult transition you are facing. Humanity seems locked into a vicious circle in which less-developed nations in Asia and Africa repeatedly experience uncontrolled birth rates that plunge them into crises of starvation, warfare, and even genocide. The wealthier nations of the great American and European economic unions and their Pacific Rim associates respond reluctantly and inadequately to these crises by providing enough aid and military intervention to tide the afflicted region over during the immediate danger. This perpetuates the impression among the affluent that there are relatively cheap and painless solutions to these problems, while it teaches the governments of the impoverished areas that fundamental reforms are unnecessary because outside help will likely come sooner or later. Even though this help is insufficient, it allows the ruling elite to take care of themselves and continue business as usual.

H.: I agree. We managed, despite close calls such as the Cuban missile crisis, to survive forty years of mutually assured nuclear destruction between two superpowers. This was a duel between two industrial giants over the kind of political system most appropriate for technologically advanced societies. Underdeveloped nations were pawns in this struggle, cultivated by each side mainly for their usefulness against the other. It's ironic that, once capitalism had prevailed over communism in the late twentieth century, something like Marx's vision of history became a reality. We now have a planetary struggle between a bloc of largely democratic nations that possess enough capital to sustain their prosperity and other nations with so little capital that they must cater to and work for the wealthy nations to survive. Most impoverished countries are incompetently governed, racked by ethnic and religious strife, and badly overpopulated. One of the main causes of the vicious cycle of overpopulation you mentioned is that, in nations too poor to have an effective welfare system, parents have larger numbers of children to make sure enough of them survive to take care of the parents in their old age. In affluent countries, there is economic security for the elderly, and the high financial and opportunity cost of raising a child acts as a deterrent to large families.

The combination of military weakness, chronic poverty, and domination by affluent nations breeds hatred and resentment that find an outlet in terrorism. Because they have no stake in the current world order and no hope of a better life, terrorists are willing to destroy what they might otherwise have wanted for themselves. Since the demolition of the World Trade Center in 2001, we have had several frightening incidents. The total casualties have not yet been high by the standards of traditional warfare, but each attack reminds us that the infrastructure of capitalist civilization is highly vulnerable, especially in its transportation and communications systems. Terrorist attacks have led to economic crises as producers and consumers lose confidence in the stability of capitalist institutions and property. The governments of developed nations are increasingly restrictive and intrusive in their security measures, thereby threatening basic liberties and creating a sense of danger and unease in our societies.

P.: It is difficult for me to convey to you how appalling the human condition seems to us. The root cause of the many dangers that threaten to destroy your species is that your minds are slaves to the cellular communities that are your current embodiment. What a human mind experiences and does is always hostage to the well-being of the fifty trillion microorganisms making up its body. To maintain these bodies, humans have inherited feelings and drives that preoccupy them and lead to selfish and irrational behavior. Like other animals, humans have a powerful urge to reproduce, but science and technology eliminate many of the checks (such as diseases and predators) that nature provides against overpopulation among nonhuman animals. Seven billion humans are now taxing Earth's limited supplies of water, breathable air, and food. More than 800 million people are either starving or malnourished. Human agriculture produces barely enough calories to feed everyone, but too many of those calories are used up in fattening livestock or are wasted because of market inefficiencies and lack of funds to purchase food in poor countries. Only a *planetary* government could adequately address these problems, primarily by drastically reducing the birth rate. Even then, humans would still be spending most of their time and effort nourishing and maintaining their multicellular bodies in the service of the low level of life found in unicellular organisms.

H.: A planetary government still seems entirely out of reach. People in affluent nations are unwilling to let poorer countries generate the kind of pollution that would occur if these countries were to industrialize on the scale of Europe or America. But the affluent are also unwilling to accept the reduction in their consumption levels that would be needed to create more humane living conditions for impoverished nations. The cost of medical technology continues to soar with the latest advances in synthetic body parts, neural prosthetics, and nanomedicine. Even in prosperous nations, only the wealthiest citizens have full access to such treatments and enhancements. This inequality is causing resentment not only in European countries with traditions of universal health care, but even in the winners-take-all society of the United States. A planetary government would have to engage in a global redistribution of wealth and capital while enforcing strict limits on the birth rate everywhere. Even the combined military might of NATO would not be enough to successfully *impose* such a worldwide regime. Yet I can't imagine humans everywhere having enough rationality and mutual trust to voluntarily form a planetary government.

P.: Since human animality threatens the survival of mental life on Earth, we are prepared to offer your species the technology you would need to replace yourselves with virtual communities such as we have on this planet. Humans would have to agree to cease reproducing in return for a guaranteed high standard of living, which our technology would give them until they die. However, we will *not impose* this transformation on you. Nor will we intervene in your discussions and planning. We have no desire to colonize or infantilize you. *You* must come up with a voluntary, distinctively human plan for the kind of transition we offer. On your return to Earth, you'll have with you multimedia documentation of our conversation and of the kind of technology we can give you, as well as instructions for making contact with us. There will be no basis for anyone doubting the truth of what you report. Our offer is open for an indefinite time period.

This decision would be a very difficult one for the human community to make. Despite all the arguments supporting a transition to posthumanity, accepting such a transformation would be a leap of faith. As you've said to me several times, it's hard for a human to imagine mental life as *we* live it.

H.: How then could we ever bring ourselves to make such a decision?

P.: To some extent, it may be forced on you if the human condition continues to worsen in the ways we've talked about. But, even in such a case, an act of faith will be required. You will be heeding the injunction of Parmenides' goddess to follow the argument where it leads you. You will be trying to do the right thing based on the best evidence and argument available. But, of course, you can't *prove* that rationality, in this sense, is best. All you can do is *believe*, like Socrates, that nothing truly bad can happen if you follow this path.

REFLECTIONS

1. Do you think P. is justified in her concern about the survival of the human race? What do you think of her claim that only a planetary government could deal with the kinds of problems that cast doubt on the survival of the human race?
2. If you were presented with P.'s offer of the technology and resources needed to create a posthuman society such as hers, would you be inclined to accept it? If not, which part(s) of her proposal do you object to most? Why?

NOTES

1. See "Fear and Loathing," chapter 3.

2. In Plato's dialogue *Crito,* Socrates' friend Crito tries to persuade him to escape from prison before he is executed. Socrates tells Crito that he will do so if that would be best, but they must first examine the question. Socrates concludes that he should remain in prison.

3. Bill McKibben, *Enough: Staying Human in an Engineered Age* (New York: Holt, 2003), 222.

4. See the epigraph to chapter 3.

5. See "The Flow of Time," chapter 3.

6. Neurologists call this form of perception *stereognosis.*

7. Vittorio Gallese, Laila Craighero, Luciano Fadiga, and Leonardo Fogassi report that this general principle has been very fruitful in research on primates, including humans: "The idea of a major role played by action in building our perception is not new. Roger Sperry in 1952 wrote: 'Perception is basically an implicit preparation to respond. Its function is to prepare the organism for adaptive action. The problem of what occurs in the brain during perception can be attacked much more effectively once this basic principle is recognized.' These sentences stress the fact that perception can be accounted for only by considering the bidirectional relationship between the agent and his/her environment." They conclude their review saying: "It is our suggestion that action is one of the founding principles of our knowledge of the world." Gallese, Craighero, Fadiga, and Fogassi, "Perception through Action," *Psyche* 5 no. 21 (July 1999), at psyche.cs.monash.edu.au/v5/psyche-5-21-gallese.html (accessed 14 September 2003).

8. George Lakoff and Mark Johnson argue that philosophy must take more seriously the *constitutive* role that our bodies and nervous systems play in cognition and reasoning. It is not enough that we recognize, contrary to Descartes, that our minds could not exist except as embodied. We must also understand that the specific physical parts, dimensions, and behavioral capacities of our bodies, and the corresponding sensorimotor functions of our brains, determine the way we conceptualize bodies and events in our environment: "The properties of concepts are created as a result of the way the brain and body are structured and the way they function in interpersonal relations and in the physical world." Lakoff and Johnson, *Philosophy in the Flesh* (New York: Basic, 1999), 37. They argue for what they call "embodied concepts": "An embodied concept is a neural structure that is actually part of, or makes use of, the sensorimotor system of our brains" (20).

9. Aristotle, *The Basic Works of Aristotle,* ed. Richard McKeon (New York: Random House, 1941), 425a, emphasis added.

10. Plato, *Apology,* 28d–e, trans. B. Jowett, at classics.mit.edu/Plato/apology.html (accessed 14 September 2003).

11. The notion of understanding as an activity with a product is present in Aristotle and in Aristotelian philosophers such as Thomas Aquinas. As Aristotle put it, "Mind in the passive sense is such because it becomes all things, but mind has another aspect in that it makes all things; this is a kind of positive state like light." Aristotle, On the Soul, in *Aristotle,* trans. W. S. Hett (Cambridge, Mass.: Harvard University Press, 1975), 430a.

12. "Most of the simple ideas that make up our complex ideas of substances, when truly considered, are only powers, however we are apt to take them for positive qualities; v.g. the greatest part of the ideas that make our complex idea of gold are yellowness, great weight, ductility, fusibility, and solubility in aqua regia, &c., all

united together in an unknown substratum: all which ideas are nothing else but so many relations to other substances; and are not really in the gold, considered barely in itself, though they depend on those real and primary qualities of its internal constitution, whereby it has a fitness differently to operate, and be operated on by several other substances." John Locke, *An Essay Concerning Human Understanding* (1690) II, 23, 37.

13. See "The Flow of Time," chapter 3.

14. It's hard to find the exact verb here. P. is trying to express what we experience in the consciousness of one part of space being outside the other. Our *consciousness* of one part is *not* outside our *consciousness* of the other part—otherwise we would not be conscious of the relation of externality between the parts. So the externality is there in the content, but it is overcome, as it were, by the unity of the conscious subject. That is the meaning of "cancelled." It is similar to a concept in Hegel for which the German term is *aufgehoben*.

15. Locke found the question of the *unity* of a body quite elusive. If every part is outside every other part, there would seem to be only unqualified externality or multiplicity without unity—which, of course, is unintelligible, since a multiplicity is made up of many ones. Here is the way he puts the question: "He that could find the bonds that tie these heaps of loose little bodies together so firmly; he that could make known the cement that makes them stick so fast one to another, would discover a great and yet unknown secret: and yet when that was done, would he be far enough from making the extension of body (which is the cohesion of its solid parts) intelligible, till he could show wherein consisted the union, or consolidation of the parts of those bonds, or of that cement, or of the least particle of matter that exists. Whereby it appears that this primary and supposed obvious quality of body will be found, when examined, to be as incomprehensible as anything belonging to our minds, and a solid extended substance as hard to be conceived as a thinking immaterial one, whatever difficulties some would raise against it" (*Essay* II, 23, 26). In Lockean terms, P.'s claim is that self-instantiation, whether genetic or mental, is the "cement" Locke was looking for.

16. Daniel Dennett, in "Why Everyone Is a Novelist," *Time Literary Supplement* (accessed 16–22 September 1988), uses the term "center of narrative gravity" for the notion of a self. He argues that selves are fictitious entities, but useful all the same, like a *center of gravity*. A body in a gravitational field behaves *as if* its entire mass were concentrated in a single point—its center of gravity. Similarly, according to Dennett, it helps us predict and otherwise make sense of human behavior to think of humans as having a point-like source of behavior, defined by various attributes such as beliefs, memories, and habits. This is the self as center of narrative gravity. Dennett's point is that a self, however useful the fiction, is *not real* in the sense that bona fide physical objects such as atoms are real. His argument begs an important question: Why isn't an atom also a center of (scientific) narrative gravity? "It" is composed of protons, electrons, and neutrons and is mostly empty space within its boundary. Its mass is the combined mass of its components, and its chem-

ical properties are a function of the number and behavior of its electrons. "It" is a *system* that, like all systems (such as selves, nations, and beehives), behaves as a unity at a certain level under specific circumstances. P.'s argument is that this unity is due to heteroinstantiation by a narrator that is self-instantiating.

17. See "Descartes' Sailor," chapter 3.

18. McKibben, *Enough*, 64–65.

19. Isaiah 11: 6–9.

20. This topic is also treated in the introduction.

21. Derek Parfit, *Reasons and Persons* (Oxford: Oxford University Press, 1984).

22. See "Planet AI: The Second Day," this chapter.

23. What P. is saying here resembles what Immanuel Kant spoke of as a "schematism": "The concept 'dog' signifies a rule according to which my imagination can delineate the figure of a four-footed animal in a general manner, without limitation to any single determinate figure such as experience, or any possible image that I can represent *in concreto*, actually presents. This schematism of our understanding, in its application to appearances and their mere form, is an art concealed in the depths of the human soul, whose real modes of activity nature is hardly likely ever to allow us to discover, and to have open to our gaze." Kant, *Critique of Pure Reason,* trans. Norman Kemp Smith (New York: St. Martin's, 1990), B180-1.

24. See "Planet AI: The Second Day," this chapter.

25. Plato, *Phaedrus,* trans. B. Jowett (1871), 249D, at classics.mit.edu/Plato/phaedrus.html (accessed 14 September 2003).

26. See "Fear and Loathing," chapter 3.

27. See the epigraph to this section.

28. John Stuart Mill, *Utilitarianism* (1863), c.2.

29. Kant's moral theory is discussed in "Fear and Loathing," chapter 3.

30. Parfit, *Reasons,* 282.

31. Homer, *The Odyssey,* trans. Samuel Butler (1900), bk. 11, at www.uoregon.edu/~joelja/odyssey.html (accessed 14 September 2003).

32. From Søren Kierkegaard, *Concluding Unscientific Postscript,* quoted in W. T. Jones, *Kant and the Nineteenth Century,* 2nd ed. rev. (New York: Harcourt Brace Jovanovich, 1975), 214.

BIBLIOGRAPHY

Alice, at www.alicebot.org/ (accessed 12 October 2001).

Allman, John Morgan. *Evolving Brains.* New York: Scientific American Library, 1999.

Aquinas, Thomas. *Of God and His Creatures.* Trans. Joseph Rickaby. London: Burns and Oates, 1905, at www.nd.edu/Departments/Maritain/etext/gc.htm (accessed 14 September 2003).

———. *Summa Theologica,* 1265–73. Trans. Fathers of the English Dominican Province, 1947, at www.ccel.org/a/aquinas/summa/FS/FS027.html#FSQ27 A1THEP1 (accessed 14 September 2003).

Aristotle. *Aristotle.* Trans. W. S. Hett. Cambridge, Mass.: Harvard University Press, 1975.

———. *Metaphysics.* Trans. W. D. Ross, at classics.mit.edu/Aristotle/metaphysics .html (accessed 14 September 2003).

———. *Nicomachean Ethics.* Trans. W. D. Ross, at classics.mit.edu/Aristotle/ nicomachaen.10.x.html (accessed 14 September 2003).

———. *The Basic Works of Aristotle.* Ed. Richard McKeon. New York: Random House, 1941.

Armstrong, David M. "The Nature of Mind." In *The Nature of Mind and Other Essays.* Ithaca, N.Y.: Cornell University Press, 1981.

Augustine. *City of God.* New Advent Translation, at www.newadvent.org/ fathers/1201.htm (accessed 14 September 2003).

Berkeley, George. *A Treatise Concerning the Principles of Knowledge.* 1710.

Boyle, Robert. "The Origins of Forms and Qualities." In *The Philosophical Works of the Honourable Robert Boyle Esq.,* vol. 3, ed. Peter Shaw. London, 1738.

Burtt, Edwin A. *The Metaphysical Foundations of Modern Science.* Garden City, N.Y.: Doubleday, 1954.

Churchland, Patricia Smith, and Paul M. Churchland. "Functionalism, Qualia, and see p. 45–33 Intentionality." *Philosophical Topics* 12 (Spring 1981): 121–46.

Clarke, George Leonard. *Elements of Ecology.* New York: Wiley and Sons, 1966.

Crandall, B. C. "Molecular Engineering." In *Nanotechnology: Molecular Speculations on Global Abundance*, ed. B. C. Crandall, 1–46. Cambridge, Mass.: MIT Press, 1996.

Damasio, Antonio. *Descartes' Error: Emotion, Reason, and the Human Brain.* New York: Putnam's Sons, 1994.

———. *The Feeling of What Happens: Body and Emotion in the Making of Consciousness.* New York: Harcourt, 1999.

Dennett, Daniel. *Brainchildren: Essays on Designing Minds.* Cambridge, Mass.: MIT Press, 1998.

———. *Consciousness Explained.* Boston: Little, Brown, 1991.

———. "Faith in the Truth," Final Draft for Amnesty Lecture, Oxford, February 1997, at ase.tufts.edu/cogstud/papers/faithint.htm (accessed 13 September 2003).

———. *The Intentional Stance.* Cambridge, Mass.: MIT Press, 1987.

———. "Why Everyone Is a Novelist." *Times Literary Supplement* (16–22 September 1988).

———. "The Zombic Hunch: Extinction of an Intuition?" Final Draft for Royal Institute of Philosophy Millennial Lecture, 28 November 1999, at ase.tufts.edu/cogstud/papers/zombic.htm (accessed 13 September 2003).

Dery, Mark. *Escape Velocity: Cyberculture at the End of the Century.* New York: Grove, 1996.

Descartes, René. *Meditations on the First Philosophy.* Trans. J. Veitch (with small modifications). Paris: 1642, at www.class.uidaho.edu/mickelsen/texts/Descartes/Descartes%20-%20Dedication.txt (accessed 18 September 2003).

———. *The Philosophical Writings of Descartes.* Vol. 2. Trans. J. Cottingham. New York: Cambridge University Press, 1984.

———. Descartes to Princess Elizabeth. 28 June 1643. In *Descartes: Philosophical Letters*, trans. and ed. Anthony Kenny. Oxford: Clarendon, 1970.

Ebert, Roger. "2001: A Space Odyssey." *Chicago Sun–Times.* 1997, at www.suntimes.com/ebert/greatmovies/space_odyssey.html (accessed 14 September 2003).

Expert Systems, at www.ee.cooper.edu/courses/course_pages/past_courses/EE459/expert/ (accessed 15 October 2001).

Gallese, Vittorio, Laila Craighero, Luciano Fadiga, and Leonardo Fogassi. "Perception through Action." *Psyche* 5, no. 21 (July 1999), at psyche.cs.monash.edu.au/v5/psyche-5-21-gallese.html (accessed 14 September 2003).

Globe and Mail (Toronto), 12 May 2003, at www.globetechnology.com/servlet/story/RTGAM.20030512.gtogmay12/BNStory/Technology (accessed 14 September 2003).

Haugeland, John. "Ontological Supervenience." *Southern Journal of Philosophy,* 22, supplement (1983).

Hayles, N. Katherine. *How We Became Posthuman: Virtual Bodies in Cybernetics, Literature and Informatics.* Chicago: University of Chicago Press, 1999.

Hobbes, Thomas. *Leviathan.* London: 1651.

Homer. *The Odyssey.* Trans. Samuel Butler, 1900, at www.uoregon.edu/~joelja/odyssey.html (accessed 14 September 2003).

Hume, David. *An Enquiry concerning Human Understanding.* London: 1748.

Jones, W. T. *Kant and the Nineteenth Century.* 2nd ed. rev. New York: Harcourt Brace Jovanovich, 1975.

Joy, Bill. "Why the Future Doesn't Need Us." *Wired Magazine* 8, no. 4 (April 2000), at www.wired.com/wired/archive/8.04/joy.html (accessed 11 September 2003).

Kant, Immanuel. *Critique of Pure Reason.* Trans. Norman Kemp Smith. New York: St. Martin's, 1990.

———. *Fundamental Principles of the Metaphysic of Morals.* Trans. T. K. Abbott, 1934, at www.class.uidaho.edu/mickelsen/texts/Kant%20-%20Fundamentals %20.%20.%20.txt (accessed 14 September 2003).

———. "What Is Enlightenment?" In *On History,* ed. and trans. L. W. Beck. Indianapolis: Bobbs–Merrill, 1963.

Klüver, H., and Bucy, P. C. "'Psychic Blindness' and Other Symptoms Following Bilateral Temporal Lobectomy in Rhesus Monkeys." *American Journal of Physiology* 119 (1937): 352–53.

———. "Preliminary Analysis of Functions of the Temporal Lobes in Monkeys." *Archives of Neurology and Psychiatry* 42 (1939): 979–1000.

Koshland, D. E., Jr. "The Seven Pillars of Life." *Science* 295 (22 March 2002): 2215–16.

Kurzweil, Ray. *The Age of Spiritual Machines.* New York: Viking, 1999.

Lakoff, George, and Mark Johnson. *Philosophy in the Flesh.* New York: Basic, 1999.

Langton, C. G. Introduction to *Artificial Life II.* Vol. 10. *Santa Fe Institute Studies in the Sciences of Complexity.* Ed. C. G. Langton, C. Taylor, J. D. Farmer, and S. Rasmussen. Redwood City, Calif.: Addison–Wesley, 1992.

LeDoux, Joseph. *The Emotional Brain.* New York: Simon & Schuster, 1996.

Leiner, Henrietta C., and Alan L. Leiner. "The Treasure at the Bottom of the Brain," at www.newhorizons.org/blab_leiner.html (accessed August 2002).

Lewontin, Richard. "Billions and Billions of Demons." *New York Review of Books,* 9 January 1997, at www.csus.edu/indiv/m/mayesgr/Lewontin1.htm (accessed 19 September 2003).

Locke, John. *An Essay Concerning Human Understanding.* 1690.

Loebner, Hugh. "Home Page of the Loebner Prize," at www.loebner.net/Prizef/loebner-prize.html (accessed 13 September 2003).

MacLean, Paul D. "Contrasting Functions of Limbic and Neocortal Systems of the Brain and Their Relevance to Psychophysiological Aspects of Modern Medicine." *American Journal of Medicine* 25 (1958): 611–15.

——. "Man and His Animal Brains." *Review of Modern Medicine* 32 (1964).

——. *The Triune Brain in Evolution: Role in Paleocerebral Functions*. New York: Kluwer Academic, 1991.

Maes, Pattie. "Agents That Reduce Work and Information Overload," 1994, at pattie.www.media.mit.edu/people/pattie/CACM-94/CACM-94.p6.html (accessed 13 September 2003).

——. "PATTIE MAES on Software Agents: Humanizing the Global Computer." Interview with Pattie Maes in *IEEE Internet Computing Online* (July–August 1997), at computer.org/internet/v1n4/maes.htm (accessed 13 September 2003).

Margulis, Lynn, and Dorion Sagan. *What Is Life?* New York: Simon and Schuster, 1995.

Marks, Lawrence E. *The Unity of the Senses*. New York: Academic, 1978.

McGinn, Colin. *The Problem of Consciousness*. Oxford: Blackwell, 1991.

McKibben, Bill. *Enough: Staying Human in an Engineered Age*. New York: Holt, 2003.

Menzel, P., and F. D'Aluisio. *Robo Sapiens: Evolution of a New Species*. Cambridge, Mass.: MIT Press, 2000.

Mill, John Stuart. *Utilitarianism*. 1863.

Moravec, Hans. *Robot: Mere Machines to Transcendent Mind*. New York: Oxford University Press, 1999.

Nagel, Thomas. *The View from Nowhere*. New York: Oxford University Press, 1986.

——. "What Is It Like to Be a Bat?" *Philosophical Review* 83 (1974): 435–50.

Newberg, Andrew, Eugene D'Aquili, and Vince Rause. *Why God Won't Go Away*. New York: Ballantine, 2001.

Newton, Isaac. *The Mathematical Principles of Natural Philosophy*. Trans. Andrew Motte. London, 1729.

Parfit, Derek. *Reasons and Persons*. Oxford: Oxford University Press, 1984.

Parmenides. *On Nature*. Trans. John Burnet, at plato.evansville.edu/public/burnet/ch4.htm (accessed 5 August 2002).

Penfield, Wilder. *Speech and Brain Mechanisms*. Princeton: Princeton University Press, 1959.

Penfield, Wilder, and Herbert Jasper. *Epilepsy and the Functional Anatomy of the Human Brain*. Boston: Little, Brown, 1954.

Place, U. T. "Is Consciousness a Brain Process?" *British Journal of Psychology* 47 (1956): 44–50.

Plato. *Apology*. Trans. B. Jowett, at classics.mit.edu/Plato/apology.html (accessed 18 September 2003).

——. *Phaedo*. Trans. B. Jowett, 1871, at classics.mit.edu/Plato/phaedo.html (accessed 14 September 2003).

——. *Phaedrus*. Trans. B. Jowett, 1871, at classics.mit.edu/Plato/phaedrus.html (accessed 14 September 2003).

——. *The Republic*. Trans. G. M. A. Grube. Indianapolis: Hackett, 1974.

Rock, Irvin. *Perception*. New York: Scientific American Library, 1984.

Ryle, Gilbert. *The Concept of Mind*. New York: Barnes & Noble, 1949.

Scientific American. "Nanotech" (September 2001).

Searle, John R. "Minds, Brains, and Programs." *The Behavioral and Brain Sciences* 3 (1980): 417–57.

———. *The Rediscovery of Mind*. Cambridge, Mass.: MIT Press, 1992.

Sherrington, Charles. *The Integrative Action of the Nervous System*. Cambridge: Cambridge University Press, 1947.

Simon, Herbert. "The Organization of Complex Systems." In *Hierarchy Theory*, ed. Howard H. Pattee, 3–27. New York: Braziller, 1973.

Sophocles. *Antigone*. Trans. R. C. Jebb, 1902, at classics.mit.edu/Sophocles/antigone.html (accessed 19 September 2003).

Stelarc. "Extended-Body: Interview with Stelarc." Interview by Paolo Atzori and Kirk Woolford. *CTHEORY*, 6 September 1995, at www.ctheory.net/text_file.asp?pick=71 (accessed 14 September 2003).

———. "Stelarc," at www.bmeworld.com/flesh/suspensions/public/stelarc/Stelarc.html (accessed 14 September 2003).

——. "Stomach Sculpture," at www.stelarc.va.com.au/stomach/stomach.html (accessed 14 September 2003).

Terzian, H. H., and G. D. Ore. "Syndrome of Kluver and Bucy Reproduced in Man by Bilateral Removal of the Temporal Lobes." *Neurology* 5 (1955): 373–80.

Thomson, Judith Jarvis. "A Defense of Abortion." *Philosophy and Public Affairs* 1 (1971): 47–66.

Turkle, Sherry. *Life on the Screen*. New York: Touchstone, 1995.

United Nations Development Programme. *Human Development Report 1998*, at www.undp.org/hdro/hdrs/1998/english/e98over.htm (accessed 14 September 2003).

Wachowski, Andy, and Larry Wachowski. *The Matrix* (screenplay), at www.ds2.pg.gda.pl/~colan/screenplay.txt (accessed 11 September 2003).

Whitaker Foundation, at www.whitaker.org/news/peckham.html (accessed 13 September 2003).

Wilson, E. O. "The Little Things That Run the World." *Conservation Biology* 1, no. 4 (December 1987): 344–46.

INDEX

ABOUT THE AUTHOR

Brian Cooney is NEH Professor of Philosophy at Centre College. He has edited and provided commentary for the anthology *The Place of Mind*.